CW01511729

IRELAND
and the
ATLANTIC
HERITAGE

E. Estyn Evans (1905-1989): photograph by William Little

IRELAND
and the
ATLANTIC HERITAGE

Selected Writings

*

EMYR ESTYN EVANS

THE LILLIPUT PRESS
MLMXCVI

Copyright © 1996 Gwyneth Evans

All rights reserved. No part of this publication
may be reproduced in any form or by any means
without the prior permission of the publisher.

First published in 1996 by
THE LILLIPUT PRESS LTD
4 Rosemount Terrace, Arbour Hill,
Dublin 7, Ireland.

A CIP record for this
title is available from
The British Library.

ISBN 1 874675 48 1

Jacket design by Jarlath Hayes
Set in 10 on 13 Janson by
mermaid turbulence
Printed in England by
Redwood Books

CONTENTS

PUBLISHER'S NOTE AND ACKNOWLEDGMENTS

This book has had a protracted genesis. It first surfaced as a proposal in discussion with Estyn Evans in 1984, when Lilliput published 'Ulster: The Common Ground' (included below). It was incorrectly listed in Evans's 1988 *Who's Who* entry as *The Irishness of the Irish*, a book of essays published in 1986. The book never appeared in this form, however, as we had decided to broaden its geographical range and to emphasize—as Evans constantly did—the significance of Ireland's setting on the Atlantic margins of the mainland of Europe (not as arrogated on occasion by our island neighbour).

A precedent exists for this decision. Following his delivery of The Frazer Lecture in 1961—on 'Atlantic Europe: The Pastoral Heritage', a major essay in the present collection—Evans was encouraged by the Vice-Chancellor of Liverpool University, and its University Press, to expand the lecture into a book, provisionally entitled 'The Atlantic Heritage'. In a letter to Evans of 4 September 1962, J.G. O'Kane, Secretary of Liverpool University Press, wrote: 'On reading The Frazer Lecture in typescript I was more than ever convinced that your theme and the outstanding way in which you have treated it in these pages would make a really fine book.' O'Kane had in mind current economic and political conditions in western Europe and referred to 'an outward-looking Atlantic Europe' in the context of 'the whole idea of the Common Market and the growth of the power of the European nations'. After some five years of desultory discussion the project came to nothing, but there is a sense in which this book, as its title suggests, fulfils an objective to which Estyn Evans gave serious consideration over thirty years ago.

The Pyrenees essay was written for Evans's BA Honours thesis before his twentieth birthday in 1925. With its reference to politically contested regions like Catalonia and the Basque country, it anticipates Evans's own preoccupations with borders and frontier, and is a unique and powerful interpretation by one so young. In general, sources are indicated either in headnotes or at the foot of each essay or article: where not attributed, it may be inferred that the work is unpublished.

The publisher is indebted to Elizabeth Purdy of Belfast for her work in typing the texts, and to John Campbell of Oxford for his invaluable advice and guidance in the work's orchestration. R.H. Buchanan, Alan Gailey and Noel Mitchel helped with the book in its early stages. The Evans family, Gwyneth, Alun and David, have been especially supportive and encouraging. I trust that *Ireland and the Atlantic Heritage* will be a fitting memorial to these labours, and to the memory of one of our immortals.

A.T. FARRELL
May 1996

His students called him the Prof., as though there were no other. I was not among that fortunate few, but I revere E. Estyn Evans, as one of my masters, and I believe him to have been one in a tiny aristocracy of the mind who created the intellectual world we inhabit and whose writings will inspire scholars yet unborn. I welcome this harvest of his effort and the cogent programme it sets before us.

Start here, he taught, in this place, muddy beneath the feet, cloudy overhead, green upon the eye. In a lecture this book includes, named for a scholar who overreached in comparative enthusiasm, Prof. Evans said we must first know the local instance. Situating ourselves on particular earth, we prevent abstractions from carrying us away and tangling us in the filaments of our obsessions. This firm place displays to us a configuration of traits, a peculiar personality. Behind the measurable, depictable face of things, lies the dynamic revealed by analysis: the dialectic of environmental and historical forces, blent by will, managed by human beings. Emplaced, they do the best they can, given their limited resources and the storms that wreck their plans and keep them poised for contingency. The locale, its personality, is the yield of human enterprise, deserving understanding and, like any work of art, appreciation.

In his book *Mourne Country*, written in and about a high corner of northeastern Ireland, Prof. Evans has provided for all time a model study of one place as the record of exchange between the environmental and the historical, mediated by the human. A taste of that grand book can be found in this volume. Every place unfolds through a particular concatenation of force and counterforce, compromise and accident. It is special in its pattern of broken rock and moulded earth. Yet all places interconnect. They meet and merge at their pervious borders. Border lands, Prof. Evans asserts, are rich in invention. Separation is defied by mobile, multicultural individuals, and his teacher, H.J. Fleure, noted that Prof. Evans was such a one, crossing in his youth the line dividing the English from the Welsh. Prof. Evans was attracted to travellers like himself—the adventurers of the Neolithic, the pioneers of the American frontier, the pedlars of Armagh—who go from place to place, inflecting the deep order with surprise.

Prof. Evans had his centres: Belfast, where he lived and taught; the Mournes, where he settled down to study; Antrim, where he was drawn by nature and tradition. But in his writings these fit as pieces into the larger puzzle of Ulster. The intransigent, fractious personality of Ulster charmed him into essays designed to capture its topographical, cultural, and political spirit in prose. Then working to establish the Ulster Folk and Transport Museum, he rendered to the people of the place a compact picture of their own complexity. It is one of the finest open-air museums in the world, where buildings, brought from throughout the province and fastidiously rebuilt, assemble for a regional portrait. Elaborated from his vision by his students G.B. Thompson and Alan Gailey, the museum reconstitutes the personality of Ulster.

Mourne Country remains the great, intense study of a single place. His museum symbolically incarnates his region. Then Prof. Evans lifts to the watery horizon to depict the regional variation within a geographical whole. Through his famed *Irish Heritage* and its noble successor *Irish Folk Ways*, details from his notebooks—lovely sketches of whitewashed farmhouses, of fields and fences and the tools used to labour the earth—combine to create an image of Ireland as both a unity and a cultural collage.

Regional diversity, the outcome of the collision of mind and matter on particular ground, should prompt in us, Prof. Evans argues, more than tolerance. Our differences should be held as precious and nurtured in education, for in providing us natural resistance to the mediocrity of the age, the diversity of our cultural inheritance holds an essential resource for adjustment to future change.

Counselling an appreciation of difference, Prof. Evans offers a liberal's solution to the ongoing problem of Ireland. The sea rolls on every side; the unity of the island is assured. Within its green space, the variety derived from environmental adaptation and historical synthesis contains the vitality people require in their quest for life. In *The Personality of Ireland*, the capstone of his achievement, Prof. Evans not only gives us the best description of Ireland, its oneness and its diversity, but as well the best description we have in any slim volume of one among the world's community of nations.

Then gently raising his gaze again, acknowledging the interactions to which archaeology attests and stressing the pastoral experience, Prof. Evans positions Ireland within the Atlantic zone, running from the Iberian peninsula up to snowy Norway. At that point, suddenly, his project soars like a skyrocket, lifting from the closely studied place to spatter the darkness with a shower of light. From the Ireland he has seen and trodden, he abruptly gestures to Japan, to Africa, to North America, collecting samples and illuminating the particular through the general and the general through the particular. The process is clear in his early piece on the Pyrenees. Prof. Evans carries us back and forth across the mountainy divide, showing how it conditioned history, and then, once we have followed him into understanding, he urges our attention to India, to Wales, to Greece, to the general traits shared by high border country. Solid and valiant at once, his work claims our attention and must continue to inspire us for generations to come. The focus of the observant scientist, secure in specialization, and the reach of the humanist, oblivious to academic boundaries, are weak in themselves, but when they combine, they produce the intelligent toughness that characterizes the *œuvre* of E. Estyn Evans. My friends, the industrious artisans of Turkey, praise the great masters by saying that, like old plane trees, they are rooted firmly in tradition, but rise up and branch wide in personal aspiration. The figure fits Prof. Evans. His work exhibits the security of one rooted in empirical study, and it displays an expansive stretch that was emboldened by the archaeologist's long view and that incorporates the humanist's brave desire to speak of what is good and true and fine.

The unity of confidence and courage, which Prof. Evans practised in public lectures, is effected in his writing by a marvellous grace of thought and elegance of style. His cadenced sentences avoid the pinched dialect of the academy, resist the tug of scholastic fashion, invite the interest of the outsider, and adhere, always, to the highest standards of his craft. Once, in reviewing a book on rural trades, he chided its author for not crafting his prose with the same precision and affection that his subjects devoted to their making of baskets and boats. Leaky, lumpy writing galled him, and he strove to make his own both useful and beautiful.

Gwyneth Evans, who knows better than anyone, saw in her handsome husband a poet struggling in the confines of an austere scholar. On occasion, the poet breaks free, and this volume includes examples of the delightful result. But I am not sorry that, in most of his work, the poet and scholar con-

tinued to battle. Ireland is blessed with poets, all of whom in recent times—
John Hewitt, Louis MacNeice, Patrick Kavanagh, Michael Longley,
Richard Murphy, Thomas Kinsella, John Montague, Seamus Heaney—
have, like Prof. Evans, found in the epiphanic moment, in the little local
instance, an excuse for a meditation on the general course of human experience. Prof. Evans saw first the metaphoric potential that lay in the bog and
that Seamus Heaney, most deservedly the recipient of the Nobel Prize,
turned then to deep verse. Brilliant poets abound in Ireland. I am grateful
that Prof. Evans chose to confine himself by the constraints of his discipline.
Within them, in the terms set by his craft, Prof. Evans was, in truth, a poet
of the land in the great Irish tradition.

To say that Prof. Evans was at once a scientist, a humanist, and a poet, is
to make a fair beginning in the assessment of the man's work. But treating
his writings as a unit, seeing them in the way he saw the land, as an expression of personality, I need to say more. For one thing, his works spray with
wit, the playful quality he enjoyed in the countryman, the good humour he
employed, especially, when meeting the reality of discord, whether in tru-
culent Ulster or in the narrow, contentious domain of the scholar. It is good
that this book includes his review of Rory de Valera's archaeological study,
and his thoughts on patriotic oratory and Parisian Orange Lodges, for they
capture the robust, amusable mood in which he confronted the difficult.

Another quality in the man that marbles his works is loyalty. Writing in
the booklet published to commemorate fifty years of geography at Queen's
University in Belfast, where he was for forty years the mainstay of the
Department, Prof. Evans emphasized the loyalty of his friends and colleagues. He praised them for a virtue that reached full tide in himself. Loyalty is built through generosity, the hospitable give and take, and it is
founded upon kindness. His kindness, his willingness to collaborate despite
differences in condition, credentials, and prestige, draws comment in the
fine essay in intellectual history with which John Campbell closes this
volume, and it was a trait of his from which I benefited over a quarter of a
century.

When I stood in the chaste, beautiful church that had been reconstructed
at the Ulster Folk and Transport Museum, my role was to represent the
scholars from abroad who had willingly received his impress, and my task
was to say a few words at the memorial service. I was compelled in the
moment to an epic trope. I thought of old Nestor upbraiding and challeng-
ing the warriors before Troy with accounts of the heroes of the past, and I
described Prof. Evans, not extravagantly, as a hero fit to inspire us in this
decadent era.

I recalled then how I was not brought into Ireland by a sentimental, genealogical search. My ancestors, many of them, were Irish, but my identity is regional, not ethnic, and Ireland beckoned me through its excellence, in particular the excellence of its writers: W.B. Yeats, J.M. Synge, Lady Gregory, Sean O'Casey, James Joyce, Samuel Beckett—and E. Estyn Evans. I spoke of the fullness of the man. He was a writer whose art could cross the Atlantic and tell a boy to study his own place with care. He was a scientist whose findings laid the foundations upon which others could build, sturdily. He was a teacher, surrounded by students who admired him so completely that four festschrifts were published to honour him. He was an administrator who could squeeze through the labyrinth of an academic bureaucracy to establish a great department. He was a man so generous that he sought through the radio and the public museum to make scholarly concerns popular. He was a man so kind that, together with Gwyneth, in a union that seemed perfect to the visitor, he could welcome me and my wild brood, muddy and chilled from the hills of Fermanagh, into a gracious home and supply us with sparkling talk, soothing drink, and clean warm beds.

Prof. Evans was a gentleman, a rigorous scientist, a witty narrator, a brave thinker, and an elegant stylist. There have been such men as E. Estyn Evans, such heroes of the intellect. They challenge us, the lesser people of later days, to do the best we can in this splendid, disappointing place.

Gwyneth Evans: drawing by Raymond Piper

ESTYN
A Biographical Memoir by Gwyneth Evans

This selection of some of Estyn Evans' many essays written over a period of fifty years has no unifying theme save a sympathetic reverence for landscape and ordinary people. It contains some serious, academic pieces, as well as what he referred to as his lighthearted and even frivolous writings, composed mostly for his own pleasure and relaxation before he discovered that through the thirties and forties, the then *Manchester Guardian* paid a much-appreciated three guineas for a short, back-page article.

I have always felt that inside the austere, disciplined academic there was a poet struggling to break free. He loved playing and experimenting with words, painting in watercolours, and he had a lively sense of the ridiculous. This is his account of his first landing in Ireland in 1928:

It was the merry month of May. The sight that greeted me that May morning as I travelled from Larne to Belfast was of hillsides 'white over' with May blossom. The whitethorn did not grow in such profusion in the even, pleached hedgerows of my native Shropshire. This was my fateful introduction to hedges which, 'like prisoners wildly overgrown with hair, put forth disordered twigs' to the fairy thorns of the pastoral Irish landscape, which was soon to become my consuming interest.

Later, he explained his emotions on first seeing the Antrim hills in May-time: 'In a similar environment Robert Burns wrote of the ecstasy of the first fine Sunday in May', and he referred to Kilvert writing on the Welsh border of 'the one day in Spring when the beauty of everything culminates and strikes one's notice and a presentiment comes that one will not see such

1

loveliness for another year'. He added, 'I confess that each May I look for that day and recognize it when it comes.'

He had come to Ireland for an interview on his twenty-third birthday (29 May), and he was appointed to take charge of the new Department of Geography at the Queen's University of Belfast.

I first met Estyn on 31 May 1928. It was my twentieth birthday, and I was feverishly revising for my finals at the University College of Wales at Aberystwyth. The late twenties and thirties were years of real depression and jobs were almost impossible to get. Estyn's friends arranged a celebration picnic to the lovely Llyfnant Valley in Cardiganshire, and one of them said, 'I will fetch that girl I know you will get along with.' Three years later we were married.

Belfast in the thirties was a pleasant place if one was fortunate enough to have a secure job. There was appalling poverty, with large numbers of barefoot urchins and women in shawls. This ubiquitous garment had diversity in its use: a weary old woman would find comfort in its enveloping warmth and anonymity, while pretty young girls would wear one provocatively as a high fashion item. To us, men and women seemed to have stereotyped roles—one seldom saw a woman on a bicycle, and never a man pushing a pram—and we were amazed at the quantities of Guinness and whiskey consumed. But Belfast had no pall of black smoke hanging over it like the South Wales coalfield—or the highly industrialized towns of the north of England. For an industrial city Belfast was so nearly in the country that one could walk out in any direction into an unspoilt landscape. Now much of that country is covered by new houses. We found its people shrewd, robust and friendly. Many were no more than second-generation city folk, and had carried their country ways of neighbourly helpfulness with them.

My Welsh-speaking father's mother (our *mamgau*) had no English and we no Welsh, but she was a loving old lady and we got on wonderfully without any language. My mother, a dynamic Scot, had come to West Wales to teach. She was always treated with respect and courtesy, but she was an interloper in a foreign country. Once a year we went north to visit relations, and felt aware of how different we were from our Scottish cousins. We realized that mother, by marrying outside her group, had lost caste. There were other differences, too. W.R. Rodgers, in his perceptive 'Black North', writes, 'Ask an Irishman how far it is to a place and the distance diminishes with your weariness.'[1] That would also be the Welshman's reaction. But to my Scottish Presbyterian mother truth was absolute, and the differences between her version of truth and mine are a vivid nightmare of my childhood. (I have since learnt that Welsh Nye Bevan and Scottish Jennie Lee based their marital harmony on a formula, 'That is my truth—now tell me yours.')

Estyn's background was equally unusual. His father, George Owen Evans, was born in 1865, and came from the Denbighshire coalfield, that narrow industrialized strip between the North Wales foothills and the English border. Orphaned when he was nine, he worked first in the local claypits; when he was twelve he was working underground, not hewing coal, but tending the fan that ventilated the mine. Because he was working underground he was eligible for three half-days' schooling a week. Through attending Sunday School and Chapel, and with the help of friends, he educated himself and was able to enter the Calvinistic Methodist College of Bala in his early twenties where he qualified as a minister. In 1906 he wrote a detailed account, now in the National Library of Wales, of his early years in his second language, English. Estyn wrote that he found little trace of proletarian revolt in the story of his father's early days: 'Of Welsh nationalism there was no trace at all.'

Estyn's father moved from a relatively comfortable living in Shrewsbury, where he ministered to a Welsh-speaking congregation, to a poor parish just across the Welsh border, so that his family should benefit from the inexpensive secondary education available in Wales following the 1889 Education Act. Unlike today, all education was through the medium of English so the parents made a firm decision to speak only English to their children, using Welsh as a secret language to speak to each other. The children had to walk a long mile over an unmarked border into England to get to the one-room Anglican primary school, with a male and female teacher. Being different, they were teased mercilessly, and as Non-Conformists they were excluded from religious education classes. Their distinctive Welsh names, Vyrnwy, Tanat, Hafryn and Estyn, were an acute embarrassment, so they became Sam, Tom, Harry and Bill. All five children (Deva was the only girl) got to secondary school and three of the four sons went to university.

Estyn completed his degree in Professor H.J. Fleure's Department of Geography and Anthropology at Aberystwyth in 1925. His external examiner, Sir John Myres of Oxford, realized that he had exceptional ability and suggested that he do graduate work under his supervision at New College Oxford. Because Geography was held in low esteem there, Estyn decided on an archaeological subject for his master's degree. But he never was to arrive: during the long summer vacation he started haemorrhaging from his lungs and ironically, on the very day when he should have gone up to Oxford, he was taken to a small sanatorium near Ironbridge.

After six months as a tuberculosis patient, Professor Fleure and friends arranged his convalescence in Wiltshire, to be cared for physically and intellectually by a keen amateur archaeologist general practitioner. Dr R.C.C. Clay was a remarkable man from a family which had been settled in Fovant as doctors for three generations. There was no Health Service in the twenties, so many doctors provided free treatment for impoverished patients and relied on fees from their more wealthy patients. Dr Clay had survived tuberculosis after losing a lung, and afterwards helped young sufferers. He was full of Downland lore. Along with poetry he wrote charming essays and a book of children's fairy stories, which our own children enjoyed. During the war he also wrote a book on first-aid. He was passionately fond of trees and indeed of all wild things. Estyn used to say that to be with him was a liberal education. They became firm friends and exchanged letters and visits regularly until Dr Clay died in 1971.

Wiltshire was and is a prehistorian's paradise. Estyn enjoyed long days helping Dr Clay with his excavations which included the avenue at Stonehenge, and visiting many famous sites such as Woodhenge, where Colonel and Mrs Cunnington were discovering the forerunner of Stonehenge, and Windmill Hill and Avebury, where Alexander Keiller was investing the profits of Dundee Marmalade in archaeological research. Through Dr Clay he met other archaeologists, among them the redoubtable O.G.S. Crawford who used to cycle over from Hampshire to visit Clay. Estyn was told that Crawford's famous brainchild, the periodical *Antiquity*, had been conceived in the inglenook of Clay's manor house. Altogether it was a first-rate crash course in archaeological techniques, and the interlude of Estyn's illness was to shape the rest of his life.

In Wales, as in Ireland earlier this century, many young people suffered from tuberculosis, and the survival rate was often less than 50 per cent. But Estyn appreciated that his illness was not an unmitigated disaster. The enforced rest enabled him to see that there was more to life than competitive exams, giving him time to think and read creatively. Tuberculosis was a great leveller and he long remembered the warm sanatorium friendships he made with both a poacher and gamekeeper, and they with each other while they were together. His close contact with archaeologists over this period made him think like an archaeologist, viewing human history against a backcloth of thousands of years. Other disciplines see man's development in a context of hundreds of years or less. Later his opponents who resisted his efforts to create a Geography Department used to say of him, 'He is not a Geographer, he is an Archaeologist', and later his warmest friendships were with archaeologists, many working in the south of Ireland.

Between moving from Wiltshire to Belfast he worked for a short time on the 14th Edition of the *Encyclopaedia Britannica* under Professor Fleure's supervision, learning to convey the maximum of meaning using the minimum of words. He used to say a spell of such work should be compulsory for aspiring politicians.

Before Estyn left for Belfast, Fleure arranged a meeting for him with his old friend Thomas Jones, who had worked in Ireland for the Barrington Trust, and had held the Chair of Economics at the Queen's University of Belfast from 1909 to 1911. Thomas Jones was then Under-Secretary to the Cabinet. He had been Lloyd George's secretary from 1916, and his advisor in the negotiations which led to the Partition of Ireland. He told Estyn that when negotiations got tough they lapsed into Welsh to the amazement of the two proud Gaels, Griffiths and Michael Collins. He briefed Estyn about Belfast, and told him something about Queen's, but the personalities he remembered best were his friends in the Workers' Educational Association.

Estyn arrived at Belfast to take up his new appointment in the late September of 1928. On his arrival in Belfast from Liverpool he was interested to see Queen's Island where so many famous ships had been built, but instead of the noise of industrial activity, there was silence, broken only by the crake of corncrakes. The migrating birds had taken possession of the silent, empty shipyard, bringing home to him the depths of the depression.

At Queen's he found the trauma of Partition and a bitter civil war still unhealed. The Establishment, wishing to be neutral or apolitical, insisted that all new members of staff sign a promise to be impartial. But that was not a new demand. When Queen's first admitted students in 1849, each professor on taking office was obliged to sign a declaration promising to 'carry out his duties faithfully' and to 'abstain from teaching or advancing any doctrine or making any statement derogatory to the truths of revealed religion, or injurious or disrespectful to the convictions of any person in any class or audience'. In addition he had to undertake not 'to discuss any subject of Politics or Polemics tending to produce contention or excitement'. One wonders how much this wording had changed down the years. I believe all signatories tried to honour the promise, but this is a place of different perceptions. When, after 1936, Estyn started taking students on fieldwork in rural Ireland it was said he sympathized with the nationalist cause. Many years later in 1949, after he had addressed a meeting of the Ulster Irish Society in New York on the theme 'Visit Ulster', a member of the Society congratulated Unionist Cabinet minister Dehra Parker on the fellow from Belfast. 'He did your cause more good', he said, 'than a dozen political agents.' Yet all Estyn had spoken about was of the complex geological structure of the country (the underlying cause of the unusual, exciting scenery), the strength and diversity of the Ulster people, and the house-types and archaic tools.

It has been said that Queen's University in 1928 was like a nineteenth-century Scottish academy, and the Arts Faculty staff were mostly dedicated Scottish academics who equated scholarship with an elitist tradition of classics, languages, mathematics, logic and metaphysics. The degree structure had been copied from Scotland when Scotland was on the point of abandoning it. Students were treated rather like schoolchildren. They had to attend lectures and sign a register to obtain class certificates, without which they were not allowed to sit examinations. Honours students were selected on school records, entrance examinations and perhaps prowess at sport. It was impossible for a pass student to move to honours.

Livingstone, the first of three Oxford Vice-Chancellors, had recently been appointed. He was resented because of his English background and for having seditious ideas: a Department of Geography, and a school of Extra Mural Studies (to link up with the Workers' Educational Association), now Continuing Education. Geography was not recognized as a university subject in Scotland and Scottish professors were reluctant to weaken the established traditions.

The University had little income and few students; new Departments would erode numbers. But Livingstone aimed to expand the University and was already persuading the District Councils to support it financially. Portadown was the first to respond with a promise of 1/4d (a farthing) on each pound of the rates. Starting a new Department against such stiff opposition was like engaging in a marathon chess game. When Estyn asked for an assistant he was told he could not have one because he did not have an honours school, and when he suggested that his student numbers merited consideration for the formation of an honours school he was told that was impossible because he did not have an assistant.

He was rescued from this difficult position by Professor H.O. Meredith, who had been appointed to the Chair of Economics when Thomas Jones moved on in 1911, and was therefore automatically Dean of the Faculty of Commerce. Meredith suggested that geography students should combine with Economics and so attain honours status. This gave the new Department some much needed respectability, but it was not until 1947, when geography was granted a single honours course, that the Department thrived and became one of the largest in the Arts Faculty. Meredith stayed at Queen's until he retired in 1942, except for the war years of 1914–18 when he was conscripted for government work. He had been a brilliant undergraduate at Cambridge, an automatic Apostle, to which select group he introduced his close friend E.M. Forster, who used to visit him in Belfast and thus became friendly with Forrest Reid.

In 1923 Meredith was a co-founder with George Buchanan of the Northern Drama League, and his main interest in the University became the production of plays, including the Greek classics (sometimes in his own translation). He had great influence among the more intelligent students, and in

1926 he took the Queen's group to the Abbey in Dublin with plays he had produced himself.

In the thirties he produced plays for groups of unemployed workers of Belfast—those produced for the shipyard workers are perhaps best remembered—the money raised being used to alleviate their poverty. Meredith was regarded by some of his scientific colleagues as a dangerous intellectual. I have heard staid academics refer to him as unreliable or a maverick, but I remember him as my husband's kindest and most distinguished colleague.

The early years from 1928 were busy years. Estyn was nursing his infant Department and building a class library of geographical books, and a map collection in the least expensive way possible. He also started the Belfast branch of the Geographical Association, thus facilitating regular meetings of Geography teachers, and at the same time was working on his MA thesis on 'Some Late Bronze Age Industries in Western Europe'. He was awarded his MA with distinction in 1931.

The new Department was housed in a cluster of wooden huts on the site of the present Whitla Hall. They had been hastily erected in 1914 to serve as a hospital for the Ulster Division of the British army, recruited from members of the Ulster Volunteer Force, who had trained illegally to fight Home Rule and afterwards suffered so tragically at the Somme. The walls of the new Department were very thin so it was possible to hear the Professor of History declaiming his beautifully polished lectures for students to take down verbatim: 'The Poles are a pack of licentious, corrupt, barbaric backwoodsmen.'

Estyn was astonished by the magnificence of the main University building. Britain has been strongly criticized for her meanness and insensitivity to Irish people during the famine in the 1840s, yet in 1845 had founded and funded three University Colleges. Wales on the other hand had been denied any third-level institution and from the mid-nineteenth century Welsh people raised subscriptions to establish their own university. The University College of Wales at Aberystwyth, which opened in 1872, was paid for entirely by public subscription.

From the tensions of nursing Geography it was a relief for Estyn to turn to Archaeology (there was no separate Department at this time—the demand for the subject came in the forties). Members of the Queen's Arts staff showed little interest in the immediate environment, but local people were aware that the stones from megaliths had been used for road metal, and farmers were spreading the soil from historic forts on their fields. Britain had had a Prehistoric Monuments Council since 1908 for the protection of prehistoric sites, but there was no such body in Ireland. Concerned members of the local Naturalists' Field Club founded a field-survey. Miss Maisie

Gaffikin, the enthusiastic amateur organizer, had heard of Estyn's Wiltshire experiences and asked him to work with her. Their survey was published under the title of 'Raths and Megaliths' in *The Irish Naturalists' Journal* in 1935, but it was incomplete. It only included the few monuments marked on Ordnance Survey maps, and other well-known, accessible sites; a co-ordinated survey was clearly necessary.

In 1930 Oliver Davies ('OD' to his friends) came to Belfast to lecture in Classical Archaeology and Ancient History. A classicist by training, he had no experience of excavating, and little knowledge of local prehistory, but he was tremendously energetic and robust—and willingly agreed to co-operate with Estyn in conducting a detailed field survey of the province's antiquities. No mountain or hill was too high or steep for OD to scale, no bog too deep or dirty for him to wade through in his quest for prehistoric sites. However, one had to suggest to him that if he phrased his question to a simple countryman, 'Do you know of any big stones or giants' graves round here?' he would get more information than to, 'Are there any megalithic monuments in the immediate vicinity?' This was a remarkable partnership, OD and Estyn, the one with his public school and Oxford background, and the other a scholarship boy from an obscure Welsh college. Together, with the help and strong support of local field-clubs, they were to revolutionize Ulster archaeology during the thirties.

Estyn and OD subdivided the province for the six-county survey: George Paterson took charge of Armagh and the south, Mr McL. May mid Ulster, while Lady Dorothy Lowry-Corry, one of the 5th Earl of Belmore's many unmarried sisters, found her vocation in locating and listing the many sites in Fermanagh. The Stormont government had promised to publish the Survey's findings, and provided some money for maps. The work could not have been done without the help of local people, doctors, postmasters, parish priests and teachers. In country interests of this sort there is little division between the people in the north of Ireland. The volunteers who participated were true amateurs doing that work at weekends, during holidays, and in the long summer evenings. In the early thirties few people had cars, though those who had were generous—but the work was mostly done by walking and cycling, and using public transport. Checks had to be made on all new sites, as well as those already recorded, and so we came to know the country and its people, from those of the big house, to the small cottage. As newcomers we were surprised by the number of charming single women we met—the spiritual widows of the Somme and other battles? Of these days Estyn wrote later,

Thus I came to know the deserted hillsides whose prehistoric sites had to be tracked down and recorded, and I fell under the spell of the Ulster countryside. I sensed a link, spiritual and vocational, between the fairy-haunted dolmens of ancient farmers, and the peasant culture still living in the hills. And I began to turn from Archaeology to Ethnology, folk-life, and to the unrecorded traces of cultural history.

In 1932 Estyn and OD decided to bolster the survey with some excavations of typical monuments, following a suggestion made to Estyn, by Sir Arthur Keith at the British Association meeting of 1928, that the prehistoric monuments of the north of Ireland differed from those of the South. They decided to excavate a cairn with a semi-circle of standing stones forming a forecourt on the infertile foothills of the Mournes at Goward near Hilltown. The paucity of the finds was reflected in the continuing poverty of the place. Only a few worked flints and shards of round-bottomed Neolithic pots were found—previous digs had been undertaken by rapacious amateurs in search of crocks of gold and spectacular finds. The Goward dig attracted much interest and many visitors. In 1960 Rory de Valera was to describe it as the beginning of 'a new approach to Irish Megalith research'. After Goward, Estyn and OD were to excavate more cairns of this type which they christened Horned Cairns (now court graves). Browndod and Ballyalton come to mind. Subsequently they realized they could do more, and train more students, if they worked separately.

Estyn's excavating culminated on Lyles Hill, a large County Antrim habitation site. It was first noticed and photographed in 1927 by Wing Commander A.C. Wright of Aldergrove Airport. Early in 1937, while measuring the site for the Archaeological Survey, Estyn picked up a large piece of Neolithic pottery complete with rim and decided to excavate later in the year. The excavation continued through the summer and in 1938, but all the excavations stopped in 1939 because of the threat of imminent war. At first Estyn and his helpers were overwhelmed at the magnitude of the site. Funds and technical assistance were woefully inadequate and they were aware of the inevitability of war with Germany. They concentrated on the small mound within the enclosure and, as at Navan, a segment was left intact, so that their findings could be checked in the future with new techniques. At most digs finds cause excitement, but at Lyles Hill they became an embarrassment. They turned up thousands of Neolithic potsherds. When Lyles Hill was first identified, R.A.S. Macalister had written, 'I do not suppose that ten pieces of Irish Neolithic pottery are known to be in existence.'[2] After Lyles Hill Estyn never excavated again, but he always tried to visit any dig in progress in any part of Ireland.

By the end of the thirties such was the proliferation of unpublished excavation reports that in 1938 Estyn and OD, despite the threat of war, decided to revive the *Ulster Journal of Archaeology* in a third series. (Until 1948 the journal was issued from Estyn's Department and it is still published.)

Broadcasting live from the Ulster countryside: taking recording equipment to the entrance of the limestone caves at Marble Arch, County Fermanagh, and in action below (see pp.188-9).

With the outbreak of war OD immediately volunteered for intelligence work. He had worked in the Balkans, but he was not called up until early in 1942, so during the early years of the war he continued his archaeological survey work. He was conspicuous with his mop of flaxen hair and individual style of dress, but his impeccable accent and exquisite good manners gave him entry, and he was a welcome guest at the large country houses of Ulster. He rode a bright green bicycle, and his favourite sites happened to be in Republican districts west of the Bann. He was often followed by a posse of police, anxious to determine if he was a spy dropped from a German plane. Once, they caught up with him and asked him where he intended to spend the night. He gave them the name of a big house. 'But where did you spend last night?' OD's naïve reply, 'I slept with Mrs Parker', greatly amused the members of the RUC. For Dame Dehra was a formidable lady—Stormont's only female Cabinet minister. Estyn was very sad that OD did not return to the north of Ireland after the war, especially as there was a growing demand for a Department of Prehistoric Archaeology. OD became Professor of Archaeology at Pietermaritzburg, but continued to return for holiday periods, and to take a lively interest in Irish prehistory. In 1987 he met a premature death when he disturbed an intruder at his house in South Africa.

Estyn was active on other fronts throughout the thirties: he produced a small textbook on France (financially his most profitable publication). After the 1937 census he worked on the demography of Belfast, and produced maps showing the distribution of the religions in the different parts of the city. He also recorded the number of persons per room in the different districts. The religious distribution maps were published in the *Ulster Journal of Archaeology* in 1944, but maps giving the number of persons per room have vanished. The outbreak of war brought new responsibilities, and time for reflection. He started his first book on Ireland, *Irish Heritage*, as an 'adventure into uncharted seas'. He felt Ireland, which had escaped the industrial revolution and the worst of repressive Puritanism, was a treasure-house of old ways, and so, excluding the more recent crafts which were already documented, he wrote of archaic practices and outdated tools that were still used. He believed that it was necessary to study the past to understand the present.

Ten years later Louis MacNeice, writing in the *New Statesman and Nation*, observed, 'Most books about Ireland are a rehash of old materials, though there are a few like E.E. Evans' *Irish Heritage* which fill a notable gap',[3] and he included Maurice Craig's *Dublin 1760–1860* in that special minority. Estyn came into contact with Louis through his involvement in a disastrous literary endeavour. In the late forties Louis and W.R. (Bertie) Rodgers decided to produce the definitive book on Ireland to be called 'The

Character of Ireland' and published by the Oxford University Press. They asked all known specialists on Irish life to contribute a chapter. Estyn was asked to write on 'The Irish Countryman', which he wrote and sent to them within a month; but not all contributors delivered. Perfectionists continued to polish, some died before delivering and some never got started. Dan Davin, the Irish New Zealander then in charge of the Oxford Press, wrote in his tragi-comic book *Closing Times* (1975) about how, over the next twenty years, MacNeice and Rodgers failed to deliver, and how he chased them through every pub in Oxford and Dublin, until finally Louis, and then Bertie, eluded him by dying.

After the despair of the war came hope for a better world afterwards. Planning committees sprang up on which Estyn was glad to participate, believing that the knowledge gained from academic research should be available for use by the community. In 1946 he wrote 'The Ulster Country-side', published in 1947 on behalf of the Northern Ireland Planning Advisory Board. This was a policy document, a blueprint for action on rural planning and landscape conservation. It advocated the need to conserve landscape and wildlife and suggested national parks and nature reserves. It was not until 1965 that the policy was incorporated in the Amenity Lands Act.

In 1945 Queen's finally created a Chair of Geography, thus giving the Department Estyn had nurtured full status. This was in response to pressure from outside opinion, for there was still opposition to it at Queen's. In 1950 he was made an honorary member of the Royal Town Planning Institute. This was in recognition that he had been a pioneer in local urban research. At about this time he was tempted to move to another job. There were opportunities to return to Wales, but ironically he was reluctant because he was not fluent in Welsh which by the 1940s had become respectable.

Estyn felt that until the Department was fully recognized he had not fulfilled the trust that had been placed in him. Had he left before his chair was established he feared the improvements he had fought for would have been lost. From 1935 the radio had made it possible to reach a larger, if unseen, audience, and perhaps persuade more people of the benefits of an education in Geography. His first radio talk in 1934 was from Radio Éireann, but after 1935 he broadcast regularly on BBC's Belfast Station and sometimes on the then National Home Service. Later in the fifties, in the early days of television, he sometimes appeared on the popular programme 'Animal, Vegetable and Mineral'.

In 1948 Estyn was invited to Bowdoin College in Maine as visiting Professor. There was no precedent for a year's sabbatical, so it caused some consternation. A colleague objected to Queen's subsidising an unknown American college, but Vice-Chancellor David Keir pointed out that Bowdoin was over a hundred years older than Queen's, was one of the famous New England Ivy League colleges, and had sent many fine graduate students to Oxford! A London University lecturer took over at Queen's for the year, while Estyn was handsomely remunerated by Bowdoin College. He left Belfast feeling content—his Department was flourishing and he felt that a new mind at the top for a year could be valuable. The very day he left Belfast a lecturer was appointed to take charge of the new Department of Prehistoric Archaeology, while OD's old lectureship continued in Ancient History.

His first visit to America was by slow boat. After several uneventful days on board, the dramatic visual impact of the New York skyline seen from the sea was an everlasting memory, as was the kindness and generous hospitality of his American friends. The brilliance of New York—the spectacular luxury of the shops—and the quality and variety of food available everywhere was incredible to Europeans who had come from post-war austerity.

Bowdoin College, in the woods of Maine, goes back to the first half of the eighteenth century. New England was not a favourite point of entry for the Scots-Irish who came to America from 1720, but the first President of the college was a Mr McKeen from the north of Ireland. A flourishing Belfast and Bangor had grown up on the coast of Maine, but Newry inland had failed to develop. It was a wonderful, enlightening year. Bowdoin was steeped in recent history. Longfellow and Hawthorne had been students, and later Elijah Kellogg; Harriet Beecher Stowe had written *Uncle Tom's Cabin* while her husband held the Chair of Divinity at the College. The 'Stowe House' remained a tourist attraction.

Estyn enjoyed teaching American students. He found them more assured and articulate than their British counterparts, though perhaps not so advanced academically. Real scholarship develops in America at graduate school. Estyn's brief, besides teaching, was to give four public lectures and he was encouraged to speak to local groups. He was invited to visit and speak at other Ivy League colleges. He visited Harvard and took part in seminars, and he gave a series of lectures at Dartmouth College. There were bizarrely named groups too: 'The Daughters of the Revolution', 'The Colonial Dames', and 'The Odd Fellows of Bowdoinham'. He remembered hearing Churchill speak at the Boston Garden on 31 March 1949. Outside, Irish-Americans carried placards: 'Send this Bundle back to Britain.'

Bowdoin was a small college where one had the assurance that one belonged to a supporting family but in 1948/49 there was an underlying tension. Estyn had heard of McCarthyism, and of how McCarthy's committee to investigate un-American activities had been the scourge of the film-makers on the West Coast, but the Committee were now targeting WASPs on the East Coast. Estyn, being a visitor from Ireland, was devastated to be told that the junior senator from Wisconsin was an Irish American and a close friend of the head of the powerful Kennedy family. Edward Kirkland, the College Professor of American History, was President of the Association of American University Teachers. He had a lecture on Academic Freedoms which was in great demand, as was his skill in defending indiscreet academics. He explained to Estyn that McCarthy's methods were like those used in the Nazi movement. Friends were encouraged to inform on friends, and members of a family on each other. One could be judged guilty by association, or an indiscreet remark could be used as evidence years later. Kirkland got so involved in the sordid business that he was everlastingly grateful to Cambridge University for inviting him to become their visiting 'Pitt' Professor for a year, thus enabling him to escape to England.

Estyn left Bowdoin in 1949 with his first honorary degree, but I doubt if he realized how much he had been adopted by the Bowdoin family. Soon after he died in 1989, exactly forty years later, I had a charming, sympathetic letter from the then secretary of the College: 'So many members of the Bowdoin family', he wrote, 'came to admire Dr Evans during his year as Tallman Professor, and will always have happy memories of his visit.' A member of the community had seen Estyn's obituary in the London *Times*. Afterwards Estyn was to regard his first year in America as a kind of watershed: before everything had to be fought for; thereafter good things happened to him.

The early fifties were fruitful years. In 1951 he wrote *A Portrait of Northern Ireland*, one of the thirteen local guides published as part of the Festival of Britain—he was also a member of the local festival planning committee and he was closely involved in *Belfast in its Regional Setting*, produced for the British Association meeting in 1952.

Mourne Country also appeared that year. Estyn had been getting to know Mourne before going to America. He had always wanted to write a geographical study of a small area and initially favoured North Antrim and the Antrim Glens. He was fascinated by the juxtaposition of the chalk and basalt, and often quoted Charles Kingsley's description of Rathlin in *Westward Ho!* 'looking like a half drowned magpie in the sea'. But Harry Tempest, publisher of *Irish Heritage*, wanted a different book. He was a keen and proficient photographer and he had some wonderful photographs of Mourne. The Kingdom of Mourne is a compact and historic region and *Mourne Country* a good title. A friend found us a very basic cottage on the lower slopes of Slieve Donard, but Tempest was not amused. 'It will all be basic chores, and no writing if you live there', he threatened, overlooking the contribution the woman is prepared to make to the partnership. Estyn enjoyed his spells of living like a Mourne countryman. He walked the length and breadth of the mountains. He got to know the farmers, the fishermen and the granite workers. Perhaps it was the latter group he most amused with his constant questions. And he enjoyed 'passing the time' leaning over the half-door of the cottage. He felt assured that he had been accepted when one Spring day he asked a friendly local shopkeeper for some new potatoes to be told that there were none. 'But there is a boat in the harbour full of Mourne potatoes,' he replied. 'Them', said the Mourne man contemptuously, 'are Pilots—they are only fit for the English.'

In his introduction to *Mourne Country* Estyn wrote, 'I have written much of it on the seaward side of Slieve Donard, where I have only to lift my eyes to see the hills and watch the coloured seasons climbing from the golden whins to the glowing heathers and the snows.' A Canadian reviewer wrote of it, 'none but an Irishman could write with such depth of feeling for the land and those that call it home',[4] while the *Dublin Magazine* of April 1952 described it as 'a scholarly and fascinating book written in rigorous and lucid language that has moments of poetry'.

In 1955 he was invited to an international symposium organized by the Wenner-Gren Foundation for Anthropological Reasearch to be held at Princeton to discuss 'Man's Role in Changing the Face of the Earth', later described as 'the first large-scale evaluation of what has happened, and what is happening, to the earth under man's impress'. The millionaire Wenner Gren was of Swedish extraction and conspicuous in Europe during the late thirties and early forties. It has been suggested that he then had Nazi sympathies, but he later moved to the USA and supported research for conservation. Carl Sauer, the geographer from Berkeley, and Lewis Mumford, the planner, arranged the meeting and chaired many of its sessions.[5] The participants were mostly American, but there were also several from Britain—two members of the Cambridge Department of Ecology, Sir Charles Galton Darwin, H.C. Darby from London University, and Fraser Darling from Scotland—as well as others from Europe, Egypt and India.

The fifties was a good decade for Queen's University: it enjoyed increased government funding and was especially fortunate in its new Vice-Chancellor, Eric Ashby (later Lord Ashby of Brandon), a man of extraordinary sympathy and vision. Many old students who spoke appreciatively of Estyn at his memorial service in December 1989 had passed through the Department in the fifties. James Hawthorne, who was to become Controller of BBC Northern Ireland, said that his batch was Geog. 1 1950, which had hoped to take a year of Geography in its stride. It was known that the Department was run with sympathetic democracy—unusual in the University at the time—and that subsidiary students of the subject were welcomed and well looked after; and he went on to list other benefits. A Planning lecturer recalled that Evans had made local studies and pride in one's 'place' respectable, while the Rev. Canon Houston McKelvey remembered how Estyn had lectured on 'The Problems of the Nomad', using the biblical text. He said that in dealing with the tensions in his parish caused by shifts of population in the early years of the Troubles, what he had learned in the Geography Department was of more use to him then than the teaching of the Theological College.

While Estyn was a student he had visited Scandinavia and had seen and been impressed by Skansen and the other Folk Parks, and he knew the Welsh Folk Museum at St Fagans near Cardiff. He had seen other examples during his year in America. Ever since his first days in Ireland he felt that Ireland had as much or even more to preserve and display, but by the early fifties many of the old ways were fast disappearing, and it was necessary to act quickly. As with the survey of Ulster's prehistoric monuments, generous help and support came from across the community. The journal *Ulster Folk-Life* (established in 1955) grew out of this effort. The Committee on Ulster Folk Life and Traditions worked through the fifties collecting suitable verbal material and artefacts, while the Folk Museum Act was passed by the Stormont Parliament in 1958 (a year after the publication of his *Irish Folk Ways*). There was much searching for a suitable museum site. The Committee favoured one to the west of the city, which would have been more accessible to people living in the province's hinterland. But the site at Cultra had many attractive features. It was the right size and being an executor's sale it came at a bargain price (less than £30,000), so was within the Committee's tight budget. Later the adjacent estate was bought to house the Transport Museum, thus extending its territory to the lough shore.

Nowadays it is customary to disparage the Stormont government. Maybe there is much to criticize, but it did contain a variety of people. Brian Maginess, who died too young, was very helpful to the early Folk Museum movement. Perhaps its strongest ally was Dame Dehra Parker, grandmother of Prime Minister James Chichester Clark. Her father, according to Ulster gossip, was a country policeman who emigrated to America and worked first as a security officer in the stockyards at Chicago. When the meat-packing industry was growing he invested his savings there, but as Chicago expanded rapidly, he invested instead in real estate. He later married an American, saw his only daughter was well educated and returned to Ulster where he bought his local Big House. Dehra Parker was formidable, elegant and intelligent, but under the assurance and sophistication were the interests of an Irish country-woman. She always took an intelligent interest in archaeological excavations and was extremely helpful with the Folk Museum effort. Her enduring concern was with how legislation would affect the welfare of ordinary people, whose opinion she was not above asking.

Estyn felt that one of Stormont's worst mistakes was to site the proposed new city between Lurgan and Portadown. He thought the money would be better spent in upgrading Derry, Omagh and Cookstown west of the Bann. Delighted with the imposition of the Matthew Stop-line around Belfast to halt its urban sprawl, he now felt it was wrong to build a new town on good rich agricultural land and uproot families who had farmed there for generations. Above all, he thought that the proposed name of Craigavon was extremely insensitive, whether it was to celebrate Northern Ireland's founding father, or the gentleman who was handling the sale of the farms on the new city's site, and suggested instead the name of Knockmena, the townland at the centre of the site. But if the name had to be political, he said, 'Why not Dehraville to celebrate that you have a woman in your Cabinet?' A Mr Copnutt, an architect planner who had worked on Cumbernauld, the satellite town outside Glasgow, was interviewed for the post of New City Planner. This flamboyant character had hired a morning suit for his interview, and was duly appointed, but after visiting the site of the new city, he decided his brief was immoral and resigned immediately.

Estyn also disagreed about the siting of the new University of Ulster at Coleraine, again on prime agricultural land. He saw the cold windy bluff site as ill-chosen, all the more so as Derry and Armagh both contained many fine old buildings and populations hungry for learning. Armagh boasted the Planetarium, the Bishop's Palace, and other fine Francis Johnston buildings besides the Anglican and Catholic cathedrals, and was thus the ecclesiastical capital of Ireland. Derry had Magee College, and with the adjacent new Altnagelvin Hospital could have taken medical students. In each city people of both traditions worked and lobbied for the location. In Derry, members of the Magee Geography Department and members of other departments worked with John Hume, and even produced a handbook for the proposed new university. Ironically, some of their ideas were adopted at Coleraine. Perhaps there could have been two campuses, with Mathematics and Humanities at Armagh, and Biomedicine and Music at Derry? Both cities felt let down afterwards. Estyn often wondered if things might have been different had the University gone to these sites.

During the fifties Estyn had campaigned for the teaching of Social Anthropology in the University. He was encouraged by the appreciative reception given to a graduate's thesis from his Department in 1954 on 'Social Relations and Attitudes in a Northern Irish Rural Area',[6] and just as earlier he had nursed the infant Archaeology Department, he now fostered Social Anthropology until a new Department was created in 1960.

After 1960 life became easier. Geography was spoken of as a happy Department. There were many visits to America and Europe and even an invitation to lecture at the Sorbonne. He was President of both Section E (Geography) and Section H (Anthropology) of the British Association annual meetings. In 1965 he was made the first Director of the Institute of Irish Studies, then the only one in the United Kingdom, and in 1971 he gave the Wiles Lectures at Queen's (later embodied in his book *The Personality of Ireland*). When in 1967 an enthusiastic group of young architects and other concerned people founded the Ulster Architectural Heritage Society, he was delighted to be asked to become its first President, and presided over its meetings for the next ten years.

In 1978, at the half-centenary celebration of the Geography Department, Eric Ashby—then Chancellor of the University—recalled Estyn's initial difficulties: 'He had to establish the discipline of Geography against material resistances such as shortage of space and cash and psychological resistances such as the assumption that Geography is to be regarded as an appendage to Geology.'[1] But Estyn was never bitter. He admitted that his early years had been full of problems, but he wrote: 'Not all were peculiar to Queen's. The battle for full recognition had to be fought almost everywhere, the fight varying in intensity according to local circumstances, academic traditions, vested interests, and the personalities involved.'

Up until the early eighties he chaired Ulster's Ancient Monuments Advisory Council (having been a member of such an advisory body since 1935) and continued to attend the meetings of a similar body in the Republic. He remained a trustee of both the Ulster Museum and the Folk Museum. There was more he wanted to do, but failing eyesight slowed him down. He was comforted by constant visits from his old staff and students, and friends from the Republic. His last visit to the United States was in April 1979. He had been invited to the 75th-anniversary celebrations of the Association of American Geographers at Philadelphia. When he arrived at the dinner he learnt that nine merit awards were to be given; of those so honoured he was the only non-American. His citation ran: 'In recognition of his outstanding multidisciplinary work on cultural landscapes, as exemplified by his remarkable multifaceted studies of the Irish people and their land.'

Maybe he wasn't such a bad Geographer after all. He was certainly a wonderful husband!

REFERENCES

1   W.R. Rodgers, 'Black North', *New Statesman and Nation* (20 November 1943), pp.331–2.
2   R.A.S. Macalister, 'Some unsolved problems of Irish Archaeology', *Proceedings of the Royal Irish Academy*, 37 Section C (1927) pp.245–67. Ref on p.249.

3   L. MacNeice, 'About Ireland', *New Statesman and Nation*, 43 (17 May 1952), pp.590–2. Ref. on p.590.

4   Review by S. Morgan Powell in *The Montreal Star*, 17 May 1952.

5   M. Williams, 'Sauer and "Man's Role in the Changing Face of the Earth" ', *Geographical Review*, 77 (1987), pp.218-31.

6   R.L. Harris, 'Social Relations and Attitudes in a Northern Irish Rural Area – Bally-gawley'. Thesis presented for the degree of MA in the University of London, 1954.

7   Lord Ashby of Brandon, Foreword in J.A. Campbell (ed.), *Geography at Queen's. An Historical Survey* (Belfast 1978).

part I

THE MAKING OF THE IRISH LANDSCAPE IN PREHISTORY

In this Thomas Davis Lecture, delivered on Radio Éireann in January 1962, Evans introduces his listeners to environmental archaeology, an approach to the study of pre-, and later, history of which he was an Irish pioneer. A little of the detail is by now out of date: we know today, for instance, that humankind probably first entered Ireland a full thousand years before Evans suggests, and that these Mesolithic peoples were not quite as confined to north-east Ireland as he maintains. Similarly, subsequent research makes it seem likely that the population of Neolithic Ireland was substantially larger—and thus its landscape impact even more dramatic—than Evans implies; and also that the growing of cereal grains at high altitudes may have been more common that he suspects. Nevertheless, in all essentials, the picture he simply and vividly portrays retains considerable validity more than a quarter of a century later.

We like to think of the wilder parts of Ireland as being little altered by the works of man; in complete contrast, say, to the landscapes of industrial England. But if a prehistoric Irishman was to return to his native land, he would find the scene almost everywhere greatly changed. No doubt the towns and their traffic and the intricate pattern of roads would startle him most, but he would be astonished also at the wide views, the farms, houses, green fields and hedges, the great stretches of treeless country and the heather-grown hills and bogs. Only the larger waterways, the open coasts and the outlines of the highest hills still crowned by his burial cairns would be familiar to him. Conversely, if we could visit prehistoric Ireland, we would look in vain for many familiar landmarks: nearly all would be blotted out by a tangle of forest inhabited by prowling animals and broken by countless lakes and waterways loud with the cries of multitudes of birds.

An imaginative picture, you say, but in fact not a few scientists are devoting a good deal of time and thought to the task of reconstructing our prehistoric landscapes. By and large the phrase which is repeated in the history books—'a land of forest and swamps'—is not far from the truth, but we are now able to picture the scene in some detail. It is a subject which interests the archaeologist because he needs to know all he can about the environments of early man. It is a matter of interest to those who investigate changes of climate. It concerns the biologist who studies the history of plants and animals and the evolution of that most precious heritage, the soil. Again, changing environmental opportunities are likely to be reflected in changing economies and resources. House-building and tool-making, for example, were limited in former times by the locally available raw materials. Different types of land-use may require different types of settlement, whether dispersed or nucleated. Moreover, the anthropologist and ethnologist, tracing the origins and growth of our institutions, folklore and material culture, seek clues in the nature of the environments in which societies lived and worked. It should be remembered that the trees, flowers, birds and animals that surrounded prehistoric man meant more to him than they do to us: his fortune, his hopes and anxieties were closely linked to them: his luck, in short, was held to depend on his relationship with the world of nature. The wealth of folk-beliefs attaching to certain plants and animals is an index of long human association. If you think of the rich lore surrounding certain trees such as the rowan, hazel and white-thorn, it will not surprise you to be told that they are venerable natives. On the other hand many of the trees in the present-day landscape—unsung in legend—are fairly recent introductions: the beech, lime, horse- and sweet-chestnut, sycamore and nearly all the conifers. We too readily speak of virgin woods and untouched nature: the truth is that it would be hard to find any landscape which has remained in its prehistoric condition.

But before I try to explain how we set about reconstructing the prehistoric landscape I must define the word *prehistoric*. The archaeologist measures human prehistory in tens and even hundreds of thousands of years. On the other hand someone has said that the end of prehistoric times in Ireland did not come until the Great Famine. What he meant was that a great deal of human history up to that time passed unrecorded among a peasant population who lived in an orally transmitted tradition. We know, however, that history of a kind has been written in Ireland for some 1500 years, though the fifth century, as the many uncertainties surrounding the figure of St Patrick remind us, strictly belongs to the protohistoric era. The last centuries before Christ mark the end of the fully prehistoric period, but for the purposes of this talk I will include the protohistoric era and end with the Anglo-Norman invasion.

If it is not easy to say when prehistory ends, it is far more difficult to say when it begins in any particular region, partly because of uncertainties of dating and partly because fresh evidence may turn up at any time. On present evidence, the older forms of Palaeolithic man who inhabited Western Europe and England, did not reach Ireland. We need not concern ourselves, then, with interglacial landscapes, or with the old Stone Age hunters who in France and Spain made their magic cave paintings.

Before man could reach this westernmost outpost of Europe, he either had to be able to cross considerable stretches of sea or he had to wait until convenient land bridges were temporarily available during the post-glacial readjustments of land and sea levels. In either case this takes us back about 8000 years to the early parts of what archaeologists call the Mesolithic period, and the probability is that man came in by boat. He came as a fisher, fowler and forest-hunter, not yet a farmer. But logically we must begin our survey of the prehistoric landscape at that time, with the first appearance of man, because with man came change. True, his influence was at first slight and restricted to that most accessible and first occupied part of Ireland, the north-east, but any human interference with the environment may have far-reaching consequences. One has only to think of the devastation that man-made forest fires can cause, even in the Irish climate.

Let us look at the country at the beginning of post-glacial time, about 10,000 years ago. The Quaternary ice-sheets which had repeatedly invaded Europe had finally melted away, leaving Ireland free of ice but encumbered with the litter of its retreat, the lowlands a tangle of lakes and water courses. In the almost treeless tundra the most conspicuous creatures were giant long-horned deer—the so-called Irish elk. Many of the lakes, reduced in size by silting, are still with us, but countless smaller stretches of water are now marked by marshy hollows or by bogs which grew as vegetation choked them. Others have been artificially drained and turned into productive meadowland. As the climate improved a scrub of birch and willow spread over the land, followed in turn by hazel, the Scots pine, oak and elm. By the time man arrived the forest was fully established, extending far up the mountain sides and flourishing, even on the edge of the Atlantic where today trees are rarely seen.

You may ask how we are able to reconstruct the composition and distribution of these ancient forests. Identifiable remains of wood are frequently preserved in peat and lake-mud, and the most common trees of successive periods can also be recognized from the charcoals left in prehistoric hearths and cremation burials. But it is mainly from the pollen grains, scattered so profusely and one would think so ephemerally from the vanished forests, that identifications of tree and plant species are made. The pollen grains of

25

successive centuries survive in enormous numbers at all depths in the bogs. Techniques of microscopic pollen analysis were first developed in Scandinavia over thirty years ago, and they have been applied to Ireland with notable success by Mr Frank Mitchell of Trinity College, Dublin. More recently the vegetation succession, established in its relative sequence by the stratification of the deep bogs, has been given an absolute chronology by means of radio-carbon dating. Not all archaeologists are convinced of the reliability of these dates, but it must be admitted that they are remarkably consistent. The most striking conclusion is that farming activities which had considerable effects on the ancient forests were already well established in many parts of Ireland over 5000 years ago, a thousand years earlier than the date accepted until recently by most archaeologists.

Botanists refer to the vegetation cover that had reached its maximum development about the fifth millennium BC as the post-glacial climax vegetation. Sea-level stood high, and maritime climatic influences remained for some 2000 years even more powerful than they are today. This climatic period is therefore termed 'Atlantic'. We can describe the vegetation as mixed oak forest. In fact, responding to the very damp conditions, the alder was one of the commonest trees, while pine was relatively restricted, though it held its own on sandy moraines and in areas of thin soil. The elm—presumably the wych-elm—was well-distributed, especially on the calcareous soils of the Central Plain, and in the west. The oak flourished best on heavy soils. Only at the thinning forest edge high up the hillsides did the birch maintain its foothold to any extent. Hazel and holly, too, found the dense high forest cover relatively inhospitable. Nor was the ash at all common. Only the highest hilltops were free of forest. The pollens of grasses are relatively scarce. That mildest corner of Ireland, Kerry and West Cork, in many ways a region on its own, was already probably distinguished by it forests of scrub oak and holly in which Lusitanian species such as the arbutus or strawberry tree flourished.

It is not to be wondered at, when one thinks of this riot of tree-growth, that man for long clung to the sea coasts and the waterways, depending on fish, fowl and game. Only by water, like the Canadian *voyageurs*, could he penetrate far inland; and from the north coast 'the fishy fruitful Bann' and Lough Neagh provided a ready highway into the interior. In time the early fisherfolk penetrated into Roscommon and the headstreams of the Shannon. Down the east coast their remains have been identified as far south as Dalkey Island. The habit of living on islands and lake-shores, which is so characteristic of Dark Age Ireland, seems to have persisted from the earliest penetration of fishers and fowlers from the north-east.

On present evidence it was well before the end of the Atlantic period that farming activities began to affect the Irish landscape. From before 3000 BC, dramatic changes began to take place in the composition of the forests and while it was fashionable until recently to attribute these changes to climatic factors—to the advent of a more continental phase—it is now thought that man was largely responsible. By the beginning of the Bronze Age, at say 1800 BC, the face of Ireland had changed considerably. No firm conclusions as to causes can yet be reached, but let me summarize the changes that took place and then give the arguments on both sides. The most significant change in the pollen counts is the decline of the elm as a constituent of the forest. There is simultaneously an increase of ivy and holly, and of oak, alder and hazel, while the light-loving ash now appears as a common tree on calcareous soils where the elm had formerly been dominant. The decline of the elm, which occurred throughout north-western Europe, has been attributed to disease, but even if this were so it could be a secondary effect, linked with the ecological disturbances carried by climatic change or by man's interference. The change to a more continental climate is implied in the term *sub-boreal* which is used for the period from 2500 to 500 BC. It is claimed that oceanic influences weakened and the temperature range increased, with warmer summers, colder winters and a lowering of mean annual temperatures. Not all those who believe that man was responsible for the landscape changes in Neolithic Ireland deny that there was climatic change or at least a temporary fluctuation—for climatic cycles are generally accepted—but they regard this factor as relatively unimportant.

It was Scandinavian workers who first advanced evidence of the consequences of human action. They observed that as the elm declined, abundant grass and weed pollens appeared, and among them they recognized the pollens of cereals, wheat and barley, neither of which is native to north-west Europe. Moreover, contemporary pottery (Neolithic), which one would anyhow expect to go with farming activities, was found not infrequently to have the impressions of grains of wheat and barley which had adhered to the pots while they were drying by the fire before being baked. Irish Neolithic pottery has also yielded impressions of wheat and barley grains. Indeed there is now pollen evidence from many parts of Ireland of extensive human interference with the forests, chronicled most abundantly by the appearance of the pollen of that most characteristic weed of cultivation, the rib-wort plantain.

Archaeologically, the Neolithic is also the period of the axe of polished stone, which was produced in great numbers in certain areas when suitable stone could be quarried, and traded far and wide. There is no longer any doubt that they were woodman's axes, used for the felling or at least the ring-barking of forest trees. I don't want to give the impression that we have a clear picture of the nature of the forest clearance or of the kind of agriculture that was practised. We do not know, for example, the part played by domestic animals, or whether, as has been suggested in Denmark, pastoral activities were supported to a large extent by leaf-fodder, of elm and ivy especially. When one recalls the almost complete absence of natural pasture land, save on the highest summits, one must reject the idea of wandering herds tended by nomadic pastoralists. On the other hand man must soon have learnt to take his domestic animals, following the example of the wild deer, to graze on the summit pastures in summer. We know that this custom of 'booleying' was very general in historic times, and its origins are presumably prehistoric. The attachment of Bronze Age man to the hills where his burial cairns commonly occur may thus be partly explained.

What is clear is that over considerable areas the forest was not able to re-establish itself or, at best, was replaced by forest of a different character. In this connection, leaving aside the question of climatic change, two factors must be borne in mind. First, the climax forest dominated by oak, elm and alder had engendered and protected a soil rich in humus. The removal of the forest cover, while making this soil available to man, exposed it to chemical leaching and to erosion, especially on the better drained slopes which early man preferred. Secondly, because of the rapid loss of fertility and because man had not the knowledge to replace it, the patches of cultivation were apparently abandoned after two or three seasons and invaded by forest weeds. Such a system of shifting cultivation would have affected a surprisingly large area in the course of hundreds of years. Many megaliths and chambered cairns, the most striking contributions of Neolithic man to the Irish landscape, now lie buried in peat bogs which grew over cultivated land. There were of course many types of forest, especially the pine groves and alder swamps, where the soils were too thin and poor or too wet to attract man. And cultivation of wheat and barley is not likely to have been attempted in the mountainous districts. There were, it seems, two types of country favoured by these first farmers, the well-drained hillslopes where the soil was fairly thin and the glacial or residual soils lying on chalk or limestone and therefore rich in lime. Both these were areas where the elm tree flourished and this may account for the rapid decline of that species as evidenced in the pollen records.

Efficient bronze axes, in the manufacture of which Irish craftsmen were highly skilled, began to be made from about 1700 BC and the spread of settlement, as indicated by finds of bronze implements and burials, into many lowland areas of dry soil shows that forest clearing continued and was extended. But it was the iron axe, adopted when the later waves of Celtic-speaking invaders brought a knowledge of this metal to Ireland, that was able to make possible the secular attack on the oak forests which culminated in the sixteenth century and left the country almost entirely stripped of high forests. In the process of forest destruction cattle, sheep and goats were great abetters, browsing off shrubs and seedlings so that regeneration was difficult and only the thorny species tended to be left—black and white thorn, holly and furze. The naked appearance of so much of Ireland in recent centuries, especially before the Great Famine, must be attributed to over-grazing.

Many of the lowland bogs had begun to grow before the Bronze Age, but the upland bogs for the most part began to form in the late Bronze Age as population moved downhill. Again we cannot separate the climatic and biological factors involved in the changing scene. Some students believe that a worsening of climate—the so-called sub-Atlantic phase—was responsible for the growth of bogland, but ecological factors were probably more important. At any rate hundreds of square miles in the west, especially in Mayo and Galway, came to be clothed in blanket bog which spread indiscriminately over lowlands and uplands alike, save where the slopes were too steep. In drier cycles many areas were subsequently invaded by birchwoods whose remains are frequently found in the bogs. These vast stretches of bog came to be utilized as summer grazing grounds.

The emphasis placed in the Irish epics on cattle and cattle raiding reminds us of the strong pastoral bias of the Celtic hierarchy. During the early Iron Age oats were introduced, and their cultivation would have helped to maintain the herds through the winter. Whitemeats were established as the staple diet, and the cult of cattle seems to have acquired a semi-religious status. Not only was cattle raiding a recognized activity, a source of wealth and prestige, but as Mr A.T. Lucas has shown, a kind of ceremonial obligation of kingship.

The keeper of livestock likes to live close to his animals, and it is to the period when the Celtic ascendancy was unchallenged, covering the first eight or nine centuries of our era, that are dated most of the many thousands of isolated farmsteads that country people know as 'forts'. These are circular enclosures—raths or duns—in which stood wattled houses surrounded by earthen banks. In stony areas they are built of stones, as were the buildings inside, and they are then known as cashels or cahers. Related to these structures, but more obviously of defensive character, are the hundreds of promontory forts around the coasts, which reach their most imposing size in Dun Aengus on Inishmore in the Aran Islands. It is to these early centuries of the Christian era also that most of the crannógs belong, and their excavation has revealed an economy similar to that of the raths: mixed farming in which cattle played a dominant role, supplemented by pigs , sheep, goats and horses. They are the homes of what we should now call strong farmers, with perhaps 60 or 100 acres of good farmland and rights of pasturage on lowland bogs or mountain grazing. We may picture the raths occupying clearings in the forest where patches of scrub alternated with enclosures of various kinds for the protection of crops or animals. We know that the Celtic overlords had chariots, and a system of roads is said to have linked their fortress-palaces, but unlike the Roman roads of England they have left little trace on the Irish landscape. The most persistent routes, to judge from the archaeological finds of many periods from river-beds, were the trackways making for fords on rivers such as the Shannon and the Bann. Of towns there was as yet none, but the functions of the later market towns were carried on at great fairs and assemblies which met at the changes of the seasons, especially in May and November, and brought great animation to hallowed sites such as Tara, Uisneach and Telltown.

Although the raths are densely clustered in some parts of the country there are some equally favoured areas which have very few although they are known to have been settled in earlier times. It is argued that such areas were left to the indigenous population, who would have lived in hamlets or clachans of kinsmen. If such bond settlements were undefended and built of clay and wattle, they would have left no visible mark on the present landscape. It may well be from the lands worked by these joint-farmers or 'ballys' (towns) that the denominations later to be known as townlands were derived, but this is a very complex problem.

When Christianity came to Ireland in the fifth century, its monastic buildings, at first made of wattle, came to be made of mortared stone in the seventh or eighth century, and made therefore a more lasting contribution to the landscape. Christianity also brought with it an incentive to agricultural expansion. Thanks to new techniques and new crops borrowed from the Roman world, and to the monastic prescription of a vegetable diet, renewed attacks were made on the forests. The pollen record shows that in the process the elm tree further declined and this time it virtually disappeared from the landscape. Instead hazel scrub spread widely, presumably on farmland as it was allowed to rest. The Irish epics relating to this period abound with references to the clearing of plains, and to the abundance of hazelnuts, blackberries and sloes, weeds of cultivation. But in the pollen record hazel gives way in turn to plantain, a characteristic meadow weed, so that a return to animal husbandry seems likely; and this is the more probable for the coastal areas at least from the end of the eighth century when the fury of the Norsemen first descended on the country.

[Thomas Davis Lecture, *Radio Éireann, January 1962*]

THE IRISHNESS OF THE IRISH

In inviting me to address you on this subject you have set me a very difficult task. No matter what I say I will offend some of you, for you would not be Irish if you were all of one mind. It would be easier if you were all from the North or all from the South; still easier if I were addressing members of the Orange Order or of Sinn Féin. This Association is forward-looking and would wish to forget recent history and heal the wounds it records. Yet I must take you into a past beyond history, because the more one looks into Irishness the more it becomes a part of the land itself, of geography. As the harassed mother remarked of her baby's nappies: 'Plus ça change, plus c'est la même chose.'

I turned first of all to Myles na Gopaleen. 'Who are the Irish?' he asks.

We Irish are simple unspoiled God-fearing sophisticated mid-Europeans, a humble community of persons drawn together in our daily round of uncomplicated agricultural tasks by the strongest traditional ties, closely woven on a diminutive leprechaun's loom, five and six a go and no coupons.

The Irish are given to self-criticism, but they do not welcome criticism from outside: I must mind my Ps and Qs. On the other hand you will not be satisfied with flattery and flannel. Nor do I intend to quote stereotypes and leave it at that. Off-the-cuff generalizations and high-sounding phrases are at best half-truths, requiring a battery of footnotes and qualifications. One could go some distance, but not all the way, with impartial statistical analysis, showing how various demographic facts are characteristic of the Irish, practising what Sir William Petty, that seventeenth-century man of parts, called 'Political Arithmetic'. This is heavy stuff, though even statistics can have their lighter side: one section of a recent census (of the USA) bore the heading: 'Figures broken down by age and sex.' I refrain from commenting on some of Ireland's demographic anomalies. But the scientist, as Blake said, has a one-eyed vision. We cannot see the truth that way. One thing is certain: that in a topic of this kind emotions are easily involved; and no matter how reasonable we pretend to be, there are few of us who are not moved to pride or anger when our national character or our patriotism is under discussion. Yet patriotism may spring from nothing more creditable than a pathetic belief in myth, and a nation has been cynically defined as a group of people bound together by a common error as to their origin and a common hatred of their neighbours. The Welsh people have no doubt as to their deep national roots, but Welsh culture has been described (by an Englishman) as '*pot-pourri* of Victorian middle-class prejudices masquerading as part of a national way of life'.

Of this I am convinced: what is called 'Irishness' can be understood only in relation to the homeland. There is a saying that you can take a boy out of Ireland but you cannot take Ireland out of the boy. In the long run, I believe geography counts for more than genes. This view recently received striking confirmation from an Irish historian, my colleague Professor J.C. Beckett:

The history of Ireland must be based on a study of a relationship between the land and the people. It is in Ireland itself, the physical conditions inspired by life in this country and the effect on those who have lived there, that the historian will find the distinct and continuing character of Irish history.[1]

Let me quote another observer, a sympathetic English geologist living in Dublin—the late Grenville Cole—who wrote a fascinating essay on the character of Ireland: 'To understand the homestead and its homefolk', he wrote, 'from the thatch of the roof to the colour of the children's hair, we must first find the locality on the domed surface of the earth.'[2]

We are dealing with an island set in warm Atlantic waters, brooding on the outermost edge of the Old World, a green pastoral island; and pastoral society and culture are very different from those associated with arable husbandry. Old pastoral habits persist among the Irish, though they may have deserted their green fields; for instance, they are among the greatest consumers of butter in the world. They are also said to be thriftless, and to love gambling, a natural response, perhaps, to the uncertainties of Irish weather. Most Irish history has been written with little sense of geography. It is part of my faith that land and people go together and have shaped each other and that you cannot understand one apart from the other. Nationalism too thrives on this identification, symbolizing the land as a person; but here the resemblance ends. For nationalism is emotional and depends on myths, and anyone who explodes myths is attempting what might be termed an antagonizing reappraisal. Just how fallacious many stereotypes of Irish history, of the Irish nation and of Irishness really are is a matter for scholarly discussion. I can only summarize some current revisions. Take first of all the question of race. One still hears talk of the Irish race, the Celtic race or the Ulster-Scot race. In the nineteenth century it was fashionable to believe in pure races. This perverted Darwinism had its home in England and received a serious setback only when other nations adopted it and the Germans pushed it to the extremes of Hitlerism. Racial Aryanism is a myth, not a scientific fact, but myths endure and facts are forgotten. When I first came to Ireland I began a programme of anthropometric research to try to identify racial types in the people of Northern Ireland. Our findings, by the way, (published by Professor Walmsley and one of my first students Mr, now Professor, John Mogey)[3] were largely substantiated by the American anthropologists, A.E. Hooton and Carleton S. Coon.[4] Needing money for our surveys, I got in touch with the then Director of the National Museum in Dublin, Dr Adolph Mahr, to see if we could tap the research funds of the Royal Irish Academy. He wrote to say that he had no faith in the measurement of race—he was in fact a fervent Nazi and believed in automatic Aryan superiority—but since I needed money, he promised me that I should have it. This, by the way, was because we had co-operated in archaeological research. Both of us newcomers to Ireland, we were deeply impressed by the vitality of its prehistoric cultures. When Professor Macalister revised his standard *Archaeology of Ireland* in 1948 he based his new assessment of early Irish culture on the views of Mahr and Evans, an Austrian and a Welshman, as to the significance of the megalithic substratum. I return to this theme later because I believe it lies near the root of your Irishness.

A pure race is a nationalist myth: indeed it is now thought that in the evolution of man the mixed breeds were the winners from the start. We are all mongrels, and should be proud of it, but the proportions of the various racial elements in the mixture vary from one region to another. Biologically, a significant strain in north-western Europe, adapted to a mild cloudy environment, has lost protective pigmentation and acquired light eyes and fair hair. From sampling, it appears that 88 per cent of the Irish have light eyes (including blue-brown); but it is strangely combined with dark hair. This is the prevailing Irish type, but there are many other strains. The darkest hair, by the way, is found in Wexford and Waterford. Many stereotypes about Irish racial characters derive from nineteenth-century theories. It used to be stated that the taller fair-haired types predominate in Ulster and down the English-settled east coast, where the conquering Nordics entered: the little dark folk, those dangerous emotional 'Iberians', predominating in the Gaelic-speaking west. In fact the mean stature of the Irish people is lowest on the east coast and highest in Kerry and Galway. The heaviest men are found in the westernmost peninsulas, and the broadest heads in Co. Kerry. These are probably relics of an ancient strain of Irishmen who took refuge there. Most paradoxical is the physical make-up of the men of Aran, one of the strongest bulwarks of Gaelic culture. Studies of both racial characters and blood-group ratios suggest that they owe much to the infusion of the blood of Cromwellian soldiers, who were recruited from the English Fenlands. But Ireland has completely absorbed them.

In general it might be said, if the subject of this address were 'Who are the Irish?', that the old strains in the population predominate—pre-plantation, pre-Norman, pre-Viking, pre-Celtic. An essential fact of Irish geography is its insular isolation: another is the proximity of Scotland. The advantage lay with the first Irishmen, some of whom arrived early enough to avoid seasickness: they could almost have walked across a narrowed North Channel some 8000 years ago, and Ulster was their first home. This has been in some ways the most Irish of the Irish provinces, certainly down to the sixteenth century. The mainly Scottish immigration into Ulster in the following centuries must of course be reckoned with, in terms of culture and religious belief, but racially it was much the same mongrel mixture: north-west European. In earlier centuries the immigrant element must always have been a minority, predominantly male, and forced to take native wives. And although most of the seventeenth-century planters brought their families with them, there was no doubt a good deal of mating with the natives, some of whom anyhow adopted the Protestant religion. On general grounds, taking Ireland as a whole, an essential continuity is inferred, and archaeology abundantly confirms this inference. This continuity is cultural as well as physical. Historical writings have, sometimes deliberately but sometimes unconsciously (because of their limited sources), obscured this fact. In any event, to depend on documentary evidence alone for an interpretation of Irish culture is to see it through the eyes of successive conquerors, whether saints or swordsmen. Records and the history that depends on them were first written down when the art of writing was introduced with Christianity, and they were naturally not without ecclesiastical bias. The Irishness of the Irish, as archaeology reveals it, was already deeply entrenched in the Middle Ages, but history ignores this fact. It is not only the fact that 80 per cent of what has been written in Irish history is based on English sources that obscures the realities of Irish cultural history—the Irish sources are equally unreliable. The English historians wanted to prove that the Irish were fit only for conquest: the Irish *Annals* which in theory record early Irish history—largely legendary as it was—were so revised by churchmen to suit their own ends that they are highly suspect. I quote Professor Kelleher of Harvard: 'Everything in the *Annals* up to 600 or 700 was largely or wholly rewritten from the late ninth century onwards.'[5] The purpose? To re-establish the prestige of the ruling families whose grip had been weakened by missionary Christianity. Kelleher compares Ireland under the revolutionary impact of early Christianity to 'a seventh-century Red China'. It gave the plebeian for the first time a place in learned society, previously a high-caste privilege among the pagan Celts. Many of the early saints later sank into local obscurity, but others were given respectable pedigrees by rewriting the records when the privileged classes took over again in the eighth century. The common people, the makers of the cultural landscape, were forgotten. Dr A.T. Lucas, Director of the National Museum, has shown how completely the church, in adjusting itself to Irish conditions, became adapted to the ethics of the ruling families. One of the main pastimes of the rival chieftains was cattle-raiding, which was as much a popular sport as modern interprovincial ballgames; and the abbots regularly claimed their tithe on the spoils of battle, so many cows from each raid.[6] Moreover, the monasteries themselves often raided each other. Dr Lucas has claimed, indeed, that at least half the burnings and pillages of churches, from the seventh century to the sixteenth century, were the work of the Irish themselves: the destruction of churches began before the Norsemen came and lasted long after they were forgotten.[7] During the Norse period the abbots would enlist their aid in raiding rival monasteries, but what they were after was lay property which the Irish chieftains placed there for safe custody. The veneration of sacred sites which gave rise to the custom of sanctuary was a carry-over from the pagan world. It was part of that universal veneration of hallowed tradition which was a bond between all classes of society and, for the ruling classes, a ready-made basis of legal order. To blame the breach on the pagan Norsemen was perhaps the easiest way to break the unwritten law.

The churchmen, of course, came to blame the Norsemen for everything, but it seems that they were, in the long run, peaceful colonizers, and in the end they were completely absorbed. It has always seemed paradoxical that some of the finest examples of Irish craftmanship date from the Norse period. Certainly the Irish had much to learn from the Norsemen. They took over their towns and markets and seafaring skills, and it is significant that Gaelic borrowed from Norse its words for such civilized cultural features as garden, hall, window and pavement.[8]

The churchmen, besides whitewashing the Irish aristocracy, invented a romantic High Kingship where none existed. That this was a falsification has generally been accepted by scholars, but it will probably take half a century before our textbooks change their tune. Revision of history is turning what seemed firm ground into a quaking bog. For most Irishmen the shining figure of St Patrick stands as the first historic Irishman—I will resist the temptation to make capital out of his Welsh origin—and the date of his arrival (AD 432) is sacrosanct. Yet Irish scholars violently disagree about Patrician chronology. Some have denied that he was ever a Bishop of Armagh, others have discovered at least two St Patricks, while others have denied his very existence.[9]

A revaluation of the Anglo-Normans is coming to be accepted, and it is a far cry from the patriots' interpretation of the role of later English conquerors implicit in John Mitchel's label of 'the Carthaginians'. The Rev Professor Martin of University College, Dublin, writes that the Normans were the first to give Ireland a centralized administration and a money economy; they introduced the jury system; they took the first steps on the road to democracy; they introduced systematic agriculture: 'the only people to be displaced were the Gaelic nobility', not the common people. They gave Ireland most of its own towns and villages, nearly all its mediaeval cathedrals and its most magnificent abbeys. 'The tragedy of the Norman invasion was not the conquest of Ireland—for that never took place—but the half-conquest'. These are the words of an Irish scholar.[10] In my view this half-conquest, tragedy or not, contributed perhaps as much as anything to the Irishness of the Irish. By failing to destroy a native culture of prehistoric antiquity, it provided the stimulus of continuing contact and initiated the enduring Anglo-Irish tradition. Moreover it gave the Irish a lasting sense of inferiority.

It will take half a century, too, for the dramatic findings of prehistoric archaeology to replace the doctored history of Celtic churchmen. The only truly impartial records of a country's story lie buried in its earth. They tell us, for instance, that the Celt was even more devoted to the business of fighting than his legendary histories imply. The Celtic aristocracy, being more barbaric, were probably more bloodthirsty than the Anglo-Norman invaders, but they were similarly a small minority.

A large part of the Irishness of the Irish is, I believe, a pre-Celtic heritage. When I came to Ireland and began recording rural folkways I was puzzled by the fact that almost nothing of this rich lore was reflected in the recorded history of Ireland, whether English or Irish. It was beneath the notice of the learned scribes, and the Irish laws ignored the common people. Failing to find in these sources the evidence I sought, I began, in 1932, a programme of excavation of prehistoric sites, starting with the megaliths, to see what evidence the spade could yield. My collaborator was Dr Oliver Davies.

I was warned off by the Belfast pundits who told me that everything that could be learned from the megaliths had already been discovered. And I may say that in my enquiries into these matters—as into rural customs and sociology—I got no encouragement from the University. Indeed I faced open hostility from professors who regarded classical and literary subjects as the only ones fit for university teachers. 'Local studies' were beneath their notice. In fact our excavations on these ritual burial sites were richly rewarding, and when I found a habitation site and began digging at Lyles Hill near Belfast in 1937, just thirty years ago, the results exceeded my wildest hopes. You may not be moved by the discovery, on that hilltop, of many thousand Neolithic potsherds where almost none had been found anywhere in Ireland before, but this was the beginning of a series of discoveries which has excited archaeologists and made Lyles Hill pottery one of the best known types of Neolithic ceramics in Western Europe. At the same time Professor Sean O'Riordain made similar discoveries at Lough Gur in County Limerick. I will not describe the many artefacts and other evidence of those ancient farming and stock-rearing Irishmen. It will suffice to say that they depended on the cultivation of wheat and barley and on cattle, pigs, and sheep or goats. Recently revised chronologies give the Irish Neolithic a total span of some 2000 years, and it was a remarkably stable culture. Gaelic scholars in general have shown little interest in these findings. Blinkered by their literary-historical training, they fail to see the significance of material culture and are critical of the work of the archaeologists; though this may simply be their Irishness, since they are no less critical of each other's theories.

I believe that in time these matters will be part of our educational system. You may say that pottery, for example, is a dull utilitarian item of culture, but for the anthropologist it is close to poetry in meaning as well as in name: pottery had great ritual significance as a part of family life. Lyles Hill pottery and other forms of Neolithic ware have since turned up in many parts of Ireland. The hundreds of megalithic sites which have been studied and classified tell us that a peasant culture deeply concerned with religious ideas, with votive offerings and magic ceremonies at wells, in lakes and on hilltops, was already established in nearly every part of Ireland well before 2000 BC. I have been preaching about this old religion with missionary zeal for nearly thirty years. (It is worth recording that among the regional variations that occur in the megalithic cultures the greatest differences were between the north—Ulster and North Connacht—and the south). The megalith-builders loved the hilltops: the older layer, hunters and fishers, preferred the lakes and rivers. After all, the two most celebrated pilgrimages of modern Ireland, Lough Derg and Croagh Patrick, terminate in a lake-island and on a hilltop! Imagine my pleasure when I read a letter in the London *Times*, from Dr Glyn Daniel, concerning Dr George Eogan's recent discoveries in the Boyne valley at Knowth: 'These great tombs are an essential part of the Irish past, and indeed perhaps one of the most important elements in the answer to the question, "Who are the Irish?"' And he quotes Professor Sean O'Riordain: 'The Irish are megalith-builders who somehow learned to speak Gaelic.'[11]

Let me bring the matter nearer home by referring to the hallowed site of Navan (Emhain Macha), the Celtic capital of ancient Ulster and the scene of a hundred heroic legends. That Armagh became the capital of Christian Ireland is surely related to its proximity to Emhain Macha whose name it shares. At the rival site of Tara, Dublin archaeologists were able to show that the Celtic fortress-palace was built on a hilltop which had been sacred to the natives for 2000 years. The Mound of the Hostages is a megalithic tomb, and in selecting the Hill of Tara as a sacred site the Celtic newcomers had continued and renewed an old Irish custom. At Navan I had long suspected something similar, for the hilltop fortress has constructional features which are pre-Celtic, and Macha was not a Celtic queen but an older goddess. This year when Mr Dudley Waterman, after four years' patient digging, had reached the base of the giant mound which traditionally covers the grave of Macha, he found it was built on a settlement at least 2000 years older. Here again the ubiquitous Lyles Hill pottery turns up. Of course this may be coincidence, but in general wherever we look we find continuity, a renewal of the old in contact with the new.

I will not weary you with more archaeology. I expect you are more interested in legendary and documentary history than in archaeology, and historians are occupationally prejudiced against the illiterates who by definition are part of prehistory. But we should not equate illiteracy with lack of intelligence. I've no doubt that because he was illiterate prehistoric man was a tremendous talker; and what could be more Irish than that? I am suggesting that many cultural features were, in Ireland, for reasons that are essentially geographical, not suppressed but renewed with each successive wave of newcomers. Refuges in mountain and bog have been ready to hand in every part of the country, and the invaders were anyhow a small minority until the seventeenth century. In an understandable reaction from centuries of political domination, nineteenth-century patriots popularized their own version of Irish history, and of Irishness. In the twentieth century Sinn Féin, in its very name, is a denial of the process of renewal under the stimulus of culture-contact which, to my mind, is the essence of Irishness. Historians, as we have seen, are revaluating the Anglo-Normans and the Vikings: prehistorians are revaluating the Celts. Should we not admit that later intruders, even the loud-mouthed English Ascendancy, are responsible for cultural innovations, some of them admirable, brought about by contact? Where in the world can the brilliant hybrid flowering of Anglo-Irish literature be matched? Again and again, I suggest, cross-fertilization has given Irish culture a touch of originality, even of genius.

I have been looking at a new book by a Russian, N.I. Konrad, called *West and East*.[12] Writing of India, which on a much vaster scale has preserved, as Professor Myles Dillon has shown, an archaic order of society which has many Irish parallels,[13] Konrad says: 'The dead cultures are constantly reborn, and transformed. Newcomers inherit the old culture. The study of this mysterious process is one of the most important tasks in the study of culture.'

Part of the process is a 'give and take', and the interpretation of ideas often brings a measure of objectivity. It is when attitudes harden under political or religious pressures and become fossilized that the genuine quality of Irishness is sacrificed.

Of course political history has left its mark. Much of what is commonly regarded as peculiarly Irish is the hang-over of colonialism: for example a certain servility, accompanied by boastfulness, which is an inverted sense of inferiority and is seen under similar circumstances in the young United States. Other culture-traits thought to be peculiarly Irish are simply old-fashioned (again as in America, with its lace-curtains, timber houses, Federal furniture, its observance of Hallowe'en and its old forms of the English language). One thinks of items of dress such as the Kinsale Cloak or of Elizabethan turns of phrase. Surviving from older times and more genuinely Irish are the melodious Irish folk songs, often composed on an archaic pentatonic scale. Sir Walford Davies, whom I am proud to claim as a Shropshire Welshman like myself, used to say they were the finest in the world. Another Welshman, Giraldus Cambrensis, gave the Irish musicians unstinted praise nearly 800 years ago: 'They seem to me to be incomparably more skilled than any other people I have seen. They harmonize at intervals of the octave and the fifth, but they always begin with B flat and with B flat end.'[14] I will refrain from quoting him on the subject of Irish morals.

In what other ways have the Irish excelled? It is not too much to say that there is a genuine concern for intellectual matters at almost all levels of society. And I would regard a certain brand of cruel wit as typically Irish. I quote two examples. First, a County Antrim man's verdict on a certain professional Irishman: 'He's the dacentest man you ever wanted to stick a graip intil.' Go back nearly five centuries and you have the delightful apology of the Earl of Kildare—more Irish than the Irish—for burning down the Round Tower at Cashel: he didn't know the Bishop wasn't inside it.

Sociologically the Irish have a strong rural heritage. They have not been given to building towns but to inhabiting towns built by others, to which they bring rural habits of mind and rural standards of hygiene. Their loyalties, as with all pastoral peoples, are to their kin rather than to the community. The bulk of them, through the centuries, have been country-dwellers who counted their wealth in livestock, living in family clusters and not in villages. The English villager's reverence for authority and his concern for the community are regarded by the Irish as signs of simple-mindedness. Gerald the Welshman said as much in 1185. I quote: 'This people has all the primitive habits of pastoral living, despises agriculture, has little use for the money-making of towns, and contemns the rights and privileges of citizenship.'[15] Pastoral living, as Giraldus calls it, had no need for elaborate capital equipment, and those who catered for its cultural needs were itinerant. Irish genius has expressed itself in individual achievement rather than in communal effort, in oratory, song, poetry (particularly national poetry) and handicraft rather than in civic architecture or orchestral music.

Its virtues sprang from poverty. I am aware that some Irish propagandists attribute almost every sign of Irish poverty and degradation to the evils of English conquest and landlordism. I give you an extreme example. It concerns the Irish habit of 'ploughing by the tail', which the English prohibited by Act of Parliament in 1635. It has been ingeniously argued that there was no such custom but that the Act was deliberately introduced in order to demonstrate how degraded the Irish were. In fact there is abundant evidence for the custom of ploughing by the tail. As a Welshman I am ready to admit that the English did incredible things to the subject peoples of these islands, often through ignorance rather than malice. But we have often been our own worst enemies. Listen to what AE (George Russell, a man of County Armagh) said of the Irish rural moneylenders—the Gombeens: 'They had the power to evict people, and they did so more than many landlords. The landlords owned the land: the Gombeen men owned the people.'[16]

I believe, as I have said, that Irishness is the product of Irish geography influencing settlers through the ages. The process of unconscious cultural cross-fertilization has operated in Ireland at many times and in many places. I could give you many examples, for instance, from Ireland's Golden Age, the Bronze Age. (My first excursions into prehistory, before I came to Ireland, were in the Irish Bronze Age.) If the process becomes overt there are protests from extremists on both sides, who protest all the louder when they are losing ground. The English in their own land, on the other hand, have been conscious compromisers. As the foreword to the 1662 English Bible has it: 'It hath been the wisdom of the Church of England to keep the mean between the two extremes.'

The contacts between native and planter, which in earlier times took place along a broad belt running down the centre of the island, have come to be concentrated in the larger urban centres within this contact belt, and it is significant that Cork in the south and Derry in the north have produced more than their share of men of great ability, who have enriched the life of Dublin and Belfast and the wider world. Potentially the men of Derry, for example, are the inheritors of two cultures, and the decay of Londonderry is one of the worst consequences of partition, which deprived it of the Celtic half of its hinterland. To many historians, fascinated by the actions and motives of outstanding individuals, these locational factors appear to have little interest. Geography is for them merely a map and a means of reference. In its own right it is a part of history, and one can be understood only in the light of the other. It is to the land that you Irish are bound: this is the one enduring fact. Who will pretend to analyse the emotional and spiritual bonds which tie people to the place of their childhood and to its local environment, and which influence them all their lives in ways they hardly suspect? The most genuine bonds are with small regions such as the Kingdom of Mourne[17] or West Cork. Here are the springs of true patriotism. But they are easily polluted and exploited by myth-makers, of one kind or another. The Irish should be proud of the antiquity and the variety of their heritage, but in my view, if Irish culture is to maintain its historic character it needs constant renewal through exposure to the outside world and to fresh cultural forces. The future must be uncertain in a rapidly changing world, but I suggest that the best way to prepare for it is to expose the myths and to try to put the historic record straight.

[*The Irish Association for Cultural, Economic and Social Relations* (Belfast 1968)]

THE COUNTRYMAN
From 'The Character of Ireland'

This essay, edited by Noel Mitchel in 1984, is a shortened version of a contribution to an ill-fated book, The Character of Ireland, *to be edited by W.R. Rodgers and Louis MacNeice and published by Oxford University Press. In* Closing Time *(1975) its Secretary, Dan Davin, tells how the book was first discussed when he met Rodgers in 1948. A list of nine chapter-headings and contributors was drawn up in 1952, but some chapters were never received, nor were the editors very active. Although Davin tried to rescue the book, it remained unpublished when he retired in 1978. MacNeice's note of acknowledgment to Evans of 21 February 1955 reads: 'It is just the sort of things we wanted, not only packed with particular information but vividly written.'*

In essentials, statistically and sociologically, Ireland is a peasant land. It is not merely that peasant proprietorship, after a long struggle, is an established fact; it is rather that the peasant gives meaning and continuity to the history and character of the country. For it is he who has fashioned the land, moulded it to his needs, and absorbed its nature in doing so. In searching for his secrets we cannot rely on written records but must turn to oral tradition and to the land itself. The peasant's ancient lore was passed on by word of mouth. He was illiterate, but with his hands he carved his rough runes on the land. His skills have resided in the craft and strength of his arms, and in remarkable faculties of speech and memory.

History can tell us little of these things. To depend on documentary evidence alone is to see Ireland through the eyes of her conquerors. The legendary histories of Gaelic Ireland no less than the countless English histories of Ireland are preoccupied with invasions and fighting heroes. Nor did the impoverished countryman leave much behind for the archaeologist to uncover. As we peer into the darkness of prehistory the glimpses we catch come from the shining panoplies of overlords, not from the earth-polished tools of the peasants who toiled to support them.

Conquering aristocracies—Bronze Age swordsmen, Gaelic warriors, Anglo-Norman earls, English and Scotch planters—have each in turn battened on those who were there before them. We seek the 'man harrowing clods' of Thomas Hardy's poem, enduring 'while dynasties pass'.

The timeless world of the peasant is of course not peculiar to Ireland and it can be matched in neighbouring islands and peninsulas throughout north-western Europe. It survives on an incomparably larger scale in other conservative corners of the Old World. A naval commander who had spent much of his life on the Yang-tse before retiring to County Kerry told me that he found in the south-west of Ireland a familiar oriental scale of values and 'all time foreshortened into a living present'. It would be instructive to draw a parallel also from the culture history of Japan, where invaders of an island world peopled by peasants had to fight for centuries on a narrow shifting frontier and where proud conquering families maintained their military codes long after they were needed. Have not the landed gentry of Ireland down to our own day contributed more than their share of generals to the British army?

But for a closer parallel within the linguistic family of western Eurasia we turn to India, standing at the extreme south-eastern end of the Indo-European world as Ireland stands at the north-western extremity. Myles Dillon has shown how certain archaic elements common to ancient Ireland and India—in language and literature and in social organization—can be explained on the theory of marginal survival. The caste system could never have reached in the confines of a small island the absurd complexities of the Indian social scene, but the three major divisions of Hindu society, *kshatriya*, *brahman* and *vaisya*, can be matched in the tripartite division of *flaith*, *fili* and *aithech* (patrons, poets and peasants) in early Celtic Ireland. This Gaelic warrior-aristocracy gave way to the Anglo-Irish Ascendancy, the poets and seers became priests and professional men, but the peasants who are older than both are with us still. They have been caught up in a money economy, in an alien urbanism and the borrowed trappings of representative government, yet their ancient familistic values are not entirely submerged. And as compared with England, where industry and urbanism are so much stronger, a simple social stratification is still in evidence; the priest, the poet and the scholar are esteemed by all and accepted by the highest in the land.

We see Ireland then as the last outpost of the Old World, the final home, until a New World was opened up across the Atlantic, of adventurers and refugees moving westwards to the very edge of Europe. Inviting enough to attract them—for it turns a fair smiling face to the east—it also provided among the marginal mountains and bleak bogs hiding places when new invaders appeared. Anthropologists have found that many ancient human stocks have lived on in Ireland. Botanists tell us that the Irish flora shows similar traits of insular survival: it is peculiarly rich in relics of former floras which in their day dominated the Irish scene. The mountains and the bogs have thus played their part in shaping and colouring Irish life. The peat bogs indeed hold the past in their depths, and from them the scientist obtains his evidence of the evolving landscape and of man's place in it. The botanist finds and counts the minute once-golden grains of pollen preserved in the peat: the archaeologist seeks rather the collars of gold which men of the Bronze Age offered to the spirits of the bog. There could be no fitter symbol of peasant Ireland, for the peasant mind too holds the past in its depths.

It would be going far beyond the evidence to suggest that the qualities of peat or granite are projected into the personalities of those who dwell among them, though I have heard it solemnly argued that the black basalts of Antrim bred the black Presbyterians of Belfast. The truth is that the mountains and boglands, the refuge areas of native stocks, are regions of poverty, of ill-drained acid soils offering poor returns to the cultivator under climatic conditions which make every grain of seed a hostage to fortune. The Irish countryman cannot be other than a gambler. We need to see how these conditions have been translated into economic action and social forms. We find that from very early times the peasant's real wealth has been in live-stock, above all in milk cattle. His arable farming was traditionally little more than was necessary to prevent his grazing grounds from deteriorating into bogland. He still measures his land, in some districts, by 'the cow's grass' rather than by the acre. His values are those of the breeder of live-stock, animal and human, of kine and kin. The bull of the herd is boss.

His aristocratic overlords were subject to the same pressures, but they could afford to be specialist ranchers, cattlemen and breeders of bloodstock. For they had seized the fattest lands, the sleek round-bellied drumlins and the lime-rich eskers which make the eastern lowlands a grazier's paradise. The fame of these pastures had reached the ears of the classical world: Mela and Solinus speak of Irish cattle as liable to burst from over-eating. And the legendary histories of Gaelic Ireland are full of the lowing of dewlapped kine and the bellowing of champion bulls. But the tribute-paying peasants needed to have their eggs in many baskets. Theirs was a small-scale pastoral economy, supplemented by the growing of a limited range of crops and by the exploitation of the food resources of the woods, waters and moorlands. In its routine the traditions of the Irish countryside are firmly fixed.

In former times the yearly cycle involved the removal of the cattle in summer, when the crops were in the ground, to common rough pasturage in the bogs or high in the valleys of the hills. This seasonal nomadism, or booleying, lingered long enough for us to obtain a glimpse of a mode of life which, like so much else in the story of common folk, has passed almost unrecorded and is therefore almost unknown to history. We can see how this mobility imposed a sturdy simplicity on dairying equipment and favoured the crafts of woodworking, basket-making and coopering rather than the fragile art of the potter. Knowledge of the territorial units within which booleying took place is important for the comprehension of local loyalties, for the study of dialects and for providing an insight into the subtle minor differences between one district and another. It seems that they were aggregated into the petty Gaelic kingdoms, areas of common tribal allegiance which were strong enough to survive the Anglo-Norman onslaught and to become fossilized as the baronies which are still the official administrative areas into which the larger, and alien, counties are divided. The smallest unit, wherein the permanent dwellings were established, has come to be known as the townland, a term of deep significance to the Irish countryman. Almost every one of the sixty or seventy thousand townlands of Ireland is, for some family, synonymous with hearth and home. It is their postal address and legal title, for the individual farm carries a family name and its postal identity is merged in that of the townland. It is the name of the family that is 'on the land'; and every effort will be made to keep it there.

The division of time no less than that of the land is determined by old custom, so that significance still attaches to the points of time which were the beginning and the end of the booleying year: the first of May and the first of November. These are the gale-days in Ireland, the times when rents fall due. For the Gaelic world they marked the beginning and the end of summer, the periods when stock was moved between seasonal grazing-grounds. One can easily see how these times of stock-taking and sorting were the seasons when dues were paid in kind to the overlord. Hallowe'en in particular is the time of preparation for the dark days ahead. It was believed that the luck of the family and farm depended on ceremonies appropriate to the occasion. Maytime observances also live on in various guises. There are many folk customs associated with it which throw light on the fears and hopes of a pastoral people. They are by no means forgotten, and even if their magic has faded, 'well, you never know; you might as well be on the safe side'. Reverence for the lone Maybush, the fairy thorn, provides a good illustration: its power, though at its greatest in May, lasts indeed throughout the year. The lone thorn is in truth a thing of fairy beauty in Maytime, massed with milk-white blossoms, but it is not for the

45

aesthetic reasons that the countryman—even many a 'strong Protestant farmer'—refuses to damage it. To interfere in any way with a fairy thorn is to invite reciprocal injury to one's family or one's cows. It is unlucky even to take its dead wood for the fire, just as in China no fallen branch may be removed from the sacred groves. We are in the presence of an antique animism.

It is worth pursuing the subject of the thorn tree a little further. Why should special sanctity attach to a bush which is nowadays, since its adoption for field-hedges, the commonest in the land? Its utilitarian function, indeed, is to protect crops from the depredations of cattle. Yet there is a very special association between the lone thorn tree—the tree growing on its own and never planted 'by the hand of man'—and the luck of the herd. I like to think the association goes back to the first forest clearings of pioneer farmers, which opened the way for woodland weeds, and that the flowering thorn tree, in all its spring glory, became linked with man's toil and the promise of summer. It was a sign that the damaging frosts were over and that the milk would soon flow from the young grass. The other forest weeds—hazel, birch and mountain ash share something of the magic of the thorn and are also associated with the lore of cattle. There is virtue in the wood of them all, but the thorn is supreme in its power of bringing luck or ill-luck. In the same way the Mayflowers which figure in the house-decking ceremonies of May Eve—the marsh marigold and the primrose—surely hold the promise of golden butter in their cups. A Gaelic name for the dandelion, which is blessed both with a golden head and a milky stem, is 'the plant of the Bride'. We recall that Brigid, the most popular of all Irish-born saints, was a cowherd, and cattle are regarded as being under her special protection.

Folklore is full of the lucky and unlucky signs with which the craft of dairying is hedged about. Butter and other milk-products, whitemeats as they were called, were formerly of vital importance and constituted, before the coming of the potato, the staple diet of the common people. Even today the Irish consumption of milk and dairy products is, per head of the population, the highest in the world. It is not merely to keep them warm and maintain their strength through the winter months that the cows, in former times, were housed with the family; it was lucky to keep them in sight of the fire, for the fire has power to dispel evil spirits. Thus the house-unit of the Irish family was standardized as a single long room which was both kitchen and byre. The farmhouse has grown in length and number of rooms with the centuries, but it has retained its simple shape and is almost invariably a single room in width. Local and regional modifications of this ground-plan, adapted to building materials and special needs, are but variations on a single theme.

Here again old custom was enforced by being linked with good luck, the all important 'luck of the house'. There is an old belief that a house should never be widened: it is frequently raised by the construction of a second storey, or lengthened by the addition of extra rooms, but it must not have living rooms built on at the back. For luck, too—in the north and west of Ireland—the old houses had two doors, a front and a back, opposite each other, and many traditions are gathered about this arrangement. Only one door was in use at any particular time, according to the way the wind blew, and the light came through it rather than through the single diminutive window. Thus one can visualize the force of the picturesque phrase about an unwanted visitor 'darkening the door'. The double doors find an explanation in the function of the original house as a dairy, and also as a threshing floor, for the corn was threshed here in the draught across the 'threshold'. The custom of milking the cow in the house is not entirely abandoned in County Kerry, that most mild and pastoral home of the Kerry cow; and in County Armagh I recently happened on a house where it used to be the custom to drive every calf and every new cow bought at the fair through the house 'for luck'. But a stranger who enters a house must not be allowed to leave by the back door lest he takes the luck of the house with him. And in the Aran Islands it was through the back door that a corpse was carried from the house. This is a practice which can be paralleled among peoples of tropical Africa: indeed almost every item of folk custom would lead us far afield into outlying corners of the Old World. There is the notion that the left-hand side of the fire is the woman's place and the right-hand side the man's, a division one finds in the Mongol yurt. What matters for us is the practical consequence—or perhaps the ultimate cause—of this belief, that the arrangement of the fireside cooking gear is such that the woman of the house has her seat to the left of the fire. The seat of honour is on the right, the male side. And it is worth noticing that the fireside and not the table is the centre of family and social life in an Irish country home. The table is a relative newcomer, pushed to one side against a wall and never occupying the centre of the room.

One might go on multiplying instances, traditional attitudes of unthinking custom and irrational bits of folklore which, trivial in themselves, add up to a way of life which is of deep significance for the older generation. It will be objected that these things are mere fossils and that for the modern countryman they can have no meaning. Admittedly alien forces such as machinery, money, urbanism, 'the fillums', and television have assaulted the old order and are changing its values. The wonder is that so much of the character of rural Ireland has survived the attack. I was reminded of this when watching a tractor-plough making awkward manoeuvres in a small field: I found it was carefully avoiding a fairy thorn growing a few yards out from the hedge. More than once, in travelling the country, I have come across implements and skills which I had been led to believe were long extinct. The countryman's heart is warmed and his eye lights up when one shares his interest in these echoes of the past.

Admittedly the famine period marked a great divide in Irish social history, and in a broad view might be described as the end of prehistoric times. In 1841, for example, nearly half the rural population of Ireland, then amounting to 87 per cent of the total, was living in single-roomed cabins. Much has changed since then, but the new pattern of country life was woven on the same loom and some of the old values were actually strengthened by the tragedy. After the famine, as economic forces broke up self-sufficiency, the urge towards the possession of land became a powerful motive force, driving the peasantry to land agitation and ultimately leading to the establishment of peasant proprietorship. The demographic pattern adjusted itself to this end. Down to famine times blind familistic forces had favoured youthful marriages, which were encouraged by the system of subdivision of holdings and also, it seems likely, by the ease with which large families could be supported on the potato. After the famine the age of marriage became higher at every successive census until to-day marriage takes place at what is probably a later age than in any other country in the world. And rural Ireland swarms with bachelors and 'incomplete families', victims of an economic and social system that attaches great prestige to the ownership of land and its identity with the family name. Yet the birth-rate has been high enough not only to keep the population fairly stable since about 1900, but also to provide some six million emigrants who have left the country since the famine.

Thus, although the numbers of children are reduced by the delayed marriage-age of women, the fertility rate remains high. Here we come once more to attitudes which are common to the world's peasantries and which are tragically evident in China and India. The regular birth of children, especially males, tends to be regarded as part of the ritual necessary to bring about a like increase in the crops and herds. For a married woman to be childless brings disgrace to her and to the whole family, and traditionally there are as many magic cures for barrenness as there are for warts or jaundice. Certain holy wells have the cure for 'the sterile curse', and a visit to one of the 'saint's beds'—stone enclosures associated with early church sites— was considered to be very effective. But there are hints that the pagan stone monuments whose thunder had been partly stolen by Christianity were even more potent. Henry Dutton writing of County Clare in 1808 notes that 'if a woman proves barren, a visit with her husband to Dermot and Grania's

Bed certainly cures her.' (Many megaliths are so named: they are explained as having been built as marriage-beds by the runaway couple.) This association between places of death and fertility may perhaps be explained by the lingering notion that spirits waiting to be reborn haunted the abodes of the dead: it is an association strikingly illustrated in the fertility games which continued to be played until recent years at funeral wakes. Again we are led back to the animist faiths of pioneer megalithic farmers, for there are abundant evidences of fertility symbolism in the construction of megalithic tombs. Standing stones, holed stones and cup-holes also have strong associations with human fertility: they are of megalithic origin, yet cup-holes were being fashioned in the stone coverings of holy wells until quite recently.

There was little room for romantic love—the luxury of a landless society—in a community which measured wealth in land and livestock. Rural society sees marriage as a social contract, not as a matter of personal preference, and in isolated areas it is still arranged by the matchmaker. There is an old belief, handed down from the days of close-knit communities, that marriages should be between distantly related partners. The purpose of marriage is to produce children to keep the land in the family, and other considerations take second place. Who is to know the potential breeding qualities of a wife chosen from an unknown stock? And, given a system of reciprocal exchanges of labour and services, what is the gain in marrying into a family beyond the reach of daily intercourse?

Arensberg has described the process of matchmaking in County Clare, from the time when the father, having selected the son who is to inherit the farm, casts around for a suitable wife, to 'the walking of the land'—its inspection by the prospective bride's parents—and the final agreement as to the amount of the dowry and the provision to be made for the old folk on the farm. The size of the dowry or marriage fortune is a matter for nice negotiation in which the values of rural living are clearly revealed. Before the introduction of a money economy the fortune was invariably measured in cows, as among simple pastoral peoples to this day. With his marriage the 'boy', who may well be up in his fifties, at last reaches adult status and acquires a new dignity. Boys and girls remain boys and girls in name and status until they marry, if they ever do. For in some parts of the country the chances of marriage for a farmer's son other than the heir, if they remain at home, are no better than fifty-fifty. John Mogey found in his survey, *Rural Life in Northern Ireland*, that the most married sections of the country population were the farm labourers and workers in rural factories. They are free of the proud bondage of the family farm.

Saddest of all is the fate of the rural craftsmen whose skills have been rendered obsolete by economic change and mass-produced goods. The hand-loom weaver was the first to go, but nearly all the others have followed—carpenter, cooper, blacksmith, shoemaker, basket-maker, tailor, thatcher—to swell the ranks of urban workers and emigrants. Once these craftsmen were numerous enough to marry among themselves. Now, unless they have a small fortune to transmit and can marry land, they cannot retain their standing and must either move out or die out. Ruined families are the result, and ruined houses are their legacy to the countryside. And among them were the craftsmen in word and song, the ballad singers and fiddlers, the story-tellers and pedlars who preserved and circulated the tales and songs of the past. Only the dregs of this fluid society are left in the tinkers who carry their homes with them. Rural life is the poorer and more earthbound for its rejection of those elements of society whose functions were not directly tied to the land.

Let us follow some of these ejected landless folk into the country towns where they find refuge in the first place. They are doing what others have done before, for the towns have a shifting population which is constantly being renewed from the countryside. Time was when they were all alien foundations. The Norsemen should be remembered not only for their wild deeds which echo through history but also as the planters of the first cities and walled towns. They were ports, and in introducing tide-water towns the Norsemen set the pattern for the future and made an inestimable contribution to Irish life. Whether it wills it or not, Ireland can never be cut off from the world so long as its cities cling to the sea. It is an astonishing fact that no inland town in Ireland has a population of as much as 20,000 and very few have 10,000. Over the entire western half of the country more than three-quarters of the people are rural dwelling. The dominance of the countryside is here almost complete. Of the cities only Belfast and Dublin are of metropolitan status.

It should never be forgotten that the urban civilization of the Mediterranean, carried north by Roman arms, stopped short of Ireland. The Irish did not learn the arts of civic life; they did not build towns but gradually took over towns built by others. Over much of the country, and throughout the provinces of Ulster and Connacht, there were very few towns until the Protestant Plantations of the sixteenth and seventeenth centuries. The new urban centres were designed as foci of anglicization and strong points to keep the Irish in subjection. Most of these small towns, or such of them as have survived—for many are today no more than a ruined castle and a cluster of houses—have been absorbed into the life of the countryside. Their functions are urban but their social pattern is rural. Family names adorn the shops and the pubs, for the familistic world of the farms has invaded the town. The small farmer aspires to marry his surplus children into business families in the town, offering in return the custom of his friends and relations scattered through the countryside.

Of course trade is not confined to kin, but it is true that business transactions tend to become social occasions. The age-old bargaining methods of the fair, inherited from a time before the use of money was adopted, tend to be practised in making shop purchases, and a man proves his adult status by his ability to hold his own in the process of bargaining. There is, however, a personal quality about business relationships which may outweigh purely financial considerations. The Irish countryman also expects to have personal relations with those who govern him, and he both detests and ignores 'form-filling'. The outside world is regarded as an extension of the kind of society he is familiar with, and should be capable of being manipulated on a personal basis. The official attitude which makes no distinction between one person and another is resented. It is therefore all important to 'know the right people'. To have friends at court is to be on the way to obtaining a job, for in Ireland friendship retains its original meaning of blood-relationship. Personal loyalties, too, may be stronger than the abstract claims of justice, as every Irish magistrate knows. Given this familistic background, and remembering that deep religious cleavages divide the urban populations, it is not to be wondered at that civic virtues are poorly developed.

In England the village community has had a profound influence on a disciplined tradition of self-government and a respect for law and order, for established institutions, which to the Irishman appear to be the mark of simple minds. Irish loyalties are to his kin and his church rather than to the community at large. In Gaelic society a man's rights and duties were essentially those connected with membership of the kin-groups. Irish law, as Binchy has shown, did not concern itself with the internal affairs of the kindred. The conflicts between members of the different groups, however, were carefully provided for in law, and no doubt their disputes were as noisy and as profitable as those which keep the swarms of Irish lawyers busy today. The Irish countryman is law conscious but hardly law-abiding. His inherent lawlessness springs from the freedom of the kin-group which was the normal co-operating economic and social unit.

Not only is this basic unit of society of high antiquity, but the local and regional varieties of landscape and life which it has helped to mould are also long established. The springs of patriotic feeling which poets and politicians have diverted towards 'the historic Irish nation' have their source in local loyalties. Study any aspect of material culture—types of thatch, shapes of spades, styles of field-fences, traditional fashions of food or dress—and you will find endless minor regional variations within what is at first sight a single homogeneous culture-province. It is these little things that identify

51

the *pays* and the *paysan*. In view of what I have said of the megalithic contribution to the elder faiths, it is significant that if one maps out the varieties of megalithic architecture and ritual as they are being revealed by current studies one becomes aware of a land already differentiated, by the beginning of the second millenium BC, into several cultural regions. The major ones, occupying the four main blocks of hilly country—north-west, north-east, south-west and south-east—foreshadow the four provinces of historic Ireland. Ulster in particular had a marked culture of its own, prophetically linked with that of south-western Scotland.

For over a thousand years, through a Bronze Age of astonishing vigour and brilliance, population expanded and new crops and domestic animals left their mark on the land. When, late in prehistoric times, oats were introduced—originating, it seems, as a weed in fields of wheat—they came to take the place of a crop which is at best risky in the climatic conditions of Ireland, and they have ever since remained the 'corn' of this cloudy land. The routine of oats cultivation is different in many important respects from that of wheat. It is spring-sown and, staying in the ground for a shorter period, takes less out of the soil than wheat. It will grow on poorer soils and ripen in all but the most extreme oceanic conditions. It demands less continuing care and less equipment than wheat cultivation, and its straw as well as its grain is useful for beasts. Moreover it leaves the fields free during the winter months for the grazing and manuring of livestock. Thus it became the medium of a system of land-use which was simpler, freer and more flexible than that of the English openfield village. It was a system which made extensive use of abundant rough pasturage and depended more on pastoral activities than on cultivation. Instead of the village with its tree-shaded green, its parish church and hierarchy, its orderly farmhouses and great open fields, the traditional unit of rural settlement in Ireland was the clustered hamlet, the bally or 'town' of perhaps a dozen thatched cabins occupied by members of a kin-group. Most of these hamlets were swept away in the agrarian revolution which brought enclosure and isolated farm-holdings, for they had never acquired the stability of the English village. A single open field—the infield—lay down-slope from the hamlet, on a patch of relatively fertile soil which had determined the choice of site. To facilitate drainage the crops were grown in high narrow ridges involving much heavy co-operative labour, and the ridges were disposed in little plots so that any one 'partner' held perhaps a score of patches scattered in all parts of the open field. As the population increased and the little patches were divided among co-heirs, the geography of the infield became an almost hopeless tangle. English observers such as Arthur Young condemned this 'rundale' system out of hand: its disorder was regarded as typically Irish, and it is worth noticing that it enriched the English language as spoken in Ireland with a most expressive epithet—the word 'throughother'.

The tools and implements of this small-scale agriculture were simple and sturdy: spades and wheel-less ploughs, flails, shovels, panniers and back-baskets, sledges and wheel-less carts, sieves, burden-ropes and rope-twisters. There was nothing that the travelling craftsman, and later the town shop, could not supply or which could not be made at home, nothing to put the peasants under an obligation to their overlord. Before the days of rack-rents they paid their taxes in the form of food-rents to a king—a custom which helps to explain the traditional lavish hospitality of Irish landlords—and they regarded themselves as tied by bonds of loyalty and blood, tenuous but invested with powerful emotional forces, to the larger kin-group or clan of which the king was leader. But this was still a small group. No complicated political institutions stood between the king and his kin, no feudal pyramid to fasten them down under its broad base. We sense the tradition of freedom and independence which the Irish countryman claims as his right. Suspicion of outside authority and resistance to oppressive laws have more than once united Irish countrymen of all creeds. Moreover the peasant's primary interest has nearly always been in livestock, whose mobility left him free to seek refuge in the hills if necessary. His system of agriculture condemned him to two periods of intense effort, in spring and harvest: for the rest of the year he was free to indulge himself without the tyranny of the soil. It was the capacity of the Irish labourer, trained to spadework, to endure periods of sustained effort without the nightly consolation of alcohol that gave him the advantage over English labourers and earned him the title of 'navvy' (navigator) in digging the canals of the eighteenth century. The Irish labourer, I am told, still prefers to save up his drinking for a periodic orgy.

It would be possible to work out the influence of long tradition on many aspects of present-day life in the Irish countryside, on the relations between the sexes, on hospitality, on 'friendliness' and co-operation, on attitudes towards the law or the weather, on the popularity of particular games and pastimes and so on. I propose to take two or three examples. Nothing could be more revealing than the geographical distribution in Ireland of the game of cricket: it is English and urban. The flannelled ritual of gentlemen and players is redolent of squires and villagers, and would be quite out of place in the Irish clachan. It is a pleasant theory, tying the game to the English openfield village, that the 22 yards of the cricket pitch owe their origin to the chain-width of furlong plough-strips across which plough-boys played ball between relict tree stumps when the day's acre was ploughed.

Or consider the countryman's attitude towards the weather; it is a matter which touches his well-being very closely, but he is not interested in climatic statistics. There is a touch of the supernatural about his respect for it, and one is reminded of the fame of Columbkille for having diverted the wind and checked the rain. It is wise neither to complain about the weather nor to tempt Providence by praising it. A day of dismal rain is merely 'soft' or 'damp'. I shouted a derogatory remark about the weather to a Donegal man one stormy harvest day. ''Tis wet', he admitted, 'but thank God 'tis windy.' Praise a spell of fine weather and you will be told, 'We'd best say nothing.' Similarly it is not wise to praise children or animals without adding a saving blessing: 'That's a right child, God bless him.' Young children are half jocularly referred to as 'wee rogues and tories'. For the fairies, it used to be said, are always on the look out to steal healthy children, especially boys. I had often heard that boys were formerly dressed as girls to deceive the fairies, but I little thought to see it for myself, as I once did in County Leitrim.

While the co-operative system which some reformers hoped would solve the economic and social problems of rural Ireland has not been a conspicuous success, various forms of small-scale co-operation are the very life of the countryside. The mutual obligations of neighbours are strong enough even in parts of Ulster to override the cleavage of religious differences. The 'swopping' of labour, the social visits at 'caileys' and wakes are characteristics of small 'neighbourhoods' of a townland or less. In the west of Ireland these co-operating units may still consist largely of blood relations, but in Ulster it is not uncommon, in areas where Protestants and Catholics live side by side, for them to share their labour or their implements. Indeed I have heard it said that members of the other religion make the best neighbours. No payments are made in these exchanges. It is characteristic of peasant societies that while money is highly esteemed as a means of bargaining with the outside world it is not used to measure work done or time spent in the circle of the family or neighbourhood. These traditional attitudes have helped to preserve a rough equality between neighbours, and the highest praise that can be given is to refer to someone as 'a modest man: you would never hear his name mentioned.' 'It is not easy', I wrote in my study of the Mourne Country, 'in a close-knit rural community of small family farms, exposed to the eye and criticism of neighbours in like circumstance, for young people to break with tradition.' It is necessary to add that conditions are different in the richer lowlands of Ulster where the population is almost exclusively Protestant. Here innovations are more readily accepted. The people may appear less friendly but their conversation, if slow beginning, is also richly rewarding.

Today, in place of the open fields, the Irish landscape is minutely divided into small fields among which the little farms lie evenly scattered, proudly isolated in their hard-won independence, their owners as jealous of their 'marches' as only men of property can be. The transformation of the land-scape was the result of new crops—potatoes, grasses and clovers especially—and of the practice of rotation agriculture involving enclosure, a movement beginning effectively in the late eighteenth century and not yet everywhere complete. But although there are thousands of miles of thorn 'ditches'—and stone dykes in the mountains and stony places—the country is singularly open and free of woodland. In destroying the last remnants of the ancient forests in the seventeenth century the invading English armies completed a process which the Irish themselves and their grazing livestock had been busy at for centuries. In the end the countryside was left almost bare, save for the planted 'demesnes' of the landlords, and even these are now being ravished. One consequence of this secular destruction of the native oak-woods is the absence of timbered or half-timbered buildings and of oaken gates and gateposts. The huge whitewashed stone gate-piers which take their place are most in evidence in the North, where folklore, indeed, hints at a venerable origin and an archaic symbolism.

One does not look for quality woodwork in furniture and the like in a land without good timber. Most peasant furniture in Ireland is made of imported deal, though one occasionally finds pleasing if rough pieces con-structed of oak dug from the bogs; and discoveries of wooden objects on sites preserved in the bogs testify to arts that deteriorated when the oak woods were lost. Such peasant arts and crafts as once existed have mostly perished. They were anyhow restricted by the absence of a complex system of agriculture and by the dominance of the simple needs of the cattle-herder. Nor do the arts of painting, sculpture, architecture or orchestral music spring from a peasant people: they demand special equipment and bourgeois capital. On the other hand the fiddle and the pipes can charm us with their traditional tunes, and the art of story-telling finds here one of its last European homes. The isolated rural communities, poor in material resources, have practised pastimes which demand little save the skills of voice and body: poetry, singing, oratory, dancing—as well as fighting and football—and raised them sometimes to a high level of art. The unlettered peasant has amazing faculties of speech and natural rhetoric and often pos-sesses very clear powers of reasoning. In these matters one man may be as good as another, whatever his station in life, and poverty goes hand in hand with a democratic spirit. To the efficiency experts the economics of hus-bandry as practised in many parts of Ireland are impossible: what economists do not take into account are the spiritual compensations of traditional ways of living.

[A.D. Kouwenhoven, G.A. de Bruijne and G.A. Hoekveld (eds),
Geplaetst in de tijd (Amsterdam 1984)]

part II

ATLANTIC EUROPE
The Pastoral Heritage

The term Atlantic Europe, in these days, has come to have implications of strategic, economic and political co-operation in Western Europe, and it carries with it a sense of an ocean wind of freedom. My use of the term, similarly, for a more restricted part of the continent, is meant to imply that, despite physical and political fragmentation, the Atlantic ends of Europe have inherited many common features of economic,[1] social and cultural life. I have attempted elsewhere to define in general terms the environmental and cultural features of this region. Here I shall try to isolate some of the factors that have given the communities of the Atlantic fringe what I have called a pastoral heritage, in which the ties of clan and kinship were strong enough to resist, in the main, the growth of feudal society. In its narrow sense the word pastoral refers to the historic preoccupation of the evergreen Atlantic coastlands with livestock and its products, above all with cattle, for which they are well adapted environmentally. (To illustrate this from current dietetic statistics, the country which has the highest per capita consumption of milk and dairy products in the world is Ireland. Or one might cite the many milky breeds of kine such as those of the Channel Islands, Kerry and Ayrshire.) But I also have in mind the extended meaning of pastoralism, the strong spiritual forces which have repeatedly welled up and flowed out to enrich the whole Western World. Again and again saints and scholars, singers and orators, preachers and teachers, poets and dramatists, political leaders and agitators have raised their voices and gone forth on their missions. British life, for example, would be much simpler but infinitely the poorer without their contribution. It is probably an oversimplification to relate this wealth of the spirit directly to the material poverty of pastoral peasants, but the association cannot be denied. The Establishment thrives on wheat, but the Evangelicals, it seems, do best on oats.

We have long been taught to see the Mediterranean lands as a cultural unit around the Great Sea. The Atlantic lands lack an African shore and we cannot nowadays think in terms of an Atlantic Sea, but until the end of the Middle Ages the European Atlantic was effectively closed to the west by a barrier of mists and myths. We must not underestimate the capacity of Atlantic seamen to break through that barrier, from Eric the Red to those many forerunners of Columbus—Irish, Welsh, Basque and Portuguese—to whose numbers Professor David Quinn[2] has recently proposed to add the bold men of Bristol. But as a navigation route the European Atlantic was until the end of the Middle Ages a closed sea in which men and their goods and ideas had circulated since prehistoric times. The sense of a closed Atlantic community is clear in the legendary histories of Ireland, for they tell of a world, the world, which extended 'from Brittany to Norway and from the Orkneys to Spain'.[3] The epics and sagas of this Western World are, by common consent, the finest examples of early medieval literature in Europe.

We have been accustomed to think of our own Highland zone—thanks to an Englishman's interpretation of the personality of Britain[4]—as a barrier against which beneficent waves of continental culture broke in vain. Detached fragments of culture that were splashed up or filtered through were soaked up by the impoverished west as by damp blotting-paper. The highlands, in this view, were a dead end, providing at best a back door into the fat English lowlands. But it is well to remind ourselves, in Stuart Piggott's graphic phrase, that the back door is often the tradesman's entrance. Through the back door, in the early days of metal, came gold and other rare metals and hard stones, commodities in which the lowlands of England were poorly endowed. The idealization of the past which is a recurrent theme in the folklore and literature of the Atlantic fringe may find some justification in the reality of a lost Golden Age. For what I have called the Atlantic ends of Europe, impoverished as they are in many material things, are rich in the old rocks where precious metals tend to be concentrated.

The Atlantic ends share a climate in which rains fall throughout the year, favouring grass rather than cereals. They extend in a broken arc of hilly peninsulas and islands through some 2000 miles, from about the mouth of the Douro to the Lofoten Islands. The granites, quartzites and other metamorphic rocks which predominate yield a thin soil which when exposed is rapidly depleted of its few plant nutrients by the leaching of heavy rains. Young soils on any scale occur only in the dune-fringed re-entrant of the Bay of Biscay. Save locally and in the south, where soils and climate are more favourable, agriculture is difficult. The Mediterranean peninsulas, on the other hand, are largely composed of sun-baked limestones, rich in plant-foods. In terms of land use the historic contrast is between intensive fruit cultivation—vine, fig and olive—on the one hand, supplemented by wheat and barley sown to catch the autumn rains, and on the other hand a pastoral economy, supplemented by spring-sown cereals, chiefly oats, which provided sustenance for man and beast.

The ancient urban settlements and civic values of Mediterranean civilization stand in contrast to the rural isolation and familial values of Atlantic culture. This is not to say that there was not, as Sir James Frazer demonstrated, a powerful undercurrent of pastoral cults in the classical world, or that strong kinship ties are not found in parts of the Mediterranean world today. Nor should it be assumed that pastoralism and its concomitant features were ever completely dominant along the Atlantic, to the exclusion of agricultural land use and settled society. Professor Parain's statement, in the *Cambridge Economic History*, that 'Fifteenth-century Ireland remained, in great part, a country of wandering pastoralists',[5] has been hotly refuted,[6] and Welsh scholars have rightly rejected the Saxon myth of Celtic cowboys who were innocent of the plough. Nor were these areas, however, as has often been assumed, immemorially enclosed and settled in single farms. It is now clear that a regional variety of openfield agriculture, involving the continuous cultivation of an infield and shifting cultivation of the outfield, was practised until recent times in all the Atlantic lands from Galicia to Norway and survives here and there, more or less modified, to this day. It was characterized by small clusters of farms occupied by close kinsmen holding the land jointly, and enjoying many common rights. It is not my purpose to discuss this system of settlement and land use save in so far as it goes with, and can be understood in the light of, a predominantly pastoral economy, but it may be noted that recent research tends to support the views of Gray and Clapham as to the important part played by Celtic systems of land use in shaping some of the varied patterns of open-field agriculture in lowland England.[7]

The historian can tell us little about medieval rural society in the pastoral west. Documents relating to the peasantries are rare even in the seventeenth century: they were too poor to be caught in the net of written contracts. The Atlantic open-field system, for example, flexible and working to unwritten rules, needed no Acts of Parliament to break it up. To supplement and extend the meagre historic records, therefore, we have to rely on other

methods of enquiry. Intensive field studies, geographical, ecological, ethno-
logical and archaeological, though not entirely respectable academically,
and often regarded indeed as parochial and pedestrian, need be neither save
in the literal sense of the words: they can be pieced together to give, within
the limitations of the evidence, a coherent picture of successive stages of
society. I believe that, in the present state of knowledge, comparative
anthropology will be better served by local field studies, investigating the
patterns of regional societies against the changing conditions of their environments, than by amassing examples of world-wide uniformities of custom
and belief such as those assembled with such consummate skill by Frazer in
his golden volumes. Now that archaeology, with the aid of novel techniques,
has revealed and measured the vast time span of human history, we can no
longer place much trust in the reconstruction of primitive religion, for
instance, from the beliefs of present-day 'primitives' in the far corners of the
world. We need to extend and intensify field observations over geographically coherent areas. As Marc Bloch insisted, the framework of institutions
within which a society lives can be understood only in the light of the whole
human environment. With this in mind, co-ordinated field studies can be
used to advance our knowledge of culture-history.

It is one of the advantages of working in the Atlantic lands that environmental conditions have themselves favoured the preservation of much valuable evidence that would otherwise be lost. The changing levels of land and
sea consequent on post-glacial readjustments are recorded in raised beaches
and submerged forests where early human remains and artefacts as well as
floristic and faunistic evidence have been saved from destruction and can be
dated with increasing accuracy. Inland, too, on plateaux and in lowland hollows, the moist Atlantic climate has cooperated by leaving behind its own
record in accumulated layers of peat. Not only do the peat bogs frequently
contain lost artefacts, or deposits—like bog butter—deliberately made for
votive or security purposes,[8] which lie in stratigraphical order century after
century, but they preserve countless billions of pollen grains from samples
of which the sequence of vegetation types and of agricultural change since
prehistoric times—even of the weeds and wild flowers—can be studied.
Carbon-14 dating, moreover, can be applied to the peat and to the fossil
wood and charcoal preserved in it. Our knowledge of the conditions of life
through several thousand years is thus greatly enlarged. The oral traditions
of the peasant, similarly, preserve memories and supernatural beliefs from
various strata of culture-history. Material poverty and the simplicity of
small-scale husbandry, moreover, have led to the survival into modern times
of many archaic types of tools, buildings and techniques. In their study the
ethnologist and the archaeologist join hands.

Many parts of the Atlantic fringe were not peopled, on present evidence, until post-glacial times, so that in peeling off, as it were, successive layers one can reach back to the regional beginnings of human history. Much information is now available on the environmental conditions and cultures of the post-glacial period. The resources of Atlantic Europe first exploited by man were the fruits of the warm waters which flooded in over coasts that were still adjusting themselves to changing levels of land and sea. The migration routes of littoral birds may well have guided fishers and fowlers along the Atlantic coasts, while the migratory fish of the Atlantic rivers, as we know from the attraction exerted by such rivers as the Bann, were a major source of food. At many points between Portugal and Scandinavia the accumulated refuse heaps of shore-dwellers testify to the long-established fishing and collecting habits of Mesolithic folk who by the middle of the fourth millennium BC were beginning to acquire some knowledge of food production and domesticated animals. By this time the pollen record shows that the dense Atlantic forests were being influenced locally by human activity. The fisherfolk already possessed dug-out and probably skin boats, and study of their tools, many of them designed for working wood, bone and skin, shows that north-east Ireland, for example, an area famous for fish and for flint, was receiving influences both from Denmark and the Asturian coast. Not a few archaic elements in Atlantic culture are derived from this oldest Mesolithic layer. There are the poaching leisters, the fishing-pots, traps, weirs and baskets, the skin boats which are still not quite extinct—and the salmon fishing coracles which derive from them—some of them archaeologically attested in the Mesolithic. More generally the making of nets, hurdles, creels and baskets, especially coiled baskets, are ancient skills, and some of the strange beliefs and tabus of Atlantic fisherfolk may have come down through seventy centuries. Until recently on some Irish lakes three-ply fishing lines were fashioned from horsehair by feeding strands of hair through goose-feather quills which were rotated in the hand. To watch this simple process, or to see a fisherman roll a hair line on his bared knee, his hand dried in wood ash from the fire, is to sense the persistence of Mesolithic habits. These are isolated traits, but I believe it may be shown that the true native stock, toughened through many millennia, has contributed much, physically and culturally, to the Atlantic heritage. Carleton Coon claims that at least half of the genetic ancestry of the composite modern Irishman is to be referred to the survival of strains from the Mesolithic sub-stratum. This has been disputed, however, by E.A. Hooton and C.W. Dupertuis.[9]

Fishing and shore collecting, though they have developed locally into profitable industries, have persisted along many Atlantic coasts among groups who combine these activities with farming and herding. Such crofting communities have immemorially gathered seaweed and shell-sand to enrich their patches of cultivation, and taken their livestock to graze on the shore in winter. (The Irish tradition of visiting the shore at Easter and feasting on shellfish is presumably of pre-Christian origin, and the morsel of tasty fish which was the relish or 'kitchen' of potato-eaters may also have been a relic feature.) A large measure of co-operation is necessary in this as in inshore fishing, and some of these coastal communities have kept themselves rather apart from those living inland.

But their partial acculturation goes back a long way, for the Mesolithic fisherfolk, living by the sea, were exposed to ideas coming by sea. Some groups early acquired a knowledge of pottery, which appears characteristically in forms lavishly decorated with cord, shell and basketry impressions or derived designs which reflect their interests and activities. Like coiled basketry or lipe-work, it is built up in coils. Such pottery, occurring in late Mesolithic horizons on sand-hill, sea-shore and lakeside sites in Ireland, for example, is interpreted as a response to the new ideas and techniques accompanying food-production which had infiltrated into Europe from the Near East. The path of diffusion which concerns us is the Atlantic route leading northwards from the Iberian peninsula. In Brittany, a site at Brasparts in Finistère which has been dated to soon after the middle of the fourth millennium is believed to have been occupied by immigrants who practised cereal cultivation and tethered grazing. Before 3000 BC classic corbelled megalithic passage graves of Portuguese type were being erected in Brittany,[10] and the associated pottery, of a kind which was soon to reach the British Isles in strength, belongs to the strikingly regional family which is known as 'western Neolithic'. In recent years this pottery has turned up in Ireland in prodigious quantities on excavated sites as far apart as Limerick and Antrim. With minor stylistic changes, it appears to have had a life of well over a thousand years, so that the Neolithic period, until lately conceived as a mere prelude to the Metal Age, is now being re-examined and re-assessed by prehistorians. It is not yet clear whether western pottery precedes the megalithic tombs with which it is most typically associated—e.g. the court cairns of the area stretching from Connacht to the Clyde—but both the megalithic habit and the pottery are clearly linked with the Atlantic route. Here I want only to refer to the evidence for the early development of pastoral activities. This western ware is well described as leathery: it is thin, hard, round-bottomed, dark brown in colour, rarely decorated but frequently burnished. It was clearly made in imitation of leather vessels, even to the sophisticated elaboration of rims and shoulders, where leather vessels require strengthening if they are to keep their shape. And it was made for suspension over an open fire. The simplicity of such cooking gear, not far removed from the bare necessities of a nomad's encampment, has proved adequate, culturally and climatically, for the simple peasant houses of the Atlantic coasts down to this day, so that the open hearth with its visible welcome and rich associations of tradition and story-telling is a link with many generations of ancestors. Nowadays of course it is the cast-iron pot (still round-bottomed) which hangs suspended from the crane: in connection with its suggested derivation there is an interesting Irish folk belief that money obtained from the sale of a cowhide should be used for the purchase of a metal vessel.

When we began turning up this pottery in quantity twenty-five years ago in Ireland, no-one would believe that it could be of high antiquity: its quality and abundance were alike astonishing, and for many later periods, even into the Middle Ages, pottery of any kind was extremely rare. With increasing pastoralism, it seems, the art of pottery-making, save for funerary purposes, declined and may even have been lost, wooden and leather vessels serving instead. The pioneer farmers, it should be remembered, brought with them cultural capital acquired in sunnier climates and they were able to exploit the untapped fertility of forest soils. So far as can be seen from the archaeological evidence, farming and stock-breeding spread hand in hand, though the Mesolithic folk may have borrowed domesticated animals— cattle, goats, sheep and pigs—before they took to arable farming. The pig, a forest animal, was perhaps the first to be adopted. We certainly cannot envisage anything like large-scale ranching, for the forest cover was almost complete. But it seems likely that the natural pastures of the higher hills, in Norway and also in the British Isles and Spain, were utilized in summer as they have been in historic times under the system of seasonal nomadism known as transhumance.[11] In south France, M. Louis regards the dolmens of Languedoc as the work of a pastoral people of Campignian culture who practised transhumance. In Ireland the carboniferous limestone plateau of the Burren in north Clare is unusually rich in gallery-graves, and Professor R. de Valera has associated them with pastoral activities. The Burren is exceptional in that its pastures are nowadays utilized in winter.[12]

Neolithic farmers favoured areas of light dry soils, typically near the coasts and on the hillslopes, where forest undergrowth was less dense. Extensive use was made, it is believed, of leaves and twigs and of elmbast for feeding livestock. In addition, the elm tree may have been used as an ecological indicator of soils suitable for clearing for temporary cultivation. At any rate the decline of elm pollen—presumably wych elm—beginning in many areas before 3000 BC, by radio-carbon dating, coincides with the beginnings of food production, which is independently recorded in the appearance of cereal and weed pollens, especially that of the ribwort plantain.[13]

That clearings were soon abandoned is shown by the pollen succession which indicates the spread of nettles and bracken, gorse and heather. Soon afterwards, pollen of the ash, a light-requiring species, occurs for the first time in any quantity, followed by hazel, alder, mountain-ash, birch and thorn. That these shrubs are old companions of man makes understandable the magic with which they are endowed. The rowan and the whitethorn, in particular, have powerful magic where cattle and milk are concerned.

This brief summary is grossly oversimplified and takes no account of climatic change or other factors affecting the changing composition of the forests. What matters for our purpose is that, from the end of the fourth millennium, animal husbandry and the shifting cultivation of wheat and barley were well established along almost the whole length of the Atlantic fringe. The spread of successive megalithic tomb types along the Atlantic route is striking evidence of its continued use throughout the third millennium. Many other archaeological distributions could be cited, stemming in particular from Spain and Portugal. The Atlantic coastlands of Iberia, the focus of many movements culminating in those associated with the cult of St James in the early Middle Ages, have strong prehistoric links with Brittany, western Britain and Ireland. There is the evidence of the cup-marks and concentric circles pecked on stone dating from the early days of metal and believed to be associated, from Galicia to Argyll, with mining activities.[14] Again there are the 'Atlantic bronzes' of the period from the eighth to the third centuries BC, when votive offerings of bronze axes in Galicia and Brittany, sometimes in enormous numbers, are characterized by bronze so adulterated with lead as to be useless.[15] Whether we regard the adulteration as evidence of pious fraud or economic necessity, the deposits demonstrate the strength and continuity of magic practices and beliefs along the Atlantic.

It was the possession of stones suitable for making axes, the woodman's tool, that brought wealth and export trade to the west in the Neolithic period. All along the fringe, fine-grained igneous or metamorphic rocks suitable for polishing were quarried, shaped and supplied to markets both at home and in the lowlands of Britain and western Europe. There are the metamorphosed tuffs of the Great Langdale group in Cumberland, the granophyre of Graig Lwyd and the dolerite of Preseli in Wales, the porcellanite of County Antrim, the greenstones of Bomlo in Norway and the varied greenstones—jadeite, chloromelanite and diorite—of Brittany. Some very localized deposits have either never been rediscovered or were worked out, as must have happened later with the gold-bearing river gravels of many Atlantic streams. Megalithic burials were frequently accompanied by polished axes of superb workmanship, and in folklore until quite recently a stone axe placed in the milking pail could work magic by increasing the flow of milk.

Whether the megaliths are to be attributed to colonists, prospectors, missionaries or chieftains—and all these theories have been advanced—their intimate association with food production, with the spirit world and with the promotion of fertility seems clear. Until recently fertility rites were still surreptitiously practised at prehistoric stone monuments in Brittany and Ireland, for example, and that such rites are ancient is shown by the many compromises the early Celtic Church had to make over their interpretation.

This continuity can be partly understood in the light of the limited sites available in the Atlantic environment for agricultural occupation, and of the enduring nature of the great stone monuments themselves. A patch of relative fertility on river estuary or raised beach, on a detritus fan or a hillslope enriched by an outcrop of limestone, is likely to display evidence of settlement at successive periods. One might cite the Carnac area in the Morbihan, the Vale in Guernsey and the Crinan district in Argyll.

On the other hand many areas of light soil, once supporting forests, rapidly lost their fertility when clearings were made and shallow cultivation introduced, a process which began in Neolithic times. It is an impressive and not uncommon sight in Ireland to see the great stone tombs erected by Neolithic farmers in their patches of cultivation now almost completely buried in peat. Pollen studies of the old soils and the basal layers of peat on such sites consistently show the deterioration of forest soils into podsols following temporary cultivation, and the subsequent growth of scrub, heather and successive bog-forming plants. Some of the characteristic types of heath vegetation, it should be observed, had been 'resident' since late glacial (Allerod) times and were able to spread as opportunity offered.

Bog and moorland vegetation came to be utilized for increasing pastoral purposes. The blanket bogs which spread in prehistoric times over plateaus and hillslopes, whether initiated by human interference or climatic change, provided extensive grazing adequate for summering stock so long as it was not enclosed, for a healthy variety of grazing grounds, topographically and botanically, would thus have been denied to the flocks and herds. It is because enclosure was unwise as well as uneconomic that common rights such as the 'souming' of the Scottish Highlands have persisted in many Atlantic environments. At lower elevations, too, the foliage of such familiar Atlantic shrubs as the evergreen gorse and broom has been utilized in place of the more abundant leaf harvest of former forests. These golden shrubs, rich in folklore, have traditionally been planted on land exhausted by cropping, to be harvested as winter fodder and for a great variety of other uses—in Galicia, in Brittany and in Ireland and west Britain. Philologists have made the interesting suggestion that among the few Basque loan-words in Gaelic are those for gorse and for a cow's hoof. Another Atlantic evergreen, the holly, was cultivated locally to feed wintering sheep, for example, in the Lake District. Thomas Pennant, writing of the same district, refers to a complaint of Elizabethan times that the new iron bloomeries were ruining the dalesmen because they consumed all the 'loppings and croppings, the sole winter food for their cattle'.[16] One finds traces of a belief in the almost magic or at least medicinal virtues of such fodder, a belief which seems to point to antiquity. I have already referred to the luck which is linked with the hazel twig and the rowan branch. The flowering whitethorn—the sacred tree of Ireland—has associations both of colour and scent with milk and with cows and similarly a host of golden wild flowers which followed in man's footsteps—gorse, primrose, marsh marigold and dandelion—were magically connected with butter and figured in the May festivals; garlands of golden flowers known as 'summer' were sometimes tied to the cows' tails. There is beauty as well as a wealth of magic in the gold of May and again in the bronze of November. The first days of May and November, the beginnings of summer and winter, were the turning points of the pastoral year, joints of time along which the supernatural could intrude. Frazer's *Golden Bough* itself has not escaped the attention of the palynologists, for mistletoe pollen has been used, with that of two other storied evergreens—the holly and the ivy—as a sensitive index of the changing frontier of the Atlantic climate in post-glacial Europe.[17]

For several reasons, the last centuries of the pre-Christian era were especially critical for the adjustment of society to environment in the areas under discussion. The effects of the climatic deterioration which is labelled sub-Atlantic have been emphasized by some writers and denied by others, but all would agree that the cultural changes which brought a knowledge of iron, a wider range of tools and weapons and new crops and agricultural techniques left a profound mark on life and landscape. The establishment of a Celtic-speaking hierarchy of warrior-chieftains from north Spain to south Scotland gave pastoral ways of life a new prestige. A correlation has been made between the climatic deterioration on the one hand and on the other the decline of wheat cultivation and the beginning of hay-making to provide winter fodder, but it is more important for our purpose to notice the first appearance of oats as a cultivated crop. The adaptation of this cereal to Atlantic conditions, ecologically and culturally, is clear. Not only did it nourish man and beast, but being spring-sown it fitted into the climatic regime of relatively dry springs and allowed the cultivated land to be utilized for the grazing of stock after their return from the hills. Beginning, it appears, as weeds in fields of wheat and barley, oats were not sown for grain on present evidence until the late Bronze Age. Their oldest known occurrence is in northern Europe, but since one of their probable homes of cultivation is the Pyrenees they may have spread thence along the Atlantic seaboard. In the Middle Ages the cider apple is believed to have been diffused by this route from north Spain to Brittany and Devon.[18] The specialized fruit-growing—apples and cherries—which has been developed on old infields in certain districts in western Norway is also said to have been a medieval introduction. From the Pyrenees could have come the sycamore which is today the commonest tree on many a wind-swept Atlantic coast where no native tree can be found. Wordsworth noted in his *Guide to the Lakes* (1810) that the sycamore had long been the favourite tree of the cottagers. Although its cultivation in Britain is said to date only from the sixteenth century, its timber has been identified in Irish bog finds and Dark Age crannógs. Not only will this tree withstand salt-laden winds but its white wood is eminently suitable for turnery and dairy utensils. Planted about the farmyard it is believed, in Montgomeryshire for instance, to protect the dairy from the fairies.[19] A Lusitanian export which is said, surprisingly, to have reached Ireland only a century and a half ago is the domesticated ass, sent in return for Irish horses exported to the Peninsular Wars.[20]

Legendary history, archaeology and forest history all point to a great expansion of economy, population and forest clearing along the fringe between the fourth and the eighth centuries AD. In the Celtic world this was the Age of the Saints whose travels renewed old contacts along the Atlantic seaboard and forged new ones reaching out to Iceland. But it was also an age when new techniques borrowed from the Roman world led to a renewal of agrarian activity which amounted to an agricultural revolution. Though milk and dairy products were at first forbidden in the monastic diet, and much forest clearing must have been in the first place for cultivation, the evidence points to increasing pastoral activity, at any rate in Ireland. In the pollen record the elm tree virtually disappears to be replaced by hazel and later by plantain and meadow weeds.[21] Single homesteads surrounded by circular farmyards—the raths—multiply throughout the lowlands. The economy revealed by the excavation of raths and crannógs was predominantly one of animal husbandry. Some 80 per cent of the enormous numbers of bones recovered from one crannóg site, Lagore in County Meath, amounting to 21 tons, belonged to cattle.[22] Pigs and sheep were relatively unimportant. We learn from the *Annals* that in the Dark and Middle Ages cattle-raiding was not merely a normal seasonal occupation and a recognized means of acquiring food, wealth and prestige but something of a ceremonial obligation laid on the leaders. So well did the Church adapt itself to the pastoral ethic that sixth-century saints of the finest quality are represented by their biographers as demanding a percentage of the takings of each successful raid. Before the power and polity of the Gaelic leaders were finally broken in early seventeenth-century Ulster, we read of the capture of 30,000 cows in a single raid.[23] There is little wonder that, as happens in parts of Africa where cattle are similarly amassed for purposes of prestige, the land was in many areas bitten bare. The nakedness of so many Atlantic landscapes is their most striking feature to this day, though they may be partly clothed with the permanent hedges, walls and earthen fences which more intensive systems of husbandry have called for.

Although cattle-raiding was the prerogative of men the milking of cows has traditionally been women's work, until mechanical aids and commercial rewards came to ease the labour and dignify the task for men. We know that the bleeding of cattle for food was practised in some parts of the fringe into last century.[24] It may be presumed that this is an older custom than the utilization of milk; and one would like to know when dairying was adopted. The oldest datable deposits of bog-butter have been placed at the very beginning of the Christian era,[25] so that we must look at latest to the early Iron Age for the full exploitation of milk and milk products as more efficient means of utilizing livestock for food. Sheep were generally of minor importance in the Atlantic tradition until commercial husbandry came in.

I should like now to consider briefly certain social and cultural traits which have persisted in these areas and which can be related in one way or another to the pastoral heritage. The use of the patronymic and the strength of familial bonds reflect the pride of blood which is characteristic of the breeder of animals. Loyalty to kin outlives changing economic conditions and persists in some degree in the world of business and local government: it can still on occasions prove itself a stronger force than truth or justice. Suspicion of external authority, especially of impersonal authority, is another factor leading to difficulties of government. The spirit of independence is notably strong in areas where the enjoyment of common pastoral rights is combined with the freedom of the sea: life on many of the smaller Atlantic islands offers a degree of freedom often amounting to lawlessness. The sea has provided opportunities not only for fishing and trading but also for escape, for raiding, piracy and smuggling. The flavour of lawlessness can indeed be tasted in Irish whiskey, for it is said that parliament whiskey, as the legitimate product was called, had to imitate the smoky flavour of home-made poteen whiskey before it could win a battle that is not yet quite over. Lawless, too, in the sense that there was no perceptible order in its plan, was the clachan or farm-town, in contrast to the more disciplined village of England or France. The word 'throughother' well expresses this characteristic. The joint tenants, too, were possessed of a fierce sense of equality which displayed itself in endless disputes and trials of strength as well as in peaceful co-operation.

Such small units of population were served by few urban centres and had to be largely self-sufficient, yet were too poor and too small to support specialist craftsmen. A proportion of the population, moreover, the more substantial farmers, have lived in single farms since later prehistoric times, and this type of scattered habitation is now widespread, for the lone steading gives the stock-breeder ready access to his animals at all times. Craftsmen such as tailors and skilled woodworkers were therefore itinerant.[26] Despised as landless men, the itinerants yet had social as well as economic functions; and their tradition persists to this day.

More obviously in the direct pastoral tradition are the cattle-drovers and seasonal migrants who followed the roads to England and paved the way for that continuing migration, from Ireland, Scotland and Wales, which has supplied London not only with labourers but with politicians, doctors, poets, preachers and teachers as well as with milkmen and drapers. The Irish summer migrants included pedlars and dealers, but they came to be mainly harvesters, young adults who, before the decline of transhumance, would have occupied themselves at home with summer herding on the hills. We might thus think of the spalpeens as practising an extended transhumance. In Spain, similarly, the wheat fields of Castile were reaped by migrant harvesters from Galicia.

Among the many elements of material culture which have an Atlantic distribution and a pastoral heritage is the long house, a house sheltering both men and beasts. The term has come to be used for a developed type now best known in parts of Wales, in which house and byre share a common entry, but the simplest type, to be found until quite recently in the Hebrides and western Ireland, consisted of a single room and had no partition between men and beasts. The traditional peasant house along the Atlantic, its walls made formerly of mud or sods, sometimes on a stone foundation, is not far removed from this ancestral long house. The rectangular house can be traced back to the Neolithic period but the circular house is of similar antiquity, and the historic rectangular house may equally well have developed from the round house through intermediate oval forms. It may be conjectured that the roof of the ancestral long house was supported on crucks, a device which restricts the width and could thus have determined the traditional size and shape of the house. It is unlucky, runs an Irish saying, to build a house more than a single room wide. It is possible indeed that such houses were so built as to be readily moved, for the crucks could be transported and we know that the turves which are still the main component of the roof of old houses—under the thatch—were in some districts cut in long strips so as to be movable, for example by Ulster transhumants in the seventeenth century.[27]

Such dual-purpose houses necessarily had the hearth towards one end—the living end—and not therefore in the centre of the building; in Ireland, for instance, the gable-chimneyed peasant long house of the north and west contrasts with the central-chimneyed house of the south and east, which betrays English influences. The open hearth, however, remained characteristic until recently, for the pastoral diet of oaten thin bread required no oven. One might cite many cultural parallels in the detail of house and furniture along the fringe, such as the falling-leaf table, the bed-alcove, roped thatch, the straw-seated chair and the half-door—designed to let in light but to exclude unwanted livestock—which is as much at home in Galicia as in Ireland.[28] One notes also the Atlantic distribution of field fences of earth and stone, the two-wheeled cart, the long-handled shovel and the single thole-pin oar which is found on fishing boats in Portugal and on the Irish rowing curragh. In many instances this cultural parallelism arises from the survival of old techniques in areas which were isolated in the impoverished Atlantic ends. In other instances it is related to the intrinsic properties, physical and social, of the Atlantic environment. Galicia, Ireland and Norway, for example, were countries which early accepted and have continued to utilize the potato, a crop well suited to areas of heavy precipitation, acid soils and small family farms. The potato, food for man and beast, came to supplement and at times dangerously to replace cereal and herbaceous crops.

This Atlantic world, with its ancient cultures and values that I have for simplicity's sake called pastoral, has played a critical role in the life of our islands. For the British Isles are distinctive among the regions of western Europe not only in being insular, but in having a fair balance, as compared say with Norway, France or Spain, between the Atlantic-highland and continental-lowland zones. The two zones have been in constant interplay, and the resurgence of nationalism in the Atlantic-highland areas has fortunately not led to their isolation. It is to be hoped that Irish exports of all kinds will continue to cross the Irish Sea, and that Welshmen will continue to supply London not only with milk but with metaphorical doses of sour milk to leaven the solid English dough. Cross-fertilization between the two cultures has led to innovations and enriched the life of our islands from early times. It is not merely that economic history can trace some of the roots of the Industrial Revolution back to the Middle Ages, when novel techniques repeatedly appeared in the intermediate belt of country from Yorkshire to Devon, in what might be called a 'zone of hybridization':[29] prehistoric archaeology tells a similar story. One thinks not only of the unique character of Stonehenge, placed between the Atlantic south-west and the English lowlands, but of the original quality of many of our prehistoric monuments, of the innovations in metal technology illustrated in the development of bronze spearhead, or again later on in the novelty of the penannular brooch which so well illustrates, besides, a continuity of native Iron Age culture which the glare of the Roman occupation has obscured.[30] We should not of course underestimate the importance of external ideas or of the many regional diversities, within each of the two broad zones of British life, of which my revered teacher Professor H.J. Fleure spoke in an earlier Frazer lecture,[31] but in assessing such British qualities as inventiveness and respect for conscience as well as what is called the genius for compromise, full weight should be given to the impact through the centuries, on the established routine of lowland life, of the roving pastoral tradition with its pride of blood, its spiritual values and oral gifts and its contemptuous impatience of external authority.

[The Frazer Lecture (1961)]

THE PYRENEES
A Geographical Interpretation of their Role in Human Times

It is a commonplace that Africa begins at the Pyrenees; and while it would be generally admitted that a good deal of truth is sacrificed to the conciseness of this phrase, it is none the less clear that physical and cultural phenomena combine to make the frontier range a barrier that is unique in modern Europe. Its separative value, however, has been variously estimated by writers who stress the importance either of the unsurmountable wall of the central Pyrenees or of the terminal passes in which such a wealth of historical and literary interest is concentrated. These views are but different aspects of the truth; and this may best be approached through a conception of distribution in time and space, which is the basis of historical geography.

This remarkably continuous range owes its features in large measure to the fact that the mountain-building forces of Tertiary times were restricted by the ancient blocks of the Central Plateau of France and the Spanish meseta. Geologically it comprises a central core of Palaeozoic rocks, together with great masses of granite, flanked by Jurassic, Cretaceous, and Eocene deposits. The last are well developed on the southern side, and Barré suggests that their virtual disappearance from the northern slopes, which altogether, indeed, comprise hardly more than a third of the total central width, is due to climatic agencies, variations in which will obviously have an important bearing on the separative function of any mountain system.

Limitation of space inhibits a detailed structural description: our first concern must be rather with general considerations. Two points worthy of emphasis are the inter-marine location of the range, and its east-to-west alignment. Connected with the former fact are the foundered areas at the seaward terminations, adjoining zones of broken topography determined by the existence of the ancient nuclei of Labourd in the west and Mouthoumet in the east, and the consequent occurrence, not only of comparatively easy coastal routes, but also of excellent harbours along the present frontier at both ends. A long tradition of seafaring life has thus played a part in binding together the coastal populations; and since it is these coastal relations which a human study serves to bring out, we shall describe the terminal features in some detail after examining the great central barrier whose role, in contrast, has been largely a negative one. A study of space-relationships is more important, for our purpose, than a restricted interpretation of intrinsic conditions.

In considering the direction of the range it must be remembered that the Cordillera Cantabrica constitutes, to all intents and purposes, a direct westward continuation, and forms, with the Pyrenees, a mountain wall over 500 miles in length, running roughly in a latitudinal direction, that is, coincident with the normal direction of boundaries between successive climatic regions. The significance of the latitude (42°–43.5°N) as a critical index of change from Mediterranean to temperate conditions serves to increase the interest of this boundary zone. It is the central section of the Pyrenees which, in all this long stretch, forms the most difficult physical obstacle and separates the most strongly contrasted regions, presenting its 150 miles of impressive peaks, from 8000 to 11,000 feet high, above the level plains of Gascony. From the Pic d'Anie (8215 feet) on the west to the abrupt end at the Canigou (9135 feet) towering above Roussillon, no pass falls below 5000 feet—the Somport (5400 feet), the Col de la Perche (5280 feet), and the Puymorens (6400 feet) being by far the lowest and most significant from an historical point of view. (The last two belong to the eastern Pyrenees, for the effective limit of our central division is Andorra.) Yet the human frontier does not lie along the crests. On the north, the *gaves*, fed by copious Atlantic rains, cut deeply through rocks of varied ages in wild ravines along which movement is still extremely difficult. This belt of steep, wooded foothills has formed, in human affairs, a greater barrier than the high mountains, where the open tracks, not the valley lines, are the traditional links in the intra-montane life. On the Spanish side lie the parallel sierras, line upon line, separated by the longitudinal headwaters of the Ebro tributaries. This régime is not sufficiently complex to provide easy passes—as it does in the Alps—but gives rise, on the other hand, to a notoriously difficult country comparable to the Jura. Here also, towards the southern boundary of the sierras, many miles from the Pyrenean crest-line, is the human frontier; and thus, as we shall see later, the unity of the central mountain mass, an inert area deflecting historic movement, is more fundamental than the location of the present political frontier along the impressively continuous crest would imply. But to stress this point is not to underestimate the significance of the mountain barrier.

Beneath the central Pyrenees, on the north, is the remarkable fan-shaped area of mountain *débris* traversed by the divergent tributaries of Garonne and Adour, which run in straight immature valleys having no lateral connections. The apex of the cone is the plateau of Lannemezan, an immense stretch of clay and rounded pebbles which forms part of the piedmont zone between the southernmost river valleys. There is a marked concentration of settlement and movement along the piedmont, where the routes have for ages been determined by the fluvial terraces of the upper Garonne and the Gave de Pau. To the south the steep calcareous foothills impede intercourse, while to the north the radiating valleys present grave obstacles to transverse communication. The lack of unity in the plains of south-west France, and the tendency for life to orient itself about more than one centre, similarly resulting in part from the disposition of the Garonne tributaries, are important factors in determining the ways of approach from the north. It will be seen that the cultural influences affecting the western Pyrenees

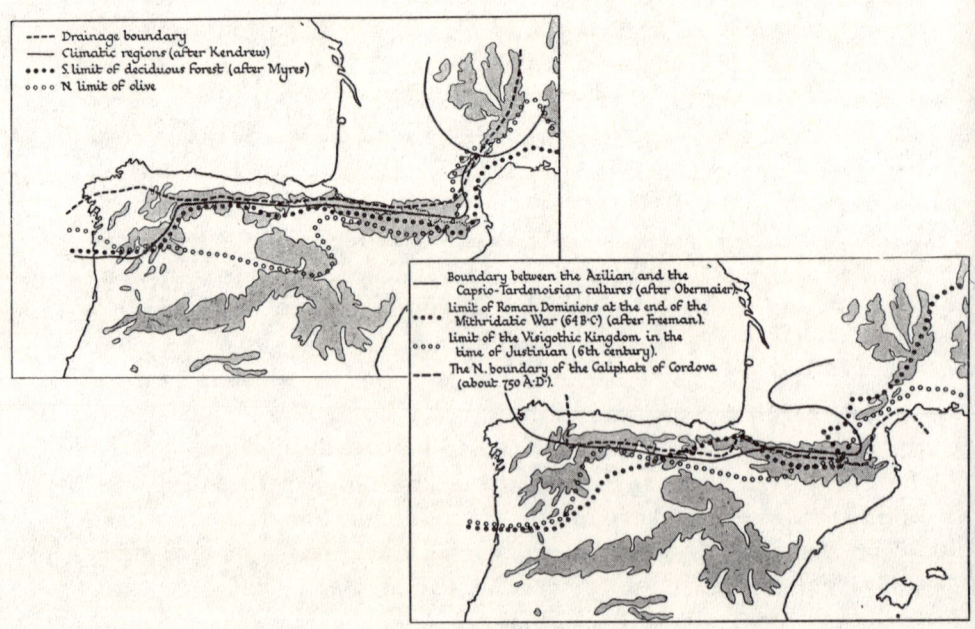

have almost invariably come from the north in a southerly and westerly direction. Historically, Bordeaux, or its predecessor on the Garonne, has stood in intimate relationship with the passes by which the central Pyrenees are turned at the west, while on the east Toulouse and Carcassonne have given access to, or more often received impulses from, the gateway of Roussillon. From earliest times, then, circulation has been thrown towards the coasts; and we must pass to a consideration of the terminal regions.

The eastern or Mediterranean Pyrenees extend from Andorra and the Carlitte (9584 feet) to the sea, and comprise the mountain line itself, here narrowed to form the Albères, together with the foundered areas of Roussillon and Ampurdan, and the bordering hills and sunken valleys—the area, in fact, where Catalan is the native tongue. The Albères end abruptly at the sea, but some fifteen miles inland an easy gap, the Col de Perthus (under 1000 feet), opens suddenly and offers a way through—by far the most inviting in the whole range—which has been utilized from the earliest times. The limits on the west are clearly defined by mountain ridges running north-east from the Carlitte to the Corbières, a line still followed by the boundary of Pyrénées-Orientales. All this country, dominated by the great pyramid of the Canigou between the Têt and the Tech, belongs to the Mediterranean, and, with the Col de Perthus and the passes of la Perche and Puymorens referred to above, provides a means of access along the shores of the inland sea from Gerona and Barcelona to Narbonne and Carcassonne. Ancient hill towns rising above stony stream-beds and parched plains lined with vines and dotted with olive-groves—these are features common to north and south of the political frontier; to southern France and eastern Spain. At the west, the geographical conditions, no less than the historical relations, offer a complete contrast. The broken country of the western or Atlantic Pyrenees, with mist-veiled hills and forested valleys, runs west from the Pic d'Anie and is continued beyond the Bidassoa, the frontier river, about the headwaters of the Ebro tributaries. In the Penas de Europa (8700 feet) the mountain lines reassert themselves and, from the hills of Leon, fan out to the Atlantic in Galicia and north Portugal. It would seem a natural and easy process to turn the Pyrenees at the coast, as the modern railway does, yet no coastal road of importance seems to have been in existence prior to the sixteenth century; and it is part of our subject to inquire why this route, and all others in a zone of easy passes between the Ebro basin and the Bay of Biscay, should have been ignored in favour of the most famous of all Pyrenean passes, that of Roncevaux. Thus Pamplona and St Jean-Pied-de-Port, not Bayonne and San Sebastian, are the ancient frontier stations; and Bayonne, secure in its seaward position between the Landes and the hills, boasts that it has never been captured. But Gerona, occupying a corresponding site south of the Albères, lying exposed to every northward movement towards the Perthus, has been the scene of terrible fighting and has been besieged no less than twenty-five times. Salses, between its *étang* and the Corbières, has a similar story.

The true border city, however, at the limit of Mediterranean conditions, is Carcassonne, at the eastern end of the long zone of boundaries which commences in far Galicia. In Santiago de Compostela, Roncevaux and Carcassonne we have three of the most renowned names of medieval Europe, names which symbolize three aspects of the varied interactions along this boundary zone. The physical differences will be briefly considered before the cultural movements are outlined in their relation to them.

The corridor of Carcassonne between block and fold, opening out very rapidly once Castelnaudary is reached, marks a change of structure as well as a change of soil, climate, drainage, vegetation and ethnic stock. In the same way, the structural plans of the French and Spanish slopes of the central Pyrenees, and of the Asturian coast and the basin of Old Castile, are strongly contrasted. With this go differences of soil, determined also by climatic and vegetational controls, north and south of the boundary zone. The critical location of the Cantabro-Pyrenean system, its continuous development, and its latitudinal alignment combine to emphasize its importance as a climatic barrier. On the south is the Spanish meseta, high and barren, with a climate marked by continental extremes and low rainfall: on the north the funnel-shaped basin of Aquitaine opens from the Bay of Biscay and has the Oceanic régime of mild winters, cool summers, and much cloud and rain throughout the year. The northern portion of the western Pyrenees, in particular, is a region of very heavy rain (over 60 inches), the eastward continuation of oceanic conditions along the Cordillera Cantabrica from the splaying valleys of Galicia, where Santiago has an average annual fall of 66 inches. Similarly the meagre remnants of the Pyrenees at the east are followed by no climatic boundary, for Mediterranean conditions are carried northwards to Carcassonne and the Cévennes. Vegetational limits follow the same path. Mediterranean types, modified on the meseta, cease in pluviose Spain north of the zone of boundaries, and give way to the deciduous forest (beech and oak) of Central Europe; while the contrast between Roussillon and Guipuzcoa is as great as that between the Ebro deserts and the well-watered poplarlined plains of Pau. Vidal de la Blache notes that there are more than fifty species of plants of Iberian origin which have spread past the Albères and persist as far as Montpellier. The northern limit of the olive, an index of Mediterranean civilization, summarizes these physical and human boundaries. The Andalusian, we are told, refers to Galicia as 'the land where there are no olives'; and this gastronomic frontier between oil and butter marks an important distinction which is paralleled by the division between the universal Spanish wine and the cider of the Basque country.

Similarly, while the fauna of Spain is in many ways more closely related to the North African than to the Alpine, the Cantabrian coast has 'northern' species, and with its increased numbers of cattle and its rich development of rural life (contrasting with the old-established urban life of the south) cannot fail to recall those Celtic lands of the north whose physical and human traits are so closely analogous. The evolution of many features of these lands falls within the scope of this essay. The Celtic affinities of pluviose Spain, which Ripley believed to be indicated by the increased headbreadth of the people, are at any rate observable in customs, in folk-music, and in musical instruments of the bagpipe kind. Travellers frequently comment on the reserve of the Galicians and Asturians 'amounting almost to moroseness, as compared with the lively peasants in Murcia and Tarragona'.

Before tracing the relations of human culture (in its initial, historic, and modern phases) to the Pyrenees, we should note the significance of the distribution of population in modern Spain. The densest areas are just those coastal strips which give access to the trans-Pyrenean zones at east and west. This concentration is one of the most permanent facts in the whole story.

Already in Palaeolithic times the boundary between the prehistoric provinces of Burkitt and Sollas follows the course of the physical boundaries; and though climatic variations must be borne in mind, yet the structural and topographical differences, strengthened by the persistence of extensive ice sheets along the boundary belt, would be of fundamental importance. The piedmont zone of the northern Pyrenees has a famous series of calcareous caves and rock-shelters, extending along the Cantabrian coast, where man spread from that 'Atlantic province' to which it is so strongly related. The reindeer, like other animals on which early man depended, in its maximum extension in Magdalenian times occupied southwest France and the Cordillera Cantabrica, but does not seem to have spread south of that range. Perhaps the most typical distribution is that of the Solutrean culture, the result of a westward invasion along the loess of Central Europe, past the western Pyrenees to Santander.

As a parallel to the rich cave art of the northern piedmont zone, we have the east Spanish art, the Palaeolithic date of which seems now to be established. Peake and Fleure regard these paintings as the work of the Capsian invaders who crossed the Straits of Gibraltar from North Africa. While the Capsian culture spreads along the northward avenue of the eastern Pyrenees, the forerunner of numerous 'African influences' (in the words of Brunhes) which followed in its path, the Middle Aurignacian, to quote Obermaier, 'coming in the opposite direction from France, enters Spain between the Pyrenees and the Atlantic and occupies the region of Cantabria'. The differentiation of direction is well illustrated here. It would be difficult to overestimate the significance of the gate of Roussillon in giving access not only to south France but also to the wide plains of western France beyond Carcassonne. Along this line the final Capsian folk (c.7000 BC) advanced northwards with the shifting of the storm zone and the spread of southern species of plants and animals, and were probably responsible—on intermingling with earlier elements—for the first representatives of the small, slight, long-headed brunette people (Mediterranean race), who still form the essential substratum of the population of south-west Europe and the British Isles.

In Cantabria, amalgamation with Magdalenian remnants produced the lower Azilian culture, while further Palaeolithic survivals in this Atlantic cul-de-sac are seen in the Asturian culture of the shell-mound period, apparently allied to others around the coasts of western Europe.

A later wave from eastern Spain introduced into France the Tardenoisian culture. The next factor to be considered is the appearance of a new broad-headed people in Europe. The Pyrenees eventually became, as it still remains, the essential southern frontier of these 'Alpine' broad heads, but, as we should expect, penetration took place along the Asturian coast; and Myres is inclined to see in the broad Mugem skulls evidence of spreads of 'lost tribes' of Alpine ancestry into Portugal.

The stage for the pageant of Pyrenean history is now set in something like permanent form, with the region of heaviest precipitation definitely fixed north of the Cantabro-Pyrenean line; and the increasing difficulty of movement in forested Europe comes to stand out in contrast to the 'opening' of the lands to the south with the establishment of those indices of climate and associated hill-top settlement and terrace cultivation which are called 'Mediterranean'. The new (Neolithic) civilization flourished and extended its influence from the Iberian coastlands—where it had a special group of domesticated animals—into south France, and prepared the way for the megalithic diffusion which was to link up the shores of western Europe by coast-wise sailing as the use of metals became know.

To the search for copper and tin we attribute the inauguration of penetration through the western Pyrenees along a line which remained in use with remarkable tenacity until a few centuries ago. The Basque provinces of Alava and Aralar contain an isolated group of rectangular dolmens which is unconnected with the Biscayan coast, but seems to stand in intimate relation to the passes north of Pamplona. These dolmens are held to be allied to those of the Pyrenees from Pau to St Gaudens and of south France in general, and may well indicate a route to the copper and tin of north-west Spain, where the rectangular form of dolmen is not uncommon—a point of great interest in connection with the medieval fame of the route south of the Cantabrian mountains.

Since the impulse seems to have come from the north, we must look to that side to examine briefly the means of approach to the hills. In the first place the coast between Bordeaux and Bayonne was inhospitable for shipping as well as for movement by land. Communications were naturally thrown inland to the eastern edge of the Landes. Between this deserted zone and the broken foothills runs the lower Adour, which, below the junction of the Gave de Pau, must have been an effective barrier in early times. Even today the marshy valley is crossed by neither road nor railway for many miles above Bayonne, and one is not surprised to find that it marks the northern limit of the Basques. The historic route from Bordeaux thus kept east of the Landes and east of the meeting of Adour and Gave de Pau. Thence it went south along the Bidouze to St Palais and so to St Jean-Pied-de-Port on the Nive. That it did not follow the lower Nive to Bayonne is explicable when a detailed map of the district is studied, for the river cuts a deep gorge in the old massif of Labourd, while the way to St Palais is open and easy. From the headwaters of the Nive the route went by Val Carlos to the Port de Roncevaux (3498 feet). The Port de Velate, some miles to the west, is much lower (2848 feet), but the means of access has to be considered. It was for this reason that the passes leading through Guipuzcoa were of little international fame. That a route should not have followed the Biscayan coast to Galicia is at first sight puzzling, but there could hardly be found a more difficult strip for movement than this. The narrow coastal plateau is very deeply dissected and ends abruptly at the sea. Railway construction was extremely difficult and costly, and there is still no continuous railway line. It was only with the greatest difficulty that a square kilometre of flat land could be found in the Asturias to serve as the base for a trigonometrical survey. Strabo's opinion summarizes the historic contrast with the rest of Spain: 'the part against the north, which borders on the ocean, is extremely cold, and besides its rugged character has no communication or intercourse with other countries.'

It is becoming increasingly clear that the peninsula did not escape the far-reaching invasions of the bronze-swordmen; and it is interesting to note that the particular variety of sword found in the Asturias and in Portugal is closely related to a type common in north France and especially in Brittany. Whether the passes of the Pyrenees played a part in its spread we cannot as yet say (the sea route was probably used), but we should observe the characteristic appearance of this north-west European type in the north and west of the Peninsula. We have more definite evidence of the penetration of the next culture-wave from Central Europe, for the late Hallstatt remains of the French Pyrenees, in the departments of Ariège, Haute-Garonne, Hautes-Pyrénées, Basses-Pyrénées and Landes, are intimately connected with those of the Jalon valley south-west of Saragossa, where settlement may have been determined by the improved conditions consequent on the rainfall maximum which occurred after 500 BC. There is little doubt that communications between these two centres were maintained by the western passes in the vicinity of Roncevaux. The relations of the Early Iron Age culture to the distribution of salt deposits have been noticed in many regions, notably at the type-site (Hallstatt) itself; but the arrangement of Iron Age tumuli along *voies de sel* is nowhere clearer than in the piedmont of the French Pyrenees. Déchelette points out that the Jalon valley is likewise rich in salt. Now the salt-mines of south-west France are all south of the Adour and east of that section of the river which runs from Dax to the confluence of the Gave de Pau, a distribution which suggests an added reason for the course the iron-sword users seem to have taken—south from Dax and not along the coast. Throughout history there has been a close connection between salt and religion (or superstition), trade and war, three essential factors in the fame of the Pyrenean passes. There is an interesting legendary association of the all-important mineral with the pass of Roncevaux, where the heart of one of the victims of the magician Merlin was salted to preserve it on its long journey to Spain. This central European Iron Age culture, which is generally regarded as Celtic (though it seems likely that the bronze-sword users also spoke a Celtic tongue), penetrated to, and established itself more firmly in, the far north-west of the Peninsula. In this way the trade connections maintained since megalithic times between north-west Spain, Brittany, south-west Britain, and Ireland fell under Celtic control, with important consequences upon subsequent movements in their contacts with the Pyrenean barrier.

We have seen that the prehistoric relations of the western Pyrenees were with Oceanic Europe. Let us turn now to the development of the eastern avenue. The rich Aeneolithic culture of south-east Spain spread along the Catalan coastlands, and a group of dolmens about Gerona indicates connections with the same area. The Balearic Islands, ever inviting exploration seawards and serving as a link in the diffusion of the megalithic idea, came to take a place in the connections between France and Spain which they have maintained throughout history. The sea route further commands interest by the establishment of Phoenician and Greek colonies along the Mediterranean coasts. It was natural that they should be planted on both sides of the Albères, for only in times of fixed policy, such as the Roman period, when regional life tended to be sacrificed to that of the larger unit, has the strategic frontier been chosen in face of the opposition of natural forces.

The Carthaginians in turn extended their control from the coasts over most of the peninsula, but the tribes who were known collectively as the Astures maintained their independence in the north. We may surmise that these included strong Celtic elements reinforced from time to time by remnants of invaders who had survived the rigours of the meseta and had retreated into pluviose Spain. In Roman times, also, the zone of boundaries exerted its influence. At the end of the Mithridatic War (64 BC) the northern limit of conquest lay from the lower Douro along the Cantabrians and the Pyrenees and thence by the Gate of Carcassonne to the central plateau of France. Though the Cantabrian tribes were eventually subdued in the time of Augustus, no effective Romanization of pluviose Spain took place. Turned seawards, with its back to the rest of the peninsula, this difficult strip had a life of its own, a life with its roots deep in a prehistoric past, destined to burst out afresh with the quickening forces of the Middle Ages. The roads along which the Romans spread their law and order followed tracks worn long before and used for long centuries afterwards; and it is of great significance that no important road followed the Biscayan coast, in the angle of which the Basques, with their non-Aryan language, were probably already fixed. The salt supplies and hot springs of the French Pyrenees were fully exploited by the Romans; and from Dax (Aquae Tarbellicae), at the crossing of the Adour, main roads ran north to Bordeaux, keeping east of the difficult Landes; south-east along the Gave de Pau and so by the Garonne to Narbonne; and south by the Port de Cize through Roncevaux to the fortress of Pamplona. Thus the Ebro basin was reached directly from Gaul, and the road to the west kept to the south side of the Cordillera Cantabrica via the gate of Burgos, along an ancient line which, thus fixed, was to be followed by all the varied forces which came from Oceanic Europe to enrich the life of trans-Pyrenean lands down to the end of the Middle Ages.

Farther east, another road—the medieval *Camino de Oloron*—crossed by the Somport to Jaca and Saragossa (then, as now, the great route-centre of the Ebro basin), a road which was resuscitated, with many other things Roman, in the eighteenth century. But between this and the Mediterranean the long Pyrenean rampart remained unsurmounted. Over the Perthus ran the Via Domitia from Tarragona to Narbonne, a 'royal road', following the *Camino de Hanibal* and the route of many other 'African' invaders.

In general, however, the Roman period was marked by no large-scale movements such as served to emphasize, before and after, the fundamental unity of the two terminal transmontane zones. It was a period of strict policy, when the influence of space-relationships ceased to be dominant, and so we find the Pyrenees, permanent and easily definable, serving throughout their length as a political boundary between Gaul and Spain. Thus the slender range of the Albères formed the southern limit of the senatorial Narbonensis, and continued to form a diocesan boundary after the reorganization of Diocletian.

Upon all the lands north and south of the range there came, after five centuries of culture of Mediterranean origin, the infiltration of barbarian peoples and the slow decline of civilization. From the dismemberment of the Empire the modern states of Europe gradually grew. It is part of our plan to trace the growth and interactions of two of these in relation to the Cantabro-Pyrenean system. Unable at first to force a way through the guarded passes of the first great obstacle in their path, one branch of these swordsmen, like their predecessors a thousand years earlier, eventually penetrated to Galicia and north Portugal, where the kingdom of the Suevi was formed in a region of mists and cool summers far more congenial to them, we may well suppose, than the rest of the peninsula. It is significant that the Vandal penetration through Roussillon was nothing like so permanent, at least in Spain. For a time, in the fifth century, the Visigoths ruled lands on both sides of the Pyrenees, but, as Frankish power spread southwards, they retained only the Mediterranean coast as far as the Rhône estuary (Septimania); and a map of the political divisions of the sixth and seventh centuries, with the Suevian kingdom long independent in the far west, and the Asturians and Basques in the north, shows a boundary which accords in a remarkable way with the accumulation of physical boundaries which we have outlined.

With the Moslem invasion in the eighth century we come to another period of African influence, and to the greatest single factor in the fame of the Pyrenees. The main waves of conquest, concentrated in the coastal track followed by all northward-flowing currents, lapped freely over the Albères into Roussillon and even reached the Loire and Rhône, but they broke impotently, save for temporary advances over the broken bulwarks in Galicia and the Basque country, against the main Pyreneo-Cantabrian wall; and it was from sections of this front that the reconquest began. As the defensive rampart of Christian civilization the Pyrenees had not failed: as the sallying post of Christian armies they occupy a position in history and legend unsurpassed by any other physical feature in western Europe. It was no accident that the Asturian coast should be one with western Europe in the struggle.

Charlemagne crossed the hills by the age-old route, the Roman road, through the defiles of the Basque country. South of the range, from Pamplona to Barcelona, he pushed his conquests and established the frontier of his Marca Hispania, the maintenance of which was facilitated by the parallel disposition of the sierras. But this main Pyrenean sector was separated from the Cantabrian front by the territory of the Basques, the utter diversity of whose tongue from Aryan speech kept them from taking active part in the Christian reconquest. The fact that this corner, containing the coastal route into Spain, became a neutral zone between the two crusading fronts, was an added reason for that concentration on the passes meeting at Pamplona which has been such a marked feature of Pyrenean history. The low pass of Idiazabal, west of the Sa. de Aralar, remained in obscurity; lateral communication between the two sectors was chiefly maintained through the gap from the upper Ebro to the Arlanzan, where Burgos was erected in AD 884 in a newly won district.

The reconquest continued during the centuries that followed Charlemagne, and Spain owes many of her national characteristics to the process. Physical controls and the accumulation of human contrasts had effected, from the earliest times, the increasing isolation of the north-west from the rest of the peninsula, but with the Moslem invasion, this section, north of the zone of boundaries, became at once the refuge of Gothic (and prehistoric) traditions and the very heart of the new growth. Territorial expansion was accompanied by the birth of an intensely Catholic and military Spain. The miraculous discovery, in the year 835, of the bones of St James at Santiago de Compostela was an event closely related to our subject. The renewed sanctity of this ancient shrine, which originated, it has been suggested, in a megalithic cult, concerns us because of its influence on Oceanic Europe; for in maintaining the long tradition of common heritages, the life of the Celtic fringe, throughout the Middle Ages, was drawn south and east over the Pyrenees and into 'foreign' territory beyond the Cantabrians. It may be permissible to see in the vigorous medieval revival—intellectual, artistic, religious, political—traces of the survival and persistence of the Celtic-Mycenaean civilization of the western Bronze Age. That the west owed much to influences from the eastern Mediterranean after the third millenium BC, influences widely reflected in Celtic folklore, is becoming increasingly appreciated. Indeed, there may be something more than structural relationships between the *Chanson de Roland* and the *Iliad*: the wonderful outburst of epic song throughout the western world was perhaps a far echo of the spread of Aegean civilization.

To all intents and purposes, French literature may be said to begin with the *Chanson de Roland* (the first and finest of the long series of Chansons de Geste) which turns about the death of Roland, the Christian Achilles, in the valley of Roncevaux. It was in the year 778 that the rearguard of Charlemagne's retiring army was overwhelmed by local tribes, an event which took hold of the popular imagination and was transformed into 'a capital incident in the secular strife between the Crescent and the Cross'. It may well be that there was a deeper reason for this wide and powerful popularity of the story of Roland's defeat, dependent perhaps—like the defeat itself—on the change that occurs thereabout between the deep, wooded, misty ravines of the north and the barren, open, sunny plains of the south. To the traveller this contrast is most striking.

The life of the Middle Ages pulsated along the pilgrim routes which met at the western passes of the Pyrenees, whence the *Camino Francès* led along Charlemagne's route to Pamplona and so through Logrono, Burgos, and Leon to Santiago. The wide attraction of the pilgrimage is shown by the frequent references to it in early English literature. It is of interest to note that the Voie St Jacques, in its long course from western France to Galicia, enforced, in the barren basin of the upper Douro, the alien hardships of a climate and environment entirely different from those of Oceanic Europe, but closely resembling those of the Holy Land. The pilgrimage grew to enormous proportions between the eleventh and fourteenth centuries. In England it ranked, in the twelfth century, with one to Rome or Jerusalem. This continued penetration of northern peoples into Spain left its mark on the life and thought of the peninsula, and was especially far-reaching because it affected, for reasons we have suggested, areas outside pluviose Spain. 'Throughout the Middle Ages', in the words of Street, 'a torrent of foreign life and art poured through the whole of the north of Spain.' We may take architectural expression as one of the more enduring results of this flood of trans-Pyrenean ideas and customs. Thus the cathedral of Santiago is 'both in plan and design a very curiously exact repetition of the church of St Sernin at Toulouse'. From the eleventh century Toulouse was a great centre of architecture, and St Sernin boasts of having the bones of St James. As a further illustration of the community of outlook which spread along the lines radiating from Roncevaux, we may observe that the ancient shrine of Rocamadour, on a pilgrim way traversing the Central Plateau of France, still treasures a copy of Roland's sword—the Durandal which wrought such havoc among the rocks of the western Pyrenees.

In fact, nearly all the fundamental ideas of Spanish architecture (and the same might be said, with the exception of its brief golden age, of Spanish literature) have been imported from without, usually from France. The Gothic style, most significant of all, spread from the basin of Paris past Bordeaux along the pilgrim way, and also reached Bayonne and Santander. The cathedrals of Leon and Burgos best show the style: the former, built about 1250, is fundamentally French, while the latter is described as 'purest thirteenth-century Gothic of France'. Merchants, scholars, soldiers, labourers, artists, pilgrims, *jongleurs*—all these types thronged the pilgrim routes and contributed to the life of the new Spain; taking back with them, also, relics of classical learning preserved by the Moslems, new arts such as the enamelling of Limoges, luxurious trade-objects such as silks, wines, oranges, and horses, and renowned weapons such as the blades of Toledo, which were damascened at Eibar near Pamplona. To what extent communications were still concentrated at the Col de Roncevaux we may gauge from the following passage from Froissart, describing the campaign of the Black Prince in 1367. 'They could not enter into Spain', he writes, 'but through the straights of Roncevaulx.' In this instance the reason was a political one, based nevertheless on geographical principles. The pass was held by the kingdom of Navarre, which, growing up in the early tenth century after the Basque lands had been won back from the Saracens, had extended its influence north of the watershed to St Palais and the crossing of the Gave de Pau. The diocese of Pamplona similarly stretched on both slopes of the range. This is no isolated occurrence. In much the same way did Savoy spread to the plains from its complex home around the St Bernard passes; and Foix command the pass of Puymorens from the Ariège valley; and Switzerland grew through its control of the passes of the central Alps. But the weakness of Navarre was revealed when the pass had lost its overwhelming importance: it was then that the northern portion split off and became part of France. For, unlike the gate of Roussillon or the coastal section of the Basque country, Navarre was traversed by the physical boundaries which run from Galicia to Carcassonne; and the two portions were bound to feel different attractions as nationality spread, cultural movements declined, and the unity of medieval Christendom ceased to be dominant.

While the western Pyrenees were winning everlasting fame because of their key position in the historic boundary zone, the eastern section was closely involved in the crisis of Christianity down to the time of the formation of Charlemagne's Spanish March. At first the frontier lay at Carcassonne; the Albères formed no barrier across this Mediterranean avenue. But, as in the west, northern peoples joined forces with the native Christians to expel the Moslems; and the Catalan tongue, derived from south France, spread in the lands gradually re-won. The spiritual and traditional forces of a region of contact were represented, as in Galicia, by a shrine of great antiquity—the pilgrim centre of Monserrat, strangely towering above the Llobregat behind Barcelona. Its fame and fascination as the legendary home of the Holy Grail grew until pilgrims to Our Lady of Monserrat numbered, it is said, half a million annually in the sixteenth century. This is but one indication that the eastern routes were becoming increasingly important as the western passes, after their burst of international life in the Middle Ages, were falling into an obscurity which lasted until a century ago. But if the collapse of the old seaboard life came later in the east, it was, as we shall see, no less effective. Meanwhile cultural affinities were multiplying in the lands on both sides of the present frontier. The brilliant Catalan genius, under the influence of the northern Gothic architecture but with inherent 'Roman' tendencies, asserted itself and produced the distinctive Catalan type of church, which is at home in Perpignan as well as in Gerona and Barcelona. Fundamental environmental controls were reflected in unity of culture under a single government, for Roussillon remained part of Aragon until the seventeenth century. While the passes of Puymorens, la Perche, and le Perthus were thronged with pilgrims, merchants, and troubadours, there was also wide extension of maritime commerce. The western Mediterranean became 'a Catalan lake', with memories, it may well be, of the period of Greek colonization seen in the revival of map-making, and of prehistoric trade as well. Coastwise communications, as in the Celtic west, were a prime factor in maintaining the common life of lands, near and remote, around the Pyrenean ends.

Before continuing our survey of the historic movement, which was largely to cease after the sixteenth century, it would be well to look at the life of the Pyrenees, considered as a natural region, during these early periods. We have pointed out that the steep-forested foothills, not the high crests, form the natural line of separation between hills and plain on the north, and, in general, higher mountain masses tend to be distinct in climate, soil, vegetation, products, and human aptitudes and outlook. An indication of the individuality of the Pyrenees is to be found in the fact that they are relatively rich in endemic species of both flora and fauna. In house types, too, Dauzat has shown that the Pyrenean zone, between the Basque country with its special type of rural habitation and the area of the *maison latine*, forms an isolated strip marked by the *maison gauloise*. This unity is the result of similar controls exerted on a pastoral people. In the High Pyrenees, distinction between the two slopes has no practical utility, for the summer pastures, *pasquiers, pla, calms, etiba*, extend on both sides of the watershed. The most natural relations are with the adjoining valleys via the open mountain paths, for example the Capcir (around the sources of the Aude) has more connections with the Cerdagne (upper Segre) than with the lower Aude. In this zone of boundaries, the limit of human life moves up the mountain with the advance of spring. Its outer limit is normally the piedmont line referred to, which is thus a cultural boundary because it is an economic one. It is the natural limit of the people of the plains, of whom the folk of the entire mountain zone show a common dislike and mistrust. The political frontier of India, until the annexation of Baluchistan, was defined by the abrupt limestone scarps of the hills which divide the settled population of Sind from the pastoral Baluchs. This natural frontier was in time superseded by the 'strategic' divide along the watershed. Similarly in north India, Mongoloid-race types are found as far as the piedmont; unity is to be referred to the High-land Zone. The fall-line of the Welsh border is likewise a cultural boundary between the pastoral hill folk and the corn-growing plainsmen. The geo-graphical truth of unity in mountain areas is, in fact, often better illustrated in ancient residual 'blocks' than in 'new fold' systems; for, in the former, unified conditions tend to be widespread without sudden changes of aspect and soil; and this is one of the many difficulties in the way of establishing a satisfactory boundary between France and Germany along the hill remnants bordering the Rhine Valley. This contrast between plains and hill core is further illustrated in ancient Greece, between the city states and the pastoral mountain area of the Peloponnese—Arcadia—which, though split up into independent hill-villages, united in face of aggression from outside. That in some areas, especially within the tropics, high plateaux have served as cen-tres of civilization is well known from the example of the native cultures of Peru, developing between 6000 and 14,000 feet, and having a downward limit at the edge of the hot forested lowlands.

The unit of organization in the mountain zone is the high valley, whose occupants were often long independent, maintaining ancient rights, and having common sympathies and strong solidarity, almost entirely cut off from outside in winter and chiefly concerned with the remote pastures in summer. The almost sovereign power of some of these Pyrenean communi-ties is shown in their treaties with other valleys. These had doubtless exist-ed from ancient times, but the general tendency of the twelfth and thir-teenth centuries towards communal organization helped the process of crystallization. The Vallées d'Ossau, Cauterets, Azun, Canfranc and Villan-ua were typical rural communes—little republics in virtue of their indepen-dence and self-government. The modern frontier has not entirely eliminat-ed the traces of cantonal autonomy in the High Pyrenees, though Andorra alone has preserved something approaching political independence. Some of the ceremonies connected with the agreements over common pasturages lasted until the end of the eighteenth century, while the treaties in certain cases became actual international agreements (*lies et passeries*) facilitating the regular practice of the mountain economy.

While the influence of Paris was spreading southwards unity of govern-ment and general law, the Pyrenees long retained their independent lord-ships, and the whole but slowly coalesced into large districts eventually owning the crests as their southern boundary. It was the eighteenth centu-ry, with the increasing interference of royal authority and the theory of 'the summit of falling waters', which witnessed the final decay of the intramon-tane life. These rural communities, possessing virtual self-government, but forming part of the mountain zone and having relations with other mountain valleys beyond the crests, must be distinguished from the more power-ful kingdoms which grew up at the Pyrenean ends in response to the historic movement. These (Roussillon, Foix, Navarre, Béarn) were born of the plain in its relations with the barrier, and tended to orient themselves about the routes and the cities at the foot of the hills. Vidal de la Blache works out the contrast between Roussillon and the Cerdagne, between plain and hill-valley. The latter escaped the devastations of the Moslems and lay off the track of all 'African' influences, but it failed to acquire, for that very reason, independent historical importance.

The ferment which was to change the medieval relations of the Pyrenees was at work from the fifteenth century. The process was slow; but by the middle of the seventeenth century the modern position was won, with the political frontier along the crests from the Bidassoa to Cape Cerbère. National consciousness was furthered by the new ideas which western Europe was learning from the classical world. The civilization of the fif-teenth century saw the beginning of the breakdown of the moral authority of the Church; the sixteenth century witnessed the collapse of the concep-tion of one Christian society in the Catholic Church. New ideas and a fresh outlook brought new lines of communication and a re-orientation of inter-national currents. The spirit of the Renaissance, in its northward course, advanced along the Rhône valley, not along the far older way by Carcas-sonne and the edge of the Central Plateau.

In Spain, national unity was virtually achieved with the fall of Granada (1492); and with the fall, peaceful trans-Pyrenean relationships decline, though Spain held for some time part of Navarre (incorporated with Castile in 1515) and the whole of Roussillon north of the watershed at the west and east. The Basque coast from Bayonne to Bilbao, which had enjoyed, from the twelfth century, a period of intense maritime activity, and had provided sailors for the voyages of discovery as well as for numerous naval wars, rapid-ly lost its leading position from the sixteenth century. Nor has the promise of renewed life given by the activity of south-west France in the eighteenth century been fulfilled. Into the causes of Spain's attitude it is unnecessary to enter in detail. She was attracted more and more to the New World; com-merce was despised and no middle class developed; she was strangled by the Inquisition; and in her wars it was the open frontier of the Netherlands, not the Pyrenees, that mattered. Under Charles V, in particular, the relations of Spain were with Naples and Flanders, and the art of those centres is strong-ly reflected in Spanish painting. By the end of the sixteenth century, shortly before Roussillon became French, the medieval tradition had gone. The knightly chronicle, with its French lineage, had degenerated into fantastic memories of a debased chivalry which Cervantes could hold up to ridicule.

The position in France was similar. 'Voici la Renaissance,' says one writer, 'notre légende va mourir.' Crusaders and pilgrims no longer came by Bordeaux and St Palais; the names of Roncevaux and Burgos were forgotten, and with them their varied literary associations. The Chansons de Geste suffered almost complete neglect from the fifteenth to the early nineteenth century. Boileau used to boast of his ignorance of Roland and his deeds, and Corneille, after bringing out *Le Cid*, was compelled by authority to turn to other sources of inspiration. Already, in the fifteenth century, 'Burgundians and Bretons, Picards and Gascons were beginning to call themselves Frenchmen.' Culture, centralized at the court, was prevented from spreading beyond the national frontiers. The splendid Gothic architecture which had been carried into Spain was forgotten or despised.

It was with Henry IV of France that the new process of frontier formation became apparent. The French crown passed in 1589 to a king of Navarre who held only the part north of the Pyrenees, which had split off when the pass whose approaches it had controlled had lost its significance. In the Wars of the Holy League it was still Pamplona that figured most prominently (1572), though San Sebastian also played a part. But the water-parting of the western Pyrenees was slowly becoming the frontier of separation it is today, and contact was being concentrated more and more at the sea coast. Basse-Navarre gave to France in Henry IV a cunning diplomat who did much to make his country unique in Europe. In his reign, and later under Richelieu and Mazarin, French culture and prosperity were carried to their highest pitch in France. With the signing of the Treaty of the Pyrenees (1659), which gave Roussillon to France, the international frontier was finally fixed along the hill-line at the east of the range; and thus were revived the conditions of that other period of 'clear administration', the Roman, which contemporary thought took as its guide. To say that 'no Spanish kingdom any longer stretched north of the great barrier of that peninsula' (Freeman) is to ignore both the geographical and historical facts with regard to the eastern frontier. It is unnecessary to point out that the principle of boundary formation actually along 'the summit of falling waters' was not everywhere adhered to. The Val d'Aran and the Cerdagne are notable exceptions, while the Basque frontier is highly irregular, and actually reaches the Bay of Biscay along the Bidassoa 'in a land where no frontier is'.

Louis XIV is reported to have said, with reference to the treaty of 1659, that the Pyrenees no longer existed. Before the seventeenth century the frontier had changed frequently to meet the changing balance of forces, but had generally been in accord with geographical distributions. Since that time there has scarcely been any tension: it has not even been thought worthwhile to correct the obvious blunders in the negotiations of the treaty.

In the sense of Louis XIV, however, the main range had never existed. Its historical role has been largely negative. It is not this Arcadian background that has become permanently enshrined in epic song, but the pathways, echoing with Spartan deeds, by which the barrier has been turned. But, with the fixing of the frontier from the Bidassoa to Cape Cerbère, even the storied valley of Roncevaux disappears, as we have seen, from literature.

The international route along the shores of the Bay of Biscay begins to figure in history with the disuse of the passes of Navarre as that kingdom fell to Castile and France. It is suggestive of the change which had taken place that while the usual name for the coast road was *el camino real*, one of the many titles of the old pilgrim road—and their very diversity attests its significance—was *le chemin de l'apostre*. Maps of the eighteenth century do not mark the road from Dax to Pamplona; while the Royal Road formed the strategic heart of Napoleon's schemes for conquering Spain. Already in the sixteenth century Charles V had a castle at Fuenterrabia guarding the crossing of the Bidassoa. St Jean-de-Luz came to replace St Jean-Pied-de-Port, and San Sebastian became more prominent than Santiago. Roncevaux declined into the miserable hamlet mentioned in our guide books, so insignificant and forgotten that Milton could make 'Charlemain with all his peerage fall by *Fontarrabia*'. Scott, too, brings Fuenterrabia into the story, for he tells us that 'a blast of the dread horn' of Roland was audible there, some forty miles from Roncevaux.

The peripheral tendencies of lines of intercourse which accompanied the establishment of a strict frontier of separation at both ends of the range were accentuated and fixed with the coming of the railway. Even today no line crosses the Pyrenees between the extreme ends, partly, no doubt, because the more abrupt slopes face the more enterprising nation. Not one of the three international lines to be constructed according to the agreement reached in 1904 has yet been completed. (This was written in 1928. The line from Jaca to Oloron now tunnels beneath the Somport, but it carries local traffic only and has no true international service. The railway from Toulouse to Barcelona via Puigcerda [opened in July 1929] marks a great advance in that the international gauge is continued from the frontier to Barcelona.) Spain's suspicions of France led her to adopt the 5ft 8.5ins gauge in place of the international one, and what this has meant in hindering communications can hardly be realized. Nor are good motoring roads common. Save at the Perthus and through St Jean-de-Luz, only four roads cross the range (all in the westernmost third), two in the neighbourhood of Roncevaux and two near the Pic du Midi, by the Somport and Pourtalet passes. The railway from Paris to Madrid follows that shortest route from Bayonne and Hendaye, over the pass of Idiazabal to Vittoria and Burgos, which had been so curiously neglected in earlier times. At the eastern frontier a remarkable divergence from the old Perthus route is observed, for the railway from Perpignan to Gerona winds along the coast through short tunnels between the series of ancient harbours from Collioure to Portbou. Northwards it follows the narrow neck of land between Salses and Leucate to link with the routes through Carcassonne and through Béziers. Along the Pyrenees the routes followed by the railways are of immense antiquity—from Toulouse along the Garonne to St Gaudens and thence by Tarbes to the Gave de Pau and Bayonne. On the south there is no such piedmont route. Saragossa concentrates railways that are of little avail for Pyrenean penetration; and the functional contrast between Aquitaine and Aragon is reflected in modern conditions of travel.

The early nineteenth century brought other factors affecting the Pyrenees besides the growth of nationalism: it brought an increase of travel and a new interest in previously little-known territories. The eighteenth century for the most part neglected the 'uncultured' medieval traditions, and found neither beauty nor interest in high mountains. But with the Romantic period a wave of admiration for the Middle Ages, on the crest of which appeared the names of Roland and Roncevaux, swept over Europe. And these names recalled a good deal of the regional life of the Pyrenees, so that *le cor* applies to the hunting horn of the mountain valleys as well as to the dread horn of Roland. The appeal of this new movement was to the north, to which the western Pyrenees belong and whence they have derived most of their life. Yet Roncevaux is in Spain. In much the same way, the deep attachment of the eastern corridor to the natural region centred about the Spanish coast is illustrated in the geographical location of the subject of the masterpiece of Catalan poetry *Lo Canigo*, north of the political boundary.

It may be permissible to see in the immense popularity of the pilgrim shrine of Lourdes a revival of the fame of ancient links along the Voie St Jacques. Increasing modern tourist traffic, too, and new methods of ex-ploitation of natural resources, bid fair to restore the international fame of that part of the range north of the boundary. But the maintenance of a strict frontier of separation has other consequences which are characteristic of a frontier location. Notably the Basques, along the coast and in the hills, still carry on illicit trade in a region where nature and culture alike recognize no division. The decay of the old towns such as Astorga, Leon, and Burgos, rich in historical memories, is also indirectly related to political unification: the castles which had given Castile its name, with all that they signified, became 'castles in Spain'. The enforcement of frontier separation in the terminal transmontane zones results, as we have seen, in the poor development of land communications. Much the larger proportion of trade between France and Spain is done by sea. The inactivity resulting from the state of equilibrium reached in the last century has its beneficial consequences, for the Franco-Spanish border has escaped the devastation of many another European frontier.

One of the lessons to be learnt from a study of the Pyrenees is the permanence of distributions and boundaries such as those of the language groups. The Catalan tongue persists in Roussillon, despite the early attempts of the French to eradicate it by improving communications and by making the Albères a strict frontier of separation against Catalonia. In the course of time, however, the Catalan in France became a confirmed Frenchman, disdainful of Spain. The most powerful contributory force was the French Revolution, with its new philosophy, a factor which Vidal de la Blache has shown to have been important in Alsace-Lorraine. (We cannot treat here of the modern regionalist movement as found, for example, in Catalonia.) The persistence of the Basque group in the west is due, in the words of Ripley, to isolation—'material, social, political, linguistic, and at last ethnic'. The limits of Basque types, for example the Adour on the north and the Sierra Longa running south and west from the Pic d'Anie on the south-east, are strikingly conservative.

The great human significance of the eastern corridor lies in the fact that it has served, from the earliest times, as an avenue along which men and their changing cultures have advanced northwards to contribute to the enrichment of the civilization of north-western Europe. At the west, the permanence of lines of penetration has been largely due to the persistence, from prehistoric times, of relationships along the Oceanic margin, with accumulated literary and social traditions that have exerted potent influences on the life of lands about the Pyrenees. Regions of contact, in more than one part of the long zone of boundaries, have seen the clash of cultures of widely differing experience, expressing itself often in a way which is symbolized by the stormy associations of the Bay of Biscay and the Gulf of Lions, between which the boundary range is thrown. The crystallization of the process of national consciousness and of the conception of strategic national frontiers after the fifteenth century, reinforced by the crisis of the French Revolution, has resulted in the obscuring of those physical traits and historical connections which gave common cultures and common languages to the lands around the Pyrenean ends and brought a measure of common pastoral life to the High Pyrenees as well. Thus do geographical distributions, interpreted on the basis of space-relationships, indicate the long and complicated evolution of the relations to environment that have come to typify on the one hand the Frenchman and on the other the Spaniard.

[I.C. Peate (ed.), *Studies in Regional Consciousness and Environment: Essays presented to H.J. Fleure* (Oxford 1930)]

IN THE MASSIF CENTRAL

I had driven north from the eastern Pyrenees on a late August day by way of Narbonne and Béziers. Even in the high Cévennes a parched northerly wind did little to temper the heat of the sun. In the *causses* the glare from the naked limestone dazzled the eye intolerably, and crossing the oven-like gorges of the Tarn and its tributaries which divide the *causses* into segments brought no relief.

Towards tea-time, dry and dusty, I pulled the car off the road along a rough track half hidden in box and juniper bushes, and in about a hundred yards, to my astonishment, came to a fortunate halt on the edge of a great gorge which, a moment before, had been entirely hidden from view. Sitting on the edge, his legs dangling into space, his eyes gazing far across the gorge to the level *causse* beyond, was an aged shepherd, crooked stick in hand and black dog by his side. Neither dog nor man took any notice of me, but when I had brewed some tea I walked over and offered him a drink. He declined with a shake of the head: he was not thirsty and, as he spoke, I sniffed the reason why. I sat down by his side and commented on his unusual perch and on the view it commanded. 'Yes,' he agreed 'it is good, but I have seen better. I am a travelled man. I am sixty-nine this year, a veteran of the '14-18 war.' He showed me a scar across the palm of his left hand. 'I got that in Italy, and good God, I also had a bullet right through me'—he pointed fore and aft—'and they gave me a pension of forty francs.'

'But you are a farmer?' I asked.

'I look after the sheep: my son and I live down there', he said pointing to a cluster of red-roofed buildings deep down in the floor of the gorge. 'We own forty hectares. I came back home when my father died. I was a *garçon de café* in Paris for twenty years. Five of my sons are there now.'

It was of this Massif Central that Stevenson wrote that all life moves downhill: 'only the fish keep their heads upstream'.

He explained that he brought the sheep up on the *causse* each day and took them down to the valley in the evening for water. I remarked, looking at the patchy brown grass bitten to the rocks, that there was little for them to eat. 'Almost nothing', he said, 'we've had four months without rain', and he held up four stubby fingers. I noticed nibbled branches of box scattered over the limestone pavement, and he told me he had cut them for the sheep. 'They like the ash best, and oak and elm when I can get them.'

I remembered the almost unrecognizable ash trees I had seen earlier by the roadside, their branches cut back to the knobbly trunk. It is a practice as old as the Neolithic, whose dolmens still stand on the *causses* to testify to ancient practices and ancient faiths. Sheep have supported the life and shaped the outlook of the *causses* for five millennia. Cloth-weaving and hosiery are part of the tradition. Millau, which I had just passed through, is called 'the town of gloves' and claims to have produced, in a recent year, half the lambskin gloves made in France. The skins are a by-product of the steady milk supply required for the making of such cheeses as Roquefort and the adjacent Causse de Larzac. Millau suffered severely—while foreign lands had profited—from the expulsion of Huguenots after the Revocation of the Edict of Nantes. Thinking also of the heresy of Albi lower down the river I wondered what religious views my shepherd held. For the men of the Massif have their own outlook on life. They despise the conformists down there in the lowlands.

Our conversation turned in this direction when I happened to remark that I had that day come from Spain. 'A poor country that is, priest-ridden and poverty striken. I lost my faith when I was thirteen, and any religion left in me was killed with thousands of my comrades in the war. The priests couldn't tell me why God allowed that. That's the trouble with de Gaulle: he's much too Catholic and will never understand Communism, in Russia or in Africa or in France.'

The men of the Massif have kept their non-conformist outlook.

'Did you suffer much in the last war?' I asked.

'The Germans often came down there', he pointed to the valley bottom, 'but this country up here belonged to the *maquis*.' He swept his arm around to the *causse* beyond on a level with us, to the junipers and box and stunted trees and bare limestone. 'It's cold up here in winter: we often have two feet of snow, and the north wind.'

The Neolithic shepherds must have wintered on the Mediterranean coast, and this transhumance is still practised in parts of the Massif Central. Another surviving custom in the *causses* is the building of corbelled stone cabins. I noticed a cluster of buildings to our right as we sat, clinging to the cliff edge, and I asked if I might examine them. They were stock shelters, roofed with large limestone slabs, and looked indeed like a cluster of mega-lithic chambered tombs. But a date on the keystone of a wide doorway told that they had been constructed in 1824. The slab roofs were not functional, but covered vaulted rooms made by limestone blocks, yet they had a purpose besides keeping the winter rains and snows out of the joints: they guided the water into a large cistern similarly constructed but half buried in the ground alongside. The cistern was lined with tiles, and after four months of drought it still contained ice-cold water which was reserved for the use of cattle. The more mobile sheep were daily transhumants, and as I left on my way north, the shepherd began rounding them up for their evening trek down the cliff edge. We shook hands, and I promised him I would return next year to these pleasant pastoral uplands. I left him gazing out over the wide horizons of the Massif, home of disbelief.

[*The Manchester Guardian*, n.d.]

THE SCOTCH-IRISH
Their Cultural Adaptation and Heritage
in the American Old West[1]

The history of the Scotch-Irish in colonial and republican North America has been written largely in terms of their individual contributions and in the light of outmoded concepts of racial distinctiveness. The older literature, at least, is strongly coloured by hero-worship or by prejudice, and paints a picture that is either white or black. While the descendants of the eighteenth-century immigrants have applauded this 'bold and hardy race' (the phrase is Theodore Roosevelt's) for its massive contributions to leadership in American life—in the political, educational, religious, military and industrial fields—some English writers have stressed the depravity of a stock which they see mainly as backwoodsmen producing little more than gangsters, hillbillies and bad whiskey. An English farmer visiting America about the year 1800 wrote:

None emigrate to the frontiers beyond the mountains, except culprits, or savage backwoodsmen, chiefly of Irish descent ... a race possessing all the vices of civilized and savage life, without the virtues of either ... the outcasts of the world, and the disgrace of it. They are to be met with, on the western frontiers, from Pennsylvania inclusive, to the furthest south.[2]

More recently Arnold Toynbee, to prove his theory of 'challenge and response', convinced himself that the Scotch-Irish 'succumbed to the barbarizing severity of their Appalachian environment' and became 'no better than barbarians, the American counterparts of the Hairy Ainu'.[3] The opinions of a contemporary observer and a theoretical historian have this in common: they are the views of Englishmen and reflect the cultural attitudes of a people accustomed to the ordered life of law-abiding villages and urban centres; and the Scotch-Irish were successful pioneers precisely because they could live without the benefits, and actively opposed the restrictions, of organized community life. Denigration of a different kind has come from the descendants of Irish Roman Catholic immigrants in the United States, though this view, too, has been coloured by the scorn of a newly urbanized stock for old rural values.

Those Americans who claim Scotch-Irish ancestry—and they are many— seem to have no doubt as to the superior qualities of their ancestors. The Proceedings of the Scotch-Irish Congress, published from 1889 onwards, are full of such immoderate self-praise and self-righteousness that one may perhaps count among the contributions of this stock the traditional boast- fulness as well as the isolationism of the American Middle West. They were not alone, however, in their extravagant ancestral claims, for other descen- dants of old immigrant groups were vociferous during the half-century before the First World War, when they felt themselves in danger of being swamped by floods of impoverished European immigrants.[4] The Scotch- Irish in particular were anxious not to be confused with the 'famine Irish', and the term Scotch-Irish significantly became popular only after 1850: before that they were usually referred to as Irish (sometimes wild Irish) or poor Scotch. But these non-English groups, and particularly the Scotch- Irish, also found a grievance in the fact that American history had been mainly written in New England[5] and that this interpretation of its course reflected the old English conviction of cultural superiority. In assessing the fundamental contributions of various immigrant cultures it must be said that the town meeting and the cherished right of free speech were essentially the gifts of the urban New Englanders.[6] The territorial unit—the township— also spread from New England.

The Scotch-Irish propagandists, in Ulster as well as in America, have weakened the force of their claims to have provided outstanding leaders in so many walks of American life by laying stress on quantity and by includ- ing in their lists of pioneers and presidents some men of doubtful virtue and others whose qualities could conceivably have been derived from a father or a mother of lesser breed.[7] If the important part played by the Scotch-Irish in the American Revolution, in the shaping of the Old Frontier and in politi- cal leadership, cannot be denied, there is equally no doubt that, ironically, Scotch-Irish relics are today a substantial element in the depressed rural population of Appalachia, which legislation inspired by the concept of the New Frontier is designed to rehabilitate.

But it is not my purpose to follow either of these historic trails or to judge which should be given greater weight in assessing the role of the Scotch-Irish in the life of the United States. It is my contention that their major lasting contribution to the American scene was their broad imprint on the American landscape and way of life. It can be fairly claimed that, all in all, the middle colonies were the most significant cultural nursery of North America, thanks to the hybridization of the various cultural groups which were attracted to Penn's colony. Growing out of it, southern and western Pennsylvania which the Scotch-Irish so largely fashioned became in turn the cradle of the Middle West. The family farm and the family Bible were the foundations of faith. The dignity of the individual was valued and distinctions of class were scorned. The cultural landscape of a large part of the United States is characterized by the single homestead and the unincorporated hamlet, and by a system of land-use dominated by a corn-and-livestock economy, which was pioneered in the Old West mainly by the Scotch-Irish. Among them the claims of family and kin were stronger than those of community. Economically, it was a wasteful system, often bringing rapid environmental deterioration. They were militant moralists, and free enterprise was raised to the level of a theological dogma. While Presbyterianism tended to become schismatic or to give way to the more emotional appeal of the Methodists and Baptists as the settlers moved ahead of established churches, its adherents clung to the ideal of an educated clergy and must be given some of the credit for the American passion for education. Of the 207 permanent colleges established in the United States before the Civil War about 50—by far the largest single group—were begun by Presbyterians, mostly of Ulster ancestry.[8] Their critics averred, however, that they believed in education only if they controlled it.

The fact that the Scotch-Irish constituted a high proportion of the first European farmers (as distinct from traders and adventurers) in the American wilderness helps to explain their formative role, for pioneers set a pattern that tends to persist. Their trails become roads: their system of settlement and land-use is stamped on the landscape. Some features of frontier life are universal, and the Scotch-Irish backwoodsmen displayed them not because of their vaunted 'racial' attributes but simply because they lived the life of the frontier. Frontier conditions make for independence, masculine dominance, lawlessness, superstition, improvisation and inventiveness. The first version of the McCormick reaper, for example, was evolved in Virginia in the early 1830s. The question that has to be asked, then, is how the Ulster immigrants came to be so numerous among the pioneers who penetrated into the wilderness.

This is explained partly by opportunity—and here the facts are not in dispute—and partly by their experience in Ulster and their cultural inheritance. Some writers lay stress on their stern Presbyterian faith and their determination to practise it without interference, but I attach more importance to their material culture and total way of life. (It must be said, however, that the ready-made organization of the Presbyterian Church was to stand them in good stead in their fight for political democracy.) The Ulstermen landed in large numbers in the Delaware ports from 1724 onwards, and since the coastal strip had been pre-empted by William Penn's Quaker followers, mainly English and Welsh, and German Protestant refugees were beginning to settle the country immediately behind, many of them crossed the Susquehanna and settled in Cumberland County, which was to become their main cradle in the New World. The townships of Antrim, Armagh, Derry, Fermanagh and Tyrone were established here. There were hostile Indians and French to the west, but the Cumberland Valley lies within the great Appalachian ridge and valley complex, so that the opportunity for linear penetration presented itself, southwards down the Shenandoah Valley into the Great Valley of Virginia and beyond. Because German settlers were already in possession of the east side of the Great Valley, they pushed down the western side. Outside southern Pennsylvania they rarely give their settlements Ulster names and cannot therefore be traced by place-names, but the name Cumberland apparently went with them, over the gap of that name, into the Cumberland Valley of Tennessee, which became their second seed-bed. Some 300,000 pioneers poured through the Cumberland Gap between 1775 and 1800.

The immigrants from Ulster had first sought refuge in New England, especially from 1717 to 1720, but they had a bad reception, and were described as 'uncleanly, unwholesome and disgusting'.[9] In New England they were a small minority, though here too they made a characteristic contribution as Indian-fighters and pioneers.[10] From 1724 onwards Philadelphia and the other Delaware ports took the bulk of the Ulster-Scots, and the tide of immigration, slackening after 1730, reached its high point in 1772–3 and thereafter ebbed away as the colonies moved towards political independence.[11] By the end of the century a quarter of a million people—one-sixth of the total European population of the USA—claimed Scotch-Irish descent, and a considerable proportion of them had already crossed the Appalachians. Even the tolerant Quakers of Philadelphia found the Ulstermen uncouth and subversive, 'a pernicious and pugnacious people',[12] but as pacifists the Quakers were willing to find room for fighters on the unsettled Indian frontier. The Ulstermen, not unwilling to go where they could take land at little or no financial cost, were also attracted by the prospect of finding freedom from established authority. And they were apparently not hindered by their women-folk, who, in patriarchal subordination, submitted to the ordeals of frontier life and repeated uprootings.

Their German neighbours, the Pennsylvania 'Dutch', already 20,000 strong by 1727, were also settled in south-eastern Pennsylvania—mainly between the Scotch-Irish and the Quakers—and some of them took part in the drive into the wilderness, but in general their attitudes were in sharp contrast to those of the Scotch-Irish. They tended to consolidate their position while the Scotch-Irish became dispersed. An extreme example of their resistance to change is provided by the Old Order Amish, a religious sect which originated in the Emmenthal and took its name from the Swiss Jacob Amman. The Amish, who first settled in Pennsylvania in 1727, still largely reject the modern world in deed as well as word, retaining almost unchanged their picturesque dress, their agricultural practices—including their horses and other farm gear—as well as the values of their eighteenth-century ancestors. Though technologically fossilized they are excellent farmers and have done so well that they now occupy much of the country around the lower Susquehanna originally settled by the Scotch-Irish.[13] All the German-speaking immigrants were Protestants of various kinds, mainly from the Rhineland and Switzerland, and the many sects formed endogamous groups which clung together and did not encourage lone rangers. Their settlements included villages such as Bethlehem and they shared with the Scotch-Irish towns such as Lancaster—which was to become by 1800 the largest 'inland' town in the United States—and though they increasingly established themselves in separate farms, these were not widely scattered and the settlements retained something of the cohesion of village communities. Like the Scotch-Irish they were much given to religion and inured to toil, but unlike them they are said to have been diligent, cheerful, well-mannered, co-operative and law abiding. Skilful farmers, they were also highly skilled in the many arts and crafts which contributed to their needs. They were accustomed to a varied diet and to oven-baked bread, to elaborate equipment for cheese-making, for smoking meat and storing fruit.[14] Their most celebrated champion was Dr Benjamin Rush who called upon the citizens of the Republic to copy the Germans in their 'knowledge and industry in agriculture and manufactures'.[15] Benjamin Rush was of Scotch-Irish background and it has been claimed that he praised the Germans in order to win them over to American nationalism.[16] Yet, partly because of their alien German tongue, their part in the affairs of the young Republic cannot be compared with that of the English planter-politicians or the Scotch-Irish backwoodsmen. Not until our own century did a Hoover or an Eisenhower become President of the United States. Their material contributions, however, were considerable, and any assessment of the role of the middle

colonies in the making of America must take account of the German element.[17] They gave the backwoods the log-cabin, the Kentucky rifle and the
Conestoga wagon. The Appalachian dulcimer and perhaps the covered
bridge were among their contributions to American 'folklore'.

In time the log-houses and barns of the early German settlements were
replaced by stone or timber-framed houses and by the vast painted barns
(the Switzer barn) which today dominate the rural landscape of the 'Dutch
Country' and by means of which German expansion in the nineteenth century can be traced through Ohio and Indiana. Almost from the beginning
the log-house, or the log-cabin as it came to be called, was adopted by the
Scotch-Irish backwoodsmen, and it is to them more than any other group of
immigrants that it owes its wide diffusion and its fame. It became so encrust-
ed with sentiment and associated with the shrines of grass-roots politicians
of the nineteenth century that one discovers with a shock that, as recently as
1939, there were over 270,000 log-houses still inhabited in the USA, mostly
in the Old West.[18] The origin of the American log-cabin has been much discussed. For long erroneously associated with early English tidewater settlements,[19] it was later attributed to the Swedes, and indeed the Swedes settled
on the Delaware were probably the first builders of log-houses in America,
but it was a German version, as might be guessed, that was taken over by the
Scotch-Irish. Henry Glassie,[20] who has made extensive field studies of log
constructions, describes the two main techniques of corner timbering used
by the Pennsylvania Dutch, leaving aside the simple saddle-notching normally employed for temporary structures. They are V-notching and full
dovetailing. The former predominates in the Shenandoah Valley, where
there were many Germans, but as one moves farther into the Appalachians
a modified dovetail—the half dovetail—makes its appearance, and beyond,
both in the Blue Ridge country and far to the west of the mountains in Kentucky, Tennessee, Ohio, Indiana, Illinois, Missouri and Arkansas, this
method of cornering predominates. Hewn hardwood logs were used, and
the interstices between them were filled by 'chinking' with mud, stones or
slivers of wood. When the filling is coated with lime-mortar the effect is that
of horizontal black-and-white half-timbering. There is a strong Ulster
flavour about the remark made by a Tennessee countryman, that 'the man
who can make mud which will stick between the logs even if thrown from a
distance is as proud as the man who is an expert with the broadaxe'.[21] In the
nineteenth century weather-boarding did away with the need for efficient
chinking or nogging, and one would not suspect that many houses so boarded over are in fact log-houses. Nearly half the rural houses in some Appalachian counties are said to be log built.

That this variety of log-house can be associated with the Scotch-Irish is attested in other ways: not only is the ground plan almost identical with that of the traditional small Ulster farmhouse, but like the north Ulster house it was generally provided with two opposite doors, and even the half-door was formerly common.[22] The chimney was placed in one of the gables, but whereas in Ireland it is invariably built inside the gable, in the log-house, probably because of the risk of fire, it was built outside in English fashion. The average internal dimensions of this type of log-house are 16 by 22 feet, which compares closely with an average of 15 by 21 feet for the traditional Ulster kitchen: the external dimensions in fact are almost identical. (The log-cabin adopted by the English settlers who spread into the mountains from tide water was typically about 16 feet square, reproducing the dimensions of the English single-bay cottage.)[23] Although the length and weight of individual logs placed a natural limit on the size of a cabin, it seems clear that the shape of these constructional units—termed pens or cribs—was partly determined by the previous experience of the builders. The immigrants from Ulster had been accustomed to live in rectangular houses whose ground plans were derived from the cruck-roofed house, presumably imported from Scotland. In the eighteenth century, when the Irish woodlands had been largely destroyed, the walls were built of mud or stone or a mixture of both, and the roof was presumably carried on composite cruck-trusses or on coupled rafters resting on the walls, but even where the roof was 'coupled' the restrictions which cruck-construction had placed on the width and height of the house persisted. The single room, though it may have had a small bedroom attached, was at once kitchen, work place, living-room and bedroom, and there is little doubt that it frequently housed some of the livestock at night. All cooking was done in the open hearth.

The log-house, like the ancestral Ulster home, was built with the clearings of the fields. Its wide open hearth was fitted with familiar gear: crane and iron pots, flesh-hook and pot-hooks, griddle and frying-pan. The crude furniture—shelves, presses and folding tables—lined the walls and left the centre of the room free.[24] An interesting variant is the double-pen log-house, consisting in its commonest form of two pens under a single roof, separated by an open passage known as the breezeway or dog trot. Originating apparently in Appalachia, it spread from the Tennessee Valley northwards into Kentucky, westwards into Missouri and Arkansas, but especially southwards into Georgia, Alabama, Mississippi and Louisiana. The dog-trot house, it has been claimed, was influenced by the through-passage of the north-west Ulster house, but its standard form owes much to Georgian fashions of symmetry and proportion. The central passage was often converted into a hall, and this style of house, translated into brick or frame, became fashionable in urban areas, for example in Tennessee. In this and other ways the log-house had a lasting effect on the traditional house-types of the Old West and beyond.

But the log-house should be seen as only one element in a complex of cultural adaptations. The Ulstermen found themselves in a land of hills and valleys, providing on the hillsides—or in the 'notches' or 'gaps'—the sites which they preferred; and although heavily forested, the 'mountain' still provided the extensive summer grazing they had been accustomed to find on the Ulster hills. It was a forest of richly varied species of trees and shrubs. The backwoodsman's principal tool, the axe, served to fell or at least to deaden the trees by girdling, but not to clear the stumps, and whereas the Germans are said to have selected level sites, grubbed up the tree roots and turned their clearings into ploughed fields, the Scotch-Irish preferred to make fresh clearings and move on once they had 'taken the good' out of the land. They were in effect practising their old 'outfield' system, adapted to a forested landscape of seemingly limitless extent. They were not tied to a plot of earth by a regular system of crop-rotation or any tradition of fruit-growing. The Indian methods of 'deadening' the woodlands served this purpose. A system of bush fallow—the equivalent of the Irish outfield—still characterizes parts of Appalachia, and even that part of the farm which is kept under cultivation is sometimes cropped in small patches which are abandoned after two or three years. Another cultural trait which characterized the backwoodsmen and which has Ulster antecedents was the practice of 'striving', the performance by rival workers of prodigious feats of strength and endurance.[25]

The Indian corn was a prolific substitute for oats and barley; and like them it was spring-sown and food for man and beast. Animal husbandry was of course an innovation, but hunting and the utilization of the forest owed much to the Indians. The 'backwoods' life which the Scotch-Irish adopted was well named, for it took shape in the shadow of the woods and derived much of its colour, sustenance and its superstitions from them. One of the subsidiary occupations of the rural population of the Old West today, from the Carolinas to Kentucky, is root digging and herb gathering to supply the crude drug houses.[26] Growing out of the backwoodsmen's use of simples and herbal cures, the industry now utilizes over a hundred plants, most of them native to the woodlands and long known to the Indians. The forest also had many species of nut- and fruit-bearing trees and supplied high quality timber in great variety—poplar, chestnut, hickory, ash, oak, dogwood and the versatile cedar—for every household use. The dogwood with its milk-white blossoms, which bring to the Old West an air of festival in May, seems to have taken the place of the Irish may tree as an ecological index, a sign of warm weather and an emblem of good luck: the tradition that corn was not planted until the dogwood flowers were fully open may well have been borrowed from the Indians.

The backwoodsmen took over not only the Indian's vast store of knowledge of plants and animals and forest lore, but his passion for hunting, and with it the deerskin shirt and the stalker's moccasins.[27] (Leather or rawhide articles of clothing would have been no novelty to the Ulster immigrants, for leather breeches were worn in some parts of the country in the eighteenth century.) Indian arrowheads provided them with gun flints.[28] They wore their hair long, Indian fashion, dressed it with bear's grease and tied it with an eel-skin or a 'whang'. Nor would Indian music, consisting of drum and flute, have been unfamiliar to Ulstermen.[29] The 'Indian fighters' took on many of the attributes of the Indian brave, and the strong silent hero of American folklore was surely born on the Old Frontier.

Few would agree with Arnold Toynbee that 'the impress of Red Indian savagery (on the Scotch-Irish) is the only social trace that has been left behind by these vanquished and vanished Redskins'.[30] Even this unfortunate judgment could be expressed differently, for a contemporary observer stated that the frontiersmen learnt the skills of concealment and surprise from their Indian enemies and turned them to good advantage in the struggle for political independence.[31] If in recent years the role of the Indian in the shaping of American life on the frontier has been re-evaluated,[32] less attention has been paid to his contributions in material culture. The first English accounts of the woodland Indians often pay high tribute to their cultural and agricultural standards, but very soon the colonists, and especially the Puritan theologians, began to stress the barbarism, tribalism and nomadism of the Indians. These were precisely the defects which the English saw in the Irish whom they were conquering at the same period.[33] In fact, the detested nomadic habits both of the Irish and the Indians were to a considerable extent the consequence of, and a defence against, foreign invasion. But leaving this aside, the main reason for the denigration was the need felt by the invaders to justify conquest. None was more zealous than the Ulster-Scot Presbyterian in 'smiting the enemies of the Lord'. The Indians, while accepting, for good or ill, the material goods of white civilization, found it so unattractive that they consciously refused to be absorbed.[34] Consequently their degraded remnants appeared to nineteenth-century historians to confirm the views of their first conquerors.

Settled agriculture had been practised in the Eastern Woodlands for millennia, and the historian's references to virgin forests are therefore as misleading as when applied to Elizabethan Ireland. Many parts of the Great Valley, for example, must have been secondary woodland, full of old clearings, and it was crossed by Indian trails. The Cherokee Indians had established a powerful 'kingdom' in the southern Appalachians,[35] and they had subsidiary hunting grounds in Shawnee territory beyond the Cumberland Mountains, their trails, which the pioneers were to follow, winding through the wind-gaps.

Other crops besides maize were taken over from the Indians: tobacco, beans of various kinds, pumpkins, squash and gourds. They all lent themselves to hand-cultivation and harvesting and demanded only the simplest of implements, spade, mattock and hoe. Like the other prolific crop of New World origin which was by this time well known in Ireland, and which the settlers took with them to North America—where it came to be known as the Irish potato—maize was cultivated by moulding or 'hilling', in the Indian fashion. It did not require a well-prepared seed-bed and its rapid growth smothered rank weeds. Moreover, the Indian methods of preparing corn for food were very similar to the Irish methods, requiring no elaborate mills or ovens. The hominy-block was a ready substitute for the knocking-stone, and hominy for porridge. Bread in cakes of many kinds (gritted bread, parched bread, corn-bread, hoe-cakes) was baked on the hearth—on a griddle, a bread-stick or a hoe—or in the pot oven; and the open hearth kept its function as the focus of the home. One item listed as the pioneer housewife's helpmeet is the bundle of turkey feathers—a ready native replacement for the goose-wing 'tidy' of the Irish hearth.[36]

A long list might be made of cultural needs which the Scotch-Irish immigrants and their descendants were able to satisfy, develop and exploit in their bountiful new environment. The dairyman's stave-built utensils, which in Ulster's deforested landscape had come to be made of bog-oak, could now be fashioned out of cedar and white oak in a variety of types: tubs, firkins, piggins, noggins, churns, pails and keelers. Pipe-staves were in great demand for the provision trade both at home and in Ireland, and no less than 1,170,384 staves where shipped from Philadelphia to Ireland in 1771.[37] Similarly the export of flax-seed to Ulster was a logical development.

The single farm, we have seen, was the characteristic pioneer settlement. It is coming to be recognized that it was the Scotch-Irish who first 'filled up the mountainsides from New Hampshire to the Great Smokies' with their solitary log-houses and their corn and woodlands-pasture culture.[38] The family farm of the Old West, surrounded by its extensive woodlands 'outfield', was an Atlantic heritage, very different both from the village system of New England and from the plantation mansions of the southern tide water. The right to claim ownership of land by possession and improvement was arrogantly assumed by colonists who had fought stubbornly for their tenant rights in Ulster; and this right was finally recognized and rationalized in the Homestead Act of 1862. Thus the single farm became the standard settlement-type of vast areas of the American heartland.

As in Atlantic Europe the communal, commercial and religious needs of scattered farms were met by small settlement clusters at crossroads, typically grouped around a mill, a post-office or a church. These 'unincorporated hamlets' are 'next to farms, the most ubiquitous of all settlement-types in the United States',[39] and they are most numerous in the region where they originated: in Pennsylvania, Maryland and Virginia, and Kentucky. At an early stage, before roads and towns were established, the pedlar must have played an important role in supplying scattered farms with news and trivial luxuries: he became a figure of American folklore and, since he had a flying start, founder of many a fortune in the new cities of the Middle West.

Of the many small towns established in Pennsylvania in the eighteenth century one type seems to have special associations with the Scotch-Irish. In plan it is a street-town resembling Cookstown, Beragh or Sixmilecross in County Tyrone, but with cross-streets spaced at fairly regular intervals. These towns were for the most part built by speculators in the late eighteenth century and their purpose is shown by the name Market Street often given to the main thoroughfare. They occasionally copy the name of an Ulster town, for example Armagh in East Wheatfield Township in Indiana County, which was laid out in 1792. In some instances, moreover, for example Rehrersburg, the street incorporates an elongated market place which is significantly known as the 'the Diamond',[40] a word which seems to be used elsewhere in this connection only in Ulster, though it is found in some American towns outside Pennsylvania, for example Cleveland, Ohio. The rectangular form of the 'square' at Rehrersburg, however, is not typical of Ulster towns. Another plan represented in Pennsylvania towns—the grid-town with central square—may also have antecedents in Ulster (for example Londonderry) though its roots lie in the common ground of Renaissance town-planning.[41] The central square is characteristic of numerous planned towns established in the late eighteenth century throughout the Old West. In the case of county seats the square contains the courthouse, one of the first examples[42] (later removed) being Lancaster in Lancaster County, where many Ulstermen settled. In towns established in the early nineteenth century, for example in Indiana, it was enlarged to comprise a complete block of the grid. The original purpose of the central square would have been to provide parking space for market wagons, but the idea of adding a central building may well have come, like the word 'diamond', from Ulster. It has been claimed that the central position of the court-house in these towns reflects the *municipio* tradition of the American South, but the evidence seems to link it with Pennsylvania, and since it was an early feature (before 1800) of trans-Appalachian settlement and is still most frequently found in Virginia,

North Carolina, Kentucky and Tennessee, there is reason to think that it was taken there by the Scotch-Irish, whose Presbyterian predilection for 'the law' was notorious.

To sum up, it is suggested that the influence of the Scotch-Irish in the making of the United States of America lay not only in their outstanding contributions to leadership in politics and education but, perhaps more significantly, in their shaping of the patterns of settlement, land-use, economy and society. They took with them the bellicose Non-conformist heritage of the Atlantic ends of Europe.[43] It is a subject that calls for investigation through the interpretation of the masses of local records surviving in the Old West; but documentary evidence alone cannot fully illuminate the largely unwritten processes of cultural adaptation that are involved in pioneer settlement. What is needed is the co-operation of the social anthropologist, the cultural geographer and the student of folk-life.

[E.R.R. Green (ed.), *Essays in Scotch-Irish History* (London 1969)]

OLD IRELAND AND NEW ENGLAND

The south-central part of the State of Maine, where the Penobscot River flows south to the sea past the cities of Bangor and Belfast,[1] will naturally hold some interest for Ulster readers. Maine, almost equal to Ireland in size, is the north-easternmost state of New England (and of the whole United States) and stands geographically in much the same relation to the rest of New England as Ulster does to Éire. Like Ulster, Maine was radical in its outlook a century and a half ago and is now strongly conservative in politics, though the label 'Republican' may seem inappropriate to the Ulsterman. Since its separation from Massachusetts in 1820 it has experienced strong currents of regionalism, expressed in literature by a long succession of prose-writers and poets. Through their work runs the spirit of the frontier, of the forest and of the sea.[2]

This, the nearest part of the United States to Europe, was one of the first coasts to be visited and, some claim, the first to be settled, but if so the early plantations were not permanent, and effective settlement, beginning in the seventeenth century as an offshoot of the Massachusetts Bay colonies, remained sparse until the early eighteenth century. The land was poor and heavily wooded, the climate harsh and the Indians hostile. The name Maine, it is believed, was given by prospecting fishermen and fur-traders who were familiar with the dark-forested 'mainland' beyond the coastal islands which they used as bases for trade and for fish-drying.

110

To this day the life of Maine clings closely to the coast, rivers and lakes. Most of the state is so rocky and infertile that having stripped the original forest-cover man finds little more use for the poor soil than did the Indians he replaced. About half of Maine is virtually unpeopled. But like the Indians, the white settlers found the coast and river estuaries more inviting. So tortuous is the outline of this sunken land, drowned across the grain of the rocks, that the coast, 250 miles long in a straight line from Kittery to Calais (that is about equal to the distance across Ireland from Fair Head to Valencia) would, if stretched out fully, measure some 2500 miles, or not much less than the distance from Maine to Ireland.

No small-scale map can do justice to the clusters of attenuated peninsulas and islands and the deep estuaries that break the line of the coast, making an amphibious fringe from ten to twenty miles wide where land and water are intermingled. As soon as one crosses the St Croix River at Calais and passes into New Brunswick the islanded coast gives way to the smooth shores of the Bay of Fundy. Between Portland and Kittery, moreover, the coast turns south parallel to the grain of the rocks, and submergence has had less effect. Inland, too, there are countless lakes totalling 2175 square miles in area, relics of the heavy glaciation which also resulted in deflected streamcourses and waterfalls, and in extensive deposits of sand and gravel. Everywhere, save where bare rock outcrops in what are called 'ledges', the land was heavily forested with a mixed growth of pine, spruce, oak, maple and birch. Owing to the lie of the land, large rivers with wide tidal estuaries are characteristic of Maine. For the Indians they were highways into the interior.

Mountains rise to four and five thousand feet about 100 miles inland, but except locally the coastal area, to a depth of thirty miles, is below 200 feet in height. Other factors have also operated at different times to keep the population concentrated near water: defence against Indians, navigation and trade, access to waterpower, the tourist industry. The growing-season is longer near the sea, and the winters, though bitterly cold, are less severe than in the hilly interior. Moreover the coast, the river estuaries and the adjacent banks provide rich fishing-grounds, and the varied shores, enriched by marine growths which a high tidal range encourages, are well stocked with lobsters, clams, and other shellfish. Oysters, formerly present in great numbers, are now rare. Sea-birds abound, and the coastal inlets are thronged with migrant species of duck and geese during spring and autumn.

All in all the natural environment of Maine, allowing for differences of climate and the frozen winter, was not unlike that of Ireland when man began his Mesolithic penetration of the island some six thousand years ago. How far back the archaeological record can be traced in Maine is not yet clear, but down to the time of white settlement native life remained essentially Mesolithic in character, modified by a partial adoption of food production and the associated arts.

The Abenaki Indians of Maine were a branch of the great Algonquin family. The name Abenaki ('Dawnlanders') may be regarded as equivalent to the term Downeasters applied to the modern people of Maine. Considerable remnants of the natives, no doubt with much mixed blood, survive in two settlements near Bangor. They are said to number about 1000, and make a living by selling baskets and bead-work. Their ancestors depended largely on fishing and hunting. A great variety of methods of fishing was practised, including weirs and traps, line-fishing, scooping and spearing. Archaeologists have mapped some 400 shellheaps along the coast of Maine: they are notably extensive at Damariscotta. Clams, oysters and lobsters were dried for winter use and packed in birch-bark boxes. Clams were apparently the favourite sea-food, as they still are throughout New England. Clam-bakes, done in layers of seaweed in Indian fashion, are a popular ingredient of summer picnics. It is a curious instance of the persistence of food-habits, perhaps not entirely accounted for by the relative abundance of species. Our prehistoric ancestors in Europe apparently preferred cockles, mussels and limpets.

The many uses to which bone, shell, sinew, bark, wood-fibre and basketry were put have their parallels in the Mesolithic culture of the Old World, traces of which may be found surviving throughout north-western Europe. Domestic potsherds which may be picked up by lakeshores and in the shell-heaps are almost indistinguishable from the heavy cord-shell-and-maggot impressed wares of the Baltic and of such Ulster sites as Island MacHugh. It seems that the Indian pottery was too porous and friable to be used as cooking vessels: they were for storage and 'pot-boiling' by means of heated stones.

Fall was the great hunting-season. Bear, beaver and the lordly moose are still found in the Maine woods, though the caribou is extinct. Something like a fever descends on the Maine folk when the 'hunting' season opens each fall. In 1948 some 36,000 deer were shot in the month of November, and the law allows each hunter to bag one deer only. During the same period there were eighteen fatal shooting accidents in the woods.

After the spring thaw, beaver and musk-rat were hunted and enormous quantities of shad and alewives (resembling a large herring) were caught as they went up the rivers to spawn. Salmon and sturgeon were also taken, and in the autumn eels were trapped on their way downstream. Sea-birds were captured during the summer and toll taken of the migrant duck and geese in spring and fall. Seals, porpoises and even whales were harpooned, ropes being made out of fir-fibre or bark. Harpoons, knives, axes, arrowheads and scrapers were fashioned out of bone, flint and stone. The sea-going Indian boat, evolved from the double-ended bark canoe, was the ancestor of the New England fisherman's 'dory'.

The native crops were corn (maize), beans and pumpkins grown in 'hills' and fertilized with the abundant alewives, a practice copied by the early white settlers. Berries were picked and dried for winter use, and the large acorns of the white oak were gathered and pounded in mortars to make flour. I have seen no large stone mortars from Maine, and it may be that wooden ones were used, but the Californian Indians used for this purpose hollowed stone-basins of the type which in Ireland are called bullauns. Like the bullauns, the Indian mortars were often clustered on large boulders or outcropping rocks. These analogies suggest that further parallels might be traced between the woodland Indians of old New England and the Mesolithic and Neolithic communities of ancient Ireland. The Abenaki lived for most of the year in bark-covered timber wigwams. Their moccasins may be compared with the raw-hide pampooties of the west of Ireland. They made much use of the perforated shell fragments for 'wampum'. As has been inferred for the early inhabitants of Ireland, the Maine Indians, like their better-known brethren in British Columbia, had a system of totems under which each group was associated with a particular species of bird, animal or fish.[3]

During the colonial period, Maine became an area of settlement of the Scotch-Irish emigrants from Ulster. It is ironic, considering the memorable part that this stock played in eighteenth-century America, that while the New World has its New England and Nova Scotia, not to mention New Hampshire and New Brunswick, the name New Ireland should be found on the map only in an obscure part of the Pacific Ocean. In the eighteenth-century parts of Maine came near to becoming a New Ireland, and it is interesting to find that during the American Revolution the name was in fact proposed for the disputed territory[4] between the Penobscot and the St John Rivers. It may be recalled that the original French colony of Acadia, part of which was given the name Nova Scotia when granted by James I to Sir William Alexander in 1621, was ceded to Britain by France in 1713. It included what is now the province of New Brunswick, and also the eastern part of Maine. With the peace of 1783 the St Croix River became the dividing line between the United States and Canada, but disputes as to the course of the inland frontier between Maine and Canada ended only in 1842.

Today of course, thanks to the Boston Irish, the name New Ireland would be more appropriate for Massachusetts, but not only did Maine attract the Scotch-Irish: it became, with New Brunswick, the first path of entry for the southern Irish on their way to Boston from the end of the eighteenth century.

It is agreed that the first considerable immigration of the Scotch-Irish took place in 1718, when five vessels from Ireland landed in Boston. Most of the newcomers moved on to the frontier districts of New Hampshire and Maine. These unsettled regions had certain attractions for the Scotch-Irish, or perhaps it would be nearer the truth to say that they seemed less unattractive to them than to the English stocks who, for a century, had been settled around Massachusetts Bay. Here the power of the Indian tribes had been broken, but further afield they remained a force to be reckoned with. The Scotch-Irish wanted freedom from interference at all costs: they had left Ulster in protest against the impositions of the established church and the landlords, and to obtain freedom they were ready to face the Indians.

It seems that the English Puritans deliberately sent them on to defend the frontiers. This, says W.F. Marshall, 'was the reason why they were at first welcomed by the earlier colonists'.[5] The harsher climate of northern New England, moreover, was more suited to oats than to wheat, and to potatoes than to oats. They also took with them their flax and spinning-wheels. Their settlements in New Hampshire and Vermont are better known than those in Maine, and Maine's Belfast was in fact a daughter-town of New Derry in New Hampshire, but it was rather by individual initiative that the Ulstermen left their mark in Maine, and something of the story may be briefly told. If Scotch-Irish family names are not much in evidence today it is because the early pioneers were not reinforced, most of the later immigrants seeking Philadelphia instead of Boston. They suffered heavily in the War of Independence, eagerly embracing an opportunity to resist oppression. Moreover, during the nineteenth century, the Scotch-Irish element in Maine was prominent in that drive towards the west which carried New England traits across the continent to the Pacific.[6] They were always the first to move on.

Among the Ulstermen who found their way into Maine from the first contingent of 1718 were several who settled in the newly founded town of Brunswick. They included the Rev. James McKeen, grandfather of the first President of Bowdoin College, Brunswick, and the Rev. James Woodside of Garvagh and Dunboe, the first resident minister of Brunswick, who was, however, dismissed. The Rev. Robert Dunlop, who came over from County Antrim in 1736, succeeded him, but was also dismissed. The Congregationalists were apparently unwilling to submit to Presbyterian ministers. But Robert Dunlap's son John became a prominent merchant in the town and built, in 1800, the first local ship to make a voyage to the West Indies. Another family of shipbuilders and sea captains were the Skolfields, whose ancestor had been a member of the garrison in Dublin Castle. His companion Joseph Orr, an Ulsterman and a weaver, is commemorated in the name Orr's Island in Casco Bay, south of Brunswick.[7]

The little town of Belfast, eighty miles east of Brunswick, was founded in 1769 by thirty-five 'proprietors' from New Derry, sons and grandsons of the original immigrants, who purchased a tract of 15,000 acres for £1500. Tradition says that the name Belfast, in preference to Londonderry, was decided on after tossing a coin. For five years in the period of the revolutionary wars the young settlement was abandoned in fear of British raiders, and when a fresh start was made in 1784 the original Scotch-Irish stock was greatly weakened.[8] The first church to be established was Congregationalist, and nearly all the Presbyterian families throughout south Maine became in the end Congregational. Scotch-Irish names, however, continue to crop up through the nineteenth century, when Maine experienced its Golden Age.

By about 1800 the main features of the settlement pattern had been established, with dozens of small towns along the coastal bays, a series of larger towns up the wide rivers at tide-limit or at falls, and smaller settlements farther upstream. The river towns are nearly always in opposite pairs, utilizing to the full favourable locations which, in most cases, had already been camp sites or carrying places of the Indians. The broad main streets of these settlements, and the timber framed houses which line them, are strongly reminiscent of the original plans of the plantation towns of seventeenth century Ulster. It is a feature of New England that, as in Ireland, the term 'town' applies both to the urban areas and to units of land. The township, several square miles in area, was the land allocated to a farm village, and was normally divided into lots of arable, pasture, upland, woodland and often shoreland.[9] In the course of time the most favourably sited villages grew into urban areas, while other villages broke up into separate farms. New immigrants tended to build isolated farm houses, most of them having access to water along coast, river or lake.

It was a combination of natural resources—the land, the sea, the rivers and the forest—that made possible Maine's Golden Age. As in the days of the Indians, communications were mostly by water, and farmers who were also fishermen built their own boats and became carriers. The forests of oak and pine from which they carved their fields were themselves carved into ships' timbers. From the end of the eighteenth century, when Massachusetts lost its best forests, Maine became the world's chief centre of merchant vessel construction, almost every bay of its immensely long coastline launching ships, barks and schooners of ever increasing size. Vessels were even built in places miles from the coast, and hauled to the launch by long yokes of oxen.

The families that built the ships also manned them and became sea captains and captains of commerce. It was a peculiarity of Maine seafaring that the captains often took their wives with them, and their children were apt to be called after some foreign port where they were born.[10] The captains' wives naturally brought back mementoes of their travels, among them pet cats from the east which are the ancestors of the countless 'shag cats' of Maine; and from Italy and India the seamen farmers of New England brought native breeds of the domestic fowl which they improved into the famous breeds named after Plymouth Rock, Rhode Island and Wyandotte.

The export cargoes were mostly lumber (cordwood, boards, shingles, pipe staves), fish (dried or salted), provisions (hay and potatoes) and bricks (burnt with timber waste and convenient for ballasting light cargoes): they were destined mainly for southern New England and the West Indies. The return cargoes were general goods from all parts of the world, but in particular plantation products from the West Indies and the Southern States— sugar, rum and molasses; tobacco and cotton. The ports of western Britain, Liverpool and Glasgow, and to a lesser extent, Belfast, received many of their colonial imports in Maine ships.

Bangor, tapping the interior up the Penobscot River, rose to be perhaps the greatest lumber market of the world by the middle of the nineteenth century, and Belfast shared in this prosperity. Already in 1816 its historian records that on a certain day in February between 300 and 400 sleds of lumber, hay and provisions reached the Belfast wharves, and a single ship's mast (83 feet long and 7 feet in diameter at the butt) required fourteen yoke of oxen to drag it.[11] Saw mills hummed on the streams and were operated by tide mills along the coast. The Penobscot claims to have evolved, for efficient 'river-driving', both the Maine 'batteaus', light yet strong boats derived from the dory, and the improved Peavey cant-dog.[12]

The effects of the American Civil War were serious for Maine. Not only was its man power drained and its commerce killed, but the days of sail were numbered, and the British tramp steamer was driving the New England schooners and clippers from the seas. The best timber, moreover, had been cut and replaced only by forest 'weeds'. Many farms had been abandoned and become overgrown with birch and juniper. The land had been devastated, not domesticated. Towards the end of the nineteenth century the river towns were driven to exploit and export the only certain harvest that remained, their ice.[13] Artificial refrigeration has now brought this trade almost to an end. But hydroelectric power brought a great increase in the pulp and textile industries, and in the twentieth century the automobile made possible a vast tourist trade. Man's greed has not been able to despoil the sea coast, except locally. The salt-water farms are the homes of wealthy city folk. The lobsters and clams which fed the Indians and sustained the first white settlers[14] are now a luxury food. A few of the lovely white towns[15] still build fishing-boats and pleasure vessels, but Bath alone has gone on to make ships of iron.

The tourist and textile industries have brought about considerable changes in the population, mainly through the influx of city folk from the New York area and of French Canadians. Today, moreover, the Irish Catholic population of Maine outnumbers the descendants of the Scotch-Irish. Already in the eighteenth century a few southern Irish immigrants had reached New England and the trickle was destined to become a flood after the Great Famine. Some of the first were deserters from the Waterford fishing fleet who joined New England boats in Newfoundland.[16] But the majority, particularly in the first half of the nineteenth century, was brought over as a return cargo in the timber vessels which sailed from New Brunswick to the ports of western and southern Ireland. Many of these immigrants drifted west through Maine towards Massachusetts, or were carried there on the gypsum boats from Nova Scotia.[17] Catholic New England, says M.L. Hansen, is largely the product of the New Brunswick timber trade.[18] It was a Nova Scotian, Sir Samuel Cunard, born in Halifax in 1785, who founded the Cunard Line of steamships and began a mail service from Liverpool to Boston in 1840. Long before this the diminishing flow of Ulster Protestants had been deflected into Philadelphia on boats which had taken flax seed, clover seed, pipe staves and tobacco to Belfast and Londonderry.

A few of the early Irish Catholic immigrants settled in Maine, and some became prominent in the lumber trade and in shipping, but most of the Irish population of the state came in with the railroad. They supplied the labour for constructional work of all kinds, and they built cabins which were as rude as those they had been forced to abandon in Ireland. Hawthorne describes their shanties as 'the very rudest that civilized men ever made for themselves', with sod-covered roofs, a board or barrel chimney, and earth two or three feet thick heaped against the walls almost to the roof.[19]

It is typical of the later Irish immigrants that, having been forced overseas by grinding rural poverty, they were reluctant to face the trials of country life. Where possible they took work as grooms and stablemen, graduating to taxi-drivers and traffic policemen, but unlike the Scotch-Irish pioneers, they are essentially urban dwellers. French Canadians also came in as labourers, especially in connexion with the lumber trade, but the great influx from Canada came after 1865: it was caused by agrarian depression in the St Lawrence Valley and by the attraction of the cotton mills. The textile towns (Lewiston, Waterville, Augusta, Biddeford, Saco and Brunswick) now have large French Catholic populations.[20]

[*Ulster Journal of Archaeology*, 3rd Series, 12 (1949)]

part III

RATHLIN ISLAND

See Rachrai Island beyont in the bay,
The dear knows what they be doin' out there
But the fishin' an' fightin' an' tearin' away.
An' what's to hinder them, and what do they care?
In Rachrai there's no Christianity there.
MOIRA O'NEILL

Known to its inhabitants as Raghery or Rachrai, the island lies four miles off
the majestic promontory of Fair Head which forms the north-eastern corner
of Ireland. Rathlin is the only sizeable, and the only inhabited, island off the
coast of Northern Ireland. About a mile wide, the island has the shape of a
short sock, with the toe pointing south to Fair Head and the leg stretching
west from the heel for some four and a half miles. This western or 'upper'
end of the island is also known as Kinramer, while the foot, the southern or
'lower end', is called Ushet, and the *Parliamentary Gazeteer of Ireland* (1844)
describes them as having 'totally dissimilar qualifications'. This is by no
means obvious, for the island is a geological unit, a severed portion of the
Antrim plateau, and consists of layers of black basalt totalling some 400 feet
in thickness overlying a foundation layer of chalk, up to 80 feet of which is
exposed on the south coast. The juxtaposition of black and white explains
the otherwise obscure reference to the island which occurs in Charles
Kingsley's *Westward Ho!*, where it is described as 'looking like a half-
drowned magpie'.

121

Rathlin Irish, now almost gone, but long preserved in the upper end, was much closer to Scottish than Irish Gaelic, and this gives a clue to the island's history, for it was a stepping-stone between the two countries and its ownership was long disputed. The tides around the island are so strong that the crossings from Scotland, the shortest of which is some fifteen miles, were often less difficult than those from Ireland. Visitors from Ballycastle, stranded on Rathlin, have been known to return to Ireland via Scotland. The islanders used to refer to Ireland as a foreign kingdom, and offenders against the unwritten island laws were punished by 'banishment to Ireland'. Probably the best-known story linking the island with Scotland has to do with the exiled King Robert the Bruce, who, in 1306, is said to have been inspired by watching the baffled spider in a cave on Rathlin. The cave, a cavern in the basalt (a photograph of the cave will be found in Mary Campbell's book of Rathlin tales, *Sea Wrack*, published at Ballycastle in 1951) is located near the so-called Bruce's Castle, which is not a castle but a walled enclosure on a rough promontory in the extreme north-east. Inside are the ruins of round corbelled structures known as Danes' Huts. They probably have no connection with the Danes, the name given to the Vikings, but these figure promi-

The south coast of Rathlin—'looking like a half-drowned magpie'—taken from near Bull Point: in the foreground is an exposure of chalk which underlies the basalt.

122

nently in the island's legends, and Rathlin is said to have been the first place in Ireland to suffer from Viking attacks, in the year 975. Caves are larger and more numerous where the softer chalk is exposed at the coast and have been very useful to fishermen. The islanders' clinker-built rowing-boats are of Viking ancestry as the name Drondhem [Trondheim, Norway?] implies. The islanders sail their boats to Ballycastle when they have livestock to sell, particularly for the Lammas Fair; and cattle as well as passengers (and formerly kelp and barley) are carried by the mail boat, in my days a two and a half ton open motor boat with an auxiliary lug sail called the 'Northern Lights' operated by the Coyles family from Ballycastle. There was also the 'lighthouse boat' captained by Paddy McQuilkin. It was said that after visiting Ballycastle for Lammas Fair, the Rathlin boats found their own way home. I remember taking a party of elegantly dressed English school teachers to Rathlin in July 1933 to make a survey of the island for the Le Play Society. They were told they would travel to the island in a motor launch, and they were taken aback when they found that the 'Northern Lights' had been carrying cattle from Rathlin and there were obvious signs of their tenancy. The trip over took two hours and because the seas were too rough for us to return the same day, we spent the night *poste restante* on the stone floor of the post office.

The 'Northern Lights', in addition to serving the lighthouse, used to supply the two island shops kept by Mrs McCuaig and Mrs McCurdy. Boyd's bakery in Ballycastle would send over tea-chests full of loaves, and they would be returned packed with eggs.

Old accounts describe the islanders as notorious smugglers and expert seamen. Well into the last century their traditional craft could still be seen: they were paddle curraghs, similar to those of Tory Island, propelled by a single paddle at the bow and very primitive compared with the rowing curraghs of the Aran Islands. They were constructed of wickerwork covered with tarred and pitched horse-hide. A painting of one done by Mrs Robert Gage in 1840 survives. Well into last century the islanders used skin-covered curraghs, and the landlord's account book of 1760 contains the entry: 'paid for one mare's hide for the boat, 1s6d.' Early last century a writer in the *Dublin Penny Journal* refers to these vessels as 'cobles covered with a tarred and pitched horse-hide'.

The sea provides much besides fish. The collection of wrack for use as manure was a winter occupation culminating in May, when storms usually brought ashore a rich harvest which was called the May-fleece. The burning of the larger stems for kelp became a considerable industry after 1774, some ninety tons a year being exported by the mid-nineteenth century. Mrs Gage comments on the dirt and stench associated with kelp burning and notes that Rathlin girls would make use of the corbelled stone sweat houses, of which several ruined examples remain, to clean themselves. Another source of income came from the collection of sea-birds' eggs, and one still comes across the iron pegs driven into the cliff tops, from which the collectors descended on ropes.

The most powerful climatic force in Rathlin is the wind, which blows from 'all arts and parts' but mainly from the south-west, though the north-westerlies are most feared. The wind shapes the island's life and landscape in many ways. The few sizeable trees have a permanent list to the east. The houses crouch down and rarely have more than one storey: when separate bedrooms became fashionable, an extra room was provided by lengthening the house. Winds and wave bring ashore not only the seaweed 'rods' but a great deal of driftwood which formerly served many purposes. It was most abundant when sailing ships coming from North America carried a deck cargo of sawn timber. The ships themselves were often wrecked on the wild shores of the island and provided more or less legitimate loot for building gates, small boats, roof frames and outbuildings while mainmasts provided roof-trees or were sawn into lengths to make gateposts or field-rollers. Portions of fishing nets washed ashore found many uses—making lobster-pots, chicken pens, or for extra cover for wind-torn thatching. A certain roughness of finish in the thatch—and indeed in many artifacts made by the islanders—is itself dictated by the wind. The thatch which projects over the eaves (easen) is not tight and neatly trimmed but loose and untidy so that the drip from the roof is broken and the wind cannot find purchase. In the mainland one may hear the saying, 'rough as Rathlin easen', and this roughness of finish colours island life in many ways. It is a wise response to wind and rain. Another example is the apparent slovenliness of field walls, which are low, loose and built of field-stones with a mortar. Not only do they allow the wind to blow through them without the eddies caused by a high solid wall—so that sheep lying against them can find comfortable shelter and at the same time dry their fleeces—but they also serve as primitive electric fences, for animals will not try to jump them once they have experienced the shower of sharp stones tumbling against their legs.

RATHLIN: AN IRISH ST KILDA?

'Where yez ever in the island afore?

'I was, but it's ten years since.' I explained the circumstances of my previous visit and he searched the past and remembered me.

'I thought I seen ye.' Then after a pause while the boat rose and staggered over an unusually large wave: 'There's great changes come over there in ten years. D'ye mind the Dornans? Paddy Joe's gone, last Easter twelvemonth,

124

Gold help'um, and his woman's far through. She'll not see another spring.' And he gave me, with the eternal interest in death that the islandman takes, an account of the casualties of a decade.

We were headed into a rising sea for the mist-shrouded island, the six of us, passengers and crew, huddled at the bottom of the boat by the tiller to escape the blown wave-tops and to give the prow better clearance. 'She's a snug wee boat since I lifted her gunwale. D'ye see the coping I put on her?' He pointed and explained that the strip of aluminium along the sides was part of a crashed German bomber which had been washed ashore.

So the island still lived on the sea and its gifts. 'There's nothing come in lately only mines, and sure they'm no use till anybody. I mind the last war; that was far better. Great timber there was come in, and drums of oil and lashings of lard and butter. It was a great time altogether for the island.' I hid my feelings of dismay at his callousness, but in answer to my unspoken thoughts he told me that his two sons had joined the Royal Navy and that one of them would never come home. I remembered that the island had given its quota of sons to the sea for generations and had always accepted in return what the sea brought in. Many a cabin had a ship's mast for its roof-pole and was furnished with teak and shining metal fittings. I remembered seeing meal-bins strangely out of keeping with the simple fireside gear— handsome brass-bound barrels that had once held salt-meat in proud three-masters. Old upturned rowing boats reared on four stout ship's timbers did duty as turf-houses or cart-sheds, and torn trawl-nets secured the rounded thatched roofs from the sea winds. Cowering for protection in little hollows, the houses were invisible as we approached the island.

To my eye nothing had changed in those ten years. Patches of oats, barley, and beans and long strips of potatoes patterned the hollows around the clustered cabins. There were the same untidy loose stone walls that looked so meaningless, for one could step over them; but they served their purpose well. No animal that had felt the tumbling cataract of sharp stones would approach too close again.

We walked the island's main road, strewn with flints and grass-grown at the sides, towards the lighthouse on the westernmost cliffs. Grass had entirely taken possession of the track as we neared the lighthouse and heard the mewing of the sea-birds. Time was when the quaint sea-parrots or puffins were caught in horsehair snares and salted down for winter proven-der, and the eggs were taken by bold cragsmen—one could still see the iron spikes where the ropes were secured at the cliff-edge—and used as food for man and beast in the lean days of early summer.

Guillemots and razor-bills launched themselves wildly from the sea-stacks, speeding seawards with outspread wings like showers of miniature flying bombs. Bright splashes on the cliffs betrayed the young fulmar petrels perched peacefully in impossible crevices, their dove-like appearance strangely out of keeping with their adult habits. And from time to time the peregrine swung past like an aerial policeman on his beat. Ravens, choughs, and hooded crows, kittiwakes and gulls of many kinds: I counted them all and found none missing. No change here, I reflected, remembering the boatman's words. And among the islandmen I recognized several whom I had known and who came up to me with a mighty handgrip and a 'Welcome back to the island.' 'Ye'd see great changes in the island', said my boatman again as we set out for the mainland that evening.

'It all looked pretty much the same as ever to me,' I replied, 'and I hope it stays that way.'

'No, it'll not stay,' he said, 'for there's nobody to come after us.' And he went on to tell me that the school had been closed 'for want of childer' and that nearly all the young folk had sought work in Scotland. 'When I was a wee lad, a man would be proud to be farming five acres of land. Now the same man has fifty acres, and it's going half wild.'

I realized that he had been looking ahead when he spoke of great changes. He saw in another generation an empty island, an island without men and women to fish and farm and gather in the wrack and the wreckage of the sea. Then I looked back at the island and saw the sea-birds everywhere, and I too saw a tenantless hulk, a larger wreck in the Western Ocean.

THE RATHLIN CROSSING: THEY'RE WHITEWASHING THE CLIFFS

The passage to Ballycastle from Rathlin Island's only harbour in Church Bay is one of 6.5 miles at the shortest, but wind and tide may double the distance if the boat is swept off course. When the tide is flooding in, the boat may, for example, reach the calmer waters of Murlough Bay on Antrim's east coast and thence creep back alongshore under Fair Head into Ballycastle harbour. I once suffered for four hours on this journey, and for a time in mid-channel, where the meeting waters seem to boil in the two 'white bushes', between which one must somehow steer, even the great cliffs of Fair Head were periodically lost from sight. The troubled waters were said by the islanders to be boiling in Breccain's Cauldron (Slough-na-Moran, the swallowing sea). The island boats, Drondhems, of Norwegian ancestry, are heavy and broad of beam; for their usual cargo is cattle, lying recumbent with their legs tied together. If they should become obstreperous they are brutally knocked senseless with the heavy starting handle. Most of the boats are now, in the 1950s, powered by ingeniously adapted ancient Morris car engines, but not very long ago they depended on long oars assisted by a small sail.

On another trip, when the waters were dead calm and shrouded in a sea fog, my boatman spoke of a different danger, the risk of being run down. The Fleetwood trawlers, rushing home to catch the market and making as little noise as possible so as not to betray their position to rival boats, would sometimes use the short-cut between Rathlin and the mainland. 'If one of them came on us now', the boatman remarked, 'we wouldn't stand an earthly chance!'

I learnt much about island life from the boatman Paddy McQuaig. He had seen many strange things in his life and was ready to believe almost anything, even improbable tales from the Bible except for parts of the story of the biblical flood. Noah could not have been the only man to escape, he complained, putting it in a characteristic negative way, 'for the McQuaigs were never without a boat.' He told me how, when he first made the crossing to Ballycastle as an apprentice oarsman, the older men in the boat encouraged him, when nearing exhaustion, to stay the course. It should be explained that the Irish coast, as seen from sea-level when leaving Rathlin harbour, is dark and forbidding, consisting of black basalt cliffs dominated towards the east by the grim majestic headland of Fair Head, but as one draws nearer one gets occasional glimpses of the gleaming white chalk which outcrops from Ballycastle westwards, generally underlying the basalt but in parts, where the basalt has been eroded or 'faulted' down, forming headlands such as Kinbane or even the whole sea cliff.

It was a dull day, with poor visibility, the tide was beginning to ebb and the boat was heading for Fair Head, some four miles to the east, to make ground before taking advantage of the full ebb tide, which would sweep it westwards. 'How shall we know where to land?' asked the boy. But the first chalk cliffs were now showing, and the older man drew the boy's attention to them. 'Look', he said 'the Ballycastle boys are whitewashing the cliffs to show us the way into port. Keep rowing, and keep an eye on the shore and we'll see how they get on.' The youngster took fresh heart and bent to his task with a will. It was soon time to run with the ebbing tide, and the boat was swiftly carried under the white chalk cliffs to the west of Ballycastle, ready to creep back inshore into harbour. From this close distance the white cliffs gleamed and glistened with spray, and the black basalts could no longer be seen. 'Look boy', said the man, 'they've finished the whitewashing, and this is where we land.'

[The second of these three pieces first appeared in
The Manchester Guardian, 24 October 1945]

Regarded in his native land by some as a traitor, by others as a martyr, Roger Casement is more widely known as the British consul who exposed the horrors of the rubber trade in the Congo and Amazon basins. Less well known are his Ulster connections, with Ballycastle and Murlough Bay. Born near Dublin, in 1864, of a Catholic mother, his father was a County Antrim Protestant from Glenshesk, where the family home, Magherintemple, was still occupied by Casements when I was last in Ballycastle. Roger himself it appears boasted that both his father and his grandfather had been citizens of Belfast.

When Roger was nine years old he was sent to live with his guardian at Magherintemple and went to school at what is now Ballymena Academy. Older people in the district still speak of his great charm—and of his mental instability. On leaving school he obtained a post as purser on a vessel trading with West Africa, where he joined H.M. Stanley's *African Association* as a volunteer, and conducted surveys in the Congo basin for King Leopold, later taking up several consular posts in the larger towns of the Belgian Congo.

He was deeply moved by the barbaric treatment of the native rubber gatherers and exposed the evils of the trade in several official reports before moving to a succession of consular posts in the Amazon basin and repeating his condemnation of the rubber traders, this time in the Putumayo territory

128

which was then claimed by both Peru and Colombia. For these great services to humanity he was knighted by the British government in 1911, but it has been said that he felt himself to be a traitor to Ireland in accepting the honour from an English king.

Meanwhile he had become interested in Irish history and in the activities of the Gaelic Athletic Association and the Gaelic League; and on visits to Ballycastle he got in touch with the Rathlin Islanders and with the remnant of Gaelic speakers in the far north-eastern corner of County Antrim, around Murlough Bay. His involvement in the Gaelic movement led to contacts with Germany and other anti-British forces. He paid several visits to Germany and after the outbreak of war in 1914 he arranged for the purchase of arms in support of the struggle for Irish independence. In 1913–14 he was chief recruiter for the Irish Volunteers and played a part in securing German guns for shipping in Erskine Childers' yacht—the *Asgard*. Returning to Ireland shortly before the Easter Rising, he was captured when landing from a German submarine at Wexford's Banna strand in Tramore Bay; and thereafter he was tried for treason, found guilty, taken to Pentonville jail and executed. Then—as subsequently—much controversy surrounded his diaries, the so-called 'Black Diaries', because of their frequent references to homosexual interests and activities. Some of the entries in the diaries were circulated to the press by the government in the hope, it is said, of discrediting him at the time of the trial, but their authenticity has been strenuously denied.

As his biographer Brian Inglis relates, when in prison in 1916 Casement told his cousin, Miss Gertrude Bannister, 'Don't let me lie in this dreadful place. Take my body back with you and let it lie in the old churchyard in Murlough Bay.' It was not, however, until 1965 that what remained of the body was taken for burial to Glasnevin where a fervid funeral oration was given by Eamon de Valera. The plot at Murlough which was his intended grave nevertheless remains marked out. Each year on 4 August the faithful have gathered there to honour his memory and on one such occasion, in 1963, I was an unintentional eavesdropper on the proceedings.

A sea mist shrouded the Scottish coast across the waters of Moyle as I walked from Ballycastle to Murlough Bay by way of the top of Fair Head. I hoped to see the golden eagles that had recently returned to the headland, but apart from the soaring and diving gannets out at sea all that stirred below me was a milk-white goat leaping from boulder to boulder—one of a feral herd that had made this wild coast its home. There was no house, no human being in sight.

I was astonished, then, to hear a voice rising loud and clear from the sea below, and the words were Gaelic, coming in impassioned phrases linked by the unmistakeable word '*agus ... agus*'. Crawling to the very edge of the cliff, which drops vertically for 300 feet, I scanned the great boulder-scree below but could see no source for the mysterious voice. The cliff, which faces north-east across an empty sea, is composed of mighty columns of dolerite; and it was their cyclopean weathered remains that had fallen to form the sprawling scree, leaving enormous vertical channels in the face of the cliff. I recalled that a similar formation of thinner basalt columns at the Giant's Causeway is known from its appearance as the Giant's Organ. The voices I heard on Fair Head were being channelled up the vertical pipes, but what was their source? Then I noticed, over half a mile away to the south, where a track dipped steeply into Murlough Bay, an assembly of cars parked at all angles in a sloping field. Nearby, gathered about a mass of boulders that had tumbled from the face of the cliff behind, was a swarm of people, a hundred or so strong, some lying on the grass, others perched among the boulders. The mysterious voice must be addressing the gathering. I could see amplifiers dotted about the field. Thanks to the topography and the direction of the wind—a light sea-breeze was blowing up the cliff-face—I could hear every word distinctly. The voice now changed to English, and the purpose of the speeches became clear. The chief orator was a devoted Irish nationalist who I met much later when he had become a professor at University College, Galway:

We are here to commemorate the forty-seventh anniversary of the murder of Roger Casement in 1916. His life story is one of the most heroic and saddest chapters in Irish history. Roger Casement was marked for assassination not only because of his devotion to the cause of Irish freedom but because of his ability and courage in defence of the unfortunate people of the trop-

Professor Keith Isles of Hobart, Tasmania, at Casement's grave, Murlough Bay, August 1963.

ics and because of his exposure of tyrannical British colonization. His captors not only tortured him, and in the end killed him, but they went to the most shameful lengths to defame and calumniate him, to destroy his name and character.

Speaker after speaker, in Irish and English, took up the theme of the unity of Ireland and the evils of partition, attacking the government of the Six Counties for its oppression and suppression. 'There is no such thing as free speech in this police-state.' I could not but reflect that the free speech denied in Northern Ireland was singularly free in this corner of the country today.

As the crowd dispersed I continued my walk down into Murlough Bay, and toward the centre-piece of the ceremony I had just witnessed, the small ruined church of Drumnakill. It stands on a promontory named from the church, of which all that survives are walls to a height of two or three feet, extending externally a mere 33 by 18 feet (a small crude stone cross which stood close by was removed or stolen in 1976). An alternative name for the church, Killemoiloge, points to a dedication to St Muloch, whose grave is said to have been near the west gable. It is remembered because until recently clay, reputed to have curative powers, was taken from there. Evidently the site was occupied in some period of the early Iron Age, possibly by Christian hermits. Roger Casement had selected this hallowed Irish site for his grave.

When I reached the field where the gathering had taken place I found a litter of papers and bottles; and Casement's designated grave strewn with fresh wreaths, their inscriptions showing that some had been placed by attending representatives of several emergent African republics. A notice board announced that a few years earlier, 'a great hosting of the Gaels' had assembled here and that a eulogy of Casement had been delivered by Eamon de Valera himself.

I made enquiries about this at the farmhouse that stands halfway up the slopes surrounding Murlough Bay. The occasion was well remembered. 'There never were such crowds at Murlough', people had come by boat from all the Glens of Antrim. Mr de Valera had been allowed to cross the border into Northern Ireland for the first time since the Irish Free State was established. I wondered if his speech had been as well heard as those I had just listened to. But no, 'nobody could hear what the great man was saying.' 'Was it a stormy day?' I asked. 'No 't'was a fine day, but the loud-speakers was put out of action.' I asked if the Orangemen had been responsible, for they were his sworn enemies, and I knew they had earlier destroyed the Casement monument, a memorial cross which had stood by the road leading into Murlough Bay. But you never know where you are in Irish politics. The loud-speakers, it seems, had been sabotaged by members of de Valera's old organization, the Irish Republican Army, which by that time was under new management.

The August Fair in Ballycastle is the most famous of the Lammas Fairs in Ulster and has been held almost without interruption for some four hundred years. Like other Lammas Fairs, of which there were at one time nearly forty in Ireland, it was originally a country fair, supplying the legitimate seasonal needs, commercial and social, of a scattered rural population. Its old name was Lewy's Fair or the Festival of Lughnasa. Máire MacNeill, in her great work of that title, lists a hundred hill-sites where festive assemblies took place on or about the beginning of August, and a further hundred gatherings at lakes or wells. Moreover they were given many different names such as Height Sunday, Lough Sunday, Blaeberry Sunday, Pilgrimage Sunday, Harvest Sunday, or the Last Sunday of Summer; and the names provide a clue both to the pre-Christian origins of the festival and to the purposes it came to serve in later times. Essentially it marked the end of summer and the beginning of harvest. Coming midway between May the first, the beginning of summer, when the hill grazings became available, and Hallowe'en, the beginning of winter, it provided the occasion for the bartering or sale of the surplus produce of summer. Sheep, lambs and wool figured prominently in some Lammas Fairs, though the popular derivation of the name from the Lambs' Fair is erroneous.

Soon after I came from Wales to Belfast as a young lecturer and began fraternizing with students—to the obvious distaste, I may say, of my senior academic colleagues—I followed the old Welsh custom of getting them to sing, more or less in harmony, as opportunity arose, for example when leading groups of different religious persuasions on field-trips. One of our most popular items, which they taught me, was 'The Ould Lammas Fair at Ballycastle'. At first I thought the fair must be a thing of the past. It was therefore with a shock of surprise that I found it, one Tuesday morning towards the end of August, in full swing under a steady soaking rain. Old folks lamented, of course, that it was not what it used to be ('Time was, when it lasted a full week') but at least the rain ran true to form. Tradition has it that it always rains for the Lammas Fair; and the country folk would not have it otherwise, for it means they can go to town with a clear conscience. A fine day for the fair is a day wasted on the farm, so by building up the legend of a wet Lammas the young folk can lay their plans ahead. 'Sure it's bound to rain and there's no cause to stay home and miss the fun.'

Pushing through the thronged main street in mid-morning is hard work for the pedestrian and almost impossible for a car. The fair is older than the town. Tight knots of country folk take complete possession of the roadway, heads close together in earnest conclave as they exchange the gossip of many months. The air is thick with glottal-stops, the accent in this north-east corner of Ireland has a strong Scottish flavour. Greetings are shouted across the street, 'How are ye doing, Pat?', 'How's the form, Andy?', 'See you at Ned's Corner.' In many a coat lapel there is a sprig of white heather, in some a harvest knot of oat-straw cunningly twisted.

At the Diamond—the Irish version of a market-square—there is much animation around the yelling cheapjacks, the stalls of the apple-women and second-hand clothes dealers, the booths where the Lammas delicacies are being sold, dulse and yellow-man: 'Did ye treat your Mary Ann', runs the chorus of the song, 'to dulse and yellow-man?'; and I had to sample them both. Dulse is a fine purple seaweed dried into rubbery curls which bounce about the mouth until the tongue has extracted the salts and you seek riddance of the limp unpalatable residue. Its chief virtue, no doubt, is that it raises a thirst that must be assuaged, and here the sweet sticky yellow-man comes powerfully to its aid. I suppose the yellow rock-like toffy was once made, like gingerbread, in human form, symbolizing some rustic deity from the Golden Bough. All that is left nowadays is the golden colour.

Competing with these age-old rites the new religion bellows its appeal across the square. An harmonium is mounted on an empty lorry, and gathered around it a seedy row of gospellers lift their voices in melodious song. I cannot catch the words, but the tune, surprisingly, is 'Drink to me only'. Ignoring the warning, a steady stream of frothy-mouthed farmers moves in and out of a nearby pub. I follow some of them down a short steep street to the Fair Green. The sloping roadway is lined with livestock; a bunch of skinny black cattle, a string of dejected donkeys, a dangerous-looking group of chestnut horses, their tails tied with straw. The surface of the road is coated with a thick layer of bright-green slime composed of miscellaneous animal droppings spread with the rain and the trampling of many feet. It is well to be on one's guard when passing the tethered beasts, warned by a red-faced 'gentleman farmer' whose smart new flannels are splashed with large green spots. Wise natives wear leggings or keep their trousers well hitched up.

A horse is led away along a side street to be put through its paces, followed by an eager throng of potential buyers and onlookers, thin-lipped, horse-toothed. A close knot of countrymen is arguing and shouting alongside a bunch of disinterested heifers: in the centre of the group is the dealer, rotund, standing firmly on his highly polished brown boots. His sly piggy eyes are almost hidden in pouches of fat, his large mouth grotesquely extended with a handful of dulse from which long streamers hang down. The fancy moustaches are mysteriously sucked in and disappear as the dealer resumes his argument. Long crafty faces peer earnestly over shoulders on the edge of the crowd. From time to time a cap is tilted back from a heated brow, revealing a surprising white expanse of forehead which has been protected from the weather. It is warm, but we must wear our raincoats. The rain falls lightly and thin twists of vapour rise to meet it from the roadway. A mighty slap of hand on hand tells of a bargain concluded not far away.

The sounds of the fair lead me to the Green where the sheep are penned. Ballycastle lies among sheepy hills, and sheep and lambs play a large part in this ancient harvest festival. Business is brisker here, for the auctioneer comes between buyer and seller; he is a thin swarthy man in black boots and leggings. Yellow-backed ewes droop under the weight of their sodden fleeces, dabbed at the neck with red or blue dye. The sour smell of sheep hangs in the damp air. As I draw away a new smell takes its place, a smell not of animals but of rotting vegetation. It is the unforgettable whiff of the flax-dams drifting from nearby fields, pleasantly nostalgic in its urban dilution, a smell recalling the olive presses of the warm South. Go nearer to the reeking hole when the lint is being taken out and you will be reminded of things less pleasant; yet there is a strange fascination about it. Humorists have called it 'Donegal violets'.

Back in the Diamond later, other smells assault me: gusts of Guinness or Bushmills as merry farmers, their bargains concluded, exude their joy, and the scent of turf as fires are set alight under kettles for the evening tea. As night falls the Diamond is lit up and shines brightly. Now the fun of the fair begins. An over-excited pair has come to blows, over a cow maybe, or a girl;

the crowd parts a little to give them fist-room and opens a pathway as their momentum carries the fighting pair into a side-street. I watch them disappear, arms flying, as the crowd closes behind them. Two tall policemen—members of the much-maligned RUC—grin at each other from opposite doorways over the bobbing heads. This is Fairday, a seasonal saturnalia when everyday laws are suspended. One of the policemen turns to me, as if to explain his inactivity: 'Ach! its only a scrap, and what's a fight, anyway? Sure it wouldn't be Lammas Fair without a few fights at the end of the day!'

An invited lecture given in the Whitla Hall, Queen's University, Belfast, on 14 May 1963, on the occasion of the presentation of a silver salver by the University to Belfast Corporation to mark the 350th anniversary of the granting of the first charter.

The Borough of Belfast, the granting of whose first charter we are commemorating today, is no chicken. I borrow this phrase, so typical of Belfast in its use of a negative to drive home a truth, from Alderman Thomas Henderson, with whom I served for several years as an added member of the Libraries, Museums and Art Committee of the Corporation. I cannot think that this slight acquaintance with the machinery of Belfast government is the reason why the University honoured me by inviting me—an English Welshman—to give this address. They may have been mindful that Belfast, like most towns in Ireland, was an English foundation, and it is a singular fact that two of its historians have been, if not Englishmen, at least Welshmen: I am not forgetting the monumental works of George Benn and R.M. Young or the more recent contributions of several Ulster authors. I have in mind Sir David Owen who wrote his *History of Belfast* in 1921 and Professor Emrys Jones whose *Social Geography of Belfast* appeared as recently as 1960. It seems right that to complete a Welsh triad an Owen and a Jones should be joined by an Evans. But I have a more personal claim to speak of the City of Belfast, now 350 years old. I have enjoyed its hospitality for exactly thirty-five years and have also enjoyed writing about the city. I recall that when, in

May 1928, I first sailed into the Lagan mouth, along Victoria Channel and past Queen's Island, on my way to an interview at this other Queen's, I was reminded that this is an eminently Victorian city. I had heard of Belfast linen, Belfast ham and the Belfast roof truss. I knew, of course, that it built ships. I expected to hear the din of the riveters among the gantries, but the only sound that fell on my puzzled ears was an ominous one—the call of a lonely corncrake in a waste of grass and thistles. Queen's Island recovered from that deep depression, but it has had its ups and downs ever since.

Now the corncrake has one annoying characteristic that it shares with some academics and some city councillors—it goes on and on, and you never know which field it's in. Let me quickly move, then, to my subject. I must try to assess the geographical personality of this many-sided city, to squeeze 350 years into an hour, knowing that it would take as long to discuss, for instance, as the town solicitor, Mr John Young, has recently done, the single tangled topic of the Belfast charters. Let me first of all refer to the general academic interest which urban studies hold for the sociologist, the geographer, the archaeologist, the historian, the engineer, the economist—in fact for students of many disciplines. The archaeologist can trace the growth of urban life in the Middle East, through layer after layer of towns turned to dust, through 7000 years.

The philosopher tells us that men came together in cities to lead the good life; but this was a precious by-product, not an original cause. Three ideas have predominated in the creation of urban settlements: the idea of defence, the idea of religion and the idea of trade. Towns can be variously classified according to their locations, forms and functions, but because every town is the product of man and nature, of various societies expressing themselves in various environments, no two are alike. The novelist has exploited the uniqueness of his own town—or of his *Five Towns*—and the urban sociologist has tried less successfully to analyse it. He sees in the texture of a town, its network of streets and buildings, a pattern which stamps itself on its citizens. Habits and gestures adapted to habitat become traits of character and bind us unconsciously to this town or that. We are not quite at home elsewhere.

Victorian as much of Belfast is, we need to go back to 1613, and indeed far beyond that, to see its ground plan taking shape. Belfast ('The way to the Crossing') owes its origin to the necessity of defending a colonial group in an alien land, and its growing point was a castle and a broad parade ground at a junction of roads, linked by High Street to the water front and by Ann Street to a ford over the Lagan that could be crossed on foot at low tide. Here a wooden bridge, the Long Bridge, was erected in 1689, to be replaced by the existing Queen's Bridge in 1841. The castle and garrison have gone, but the chief point of reference for citizens of Belfast is still Castle Junction. There we know where we stand; we can orientate ourselves historically and geographically. This ease of orientation, of identifying our location and picking out familiar landmarks, whether it be Cave Hill or the Gas Works, is part of the Belfast inheritance and it has been contended that it produces a logical attitude of mind. The American's first question in a strange city is: 'Say, which direction does this street run?' If, as often as not in an old European town, it should curve, he is stumped. A Parisian writer forced to live for a time in Manchester described that city as utterly directionless, and claimed that the experience led to the temporary disorganization of his logical nature.

The River Lagan and the surrounding hills were here in all their grandeur 350 years ago, and indeed 7000 years ago, when Jericho was a-building; and already man was making use of their resources, their fish, shellfish and woodland game. What was he doing, that distant Ulsterman, among the oak woods and down in the reeds by the river? He may have been, in Dryden's graphic phrase, 'loud with acorns', but I suspect he was also loud with primitive music, with fife and drum and with the noise of family feuds. He fished for salmon, the archaeologists tell us, and he left behind his flint fishing spears where other sportsmen now play cricket near the Ormeau Bridge: but soon he was herding his cattle and growing his crops in clearings among the woods. The herdsman has left his mark on the town in more ways than one. He was a commuter, a seasonal nomad. In this month of May he would drive his livestock through the flowering thorns to the Antrim Hills, along Stockman's Lane, using the first dry ground at the end of the Bog Meadows. The suggestively named lane now hides its bucolic past under the

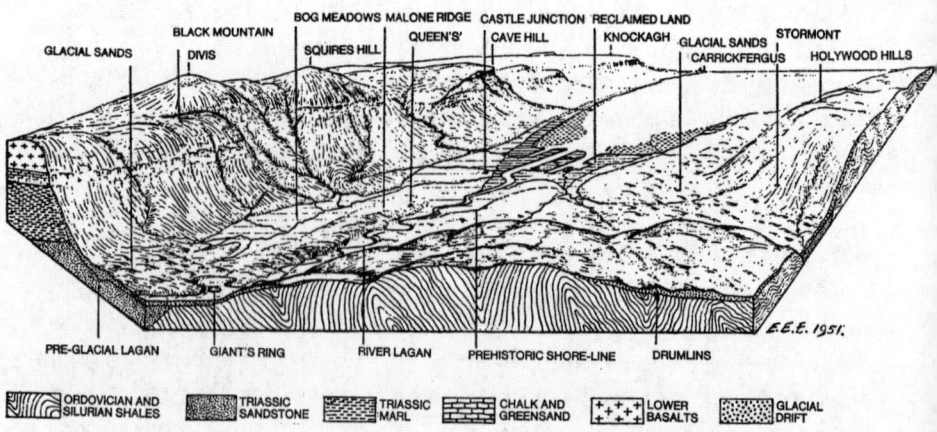

Block-diagram of the site of Belfast, looking north from the Castlereagh Hills

respectability of Balmoral Avenue. He would bring his stock back to the valley at Hallowe'en. Gaelic society was pastoral and familial in organization. It excelled in personal skills rather than communal achievement and flourished without benefit of urban centres. It has been said with some truth that the Irish do not build cities but turn those built by others into slums. Though by early medieval times the idea of religion had brought with it to Ireland some monumental architecture (in the form of churches, round towers and high crosses), the idea of trade had brought no buildings or monuments in stone, for it was conducted at temporary fairs on sites hallowed by long custom. One such site was, very probably, the pre-historic Giant's Ring, which was still a place of popular assembly in the eighteenth century, and may have served in this way since the earliest times. It is placed well back from the river mouth at the south end of the Malone Ridge, for the site of Belfast was then almost awash and probably invaded by tides. The Giant's Ring in its day would have served much the same region as the present city. There has been much more continuity than our history books allow. Belfast, an English plantation, owes much of its character to the landscape that was fashioned earlier by generations who gave each hill and stream and meadow—Divis and Farset and Stranmillis—those Gaelic names that are preserved in singularly uncorrupted forms. The citizens of Belfast, whatever their creed, are unconsciously proud of this heritage; witness the scorn they reserve for the Englishman who fails to get the correct stress on Ligoniel or Ballymacarrett. But the Gaelic past has contributed to the present scene more than the poetry of its place-names or the lines of cattle-tracks that have hardened into Stockman's Lane, Shankill Road and Sandy Row. It touches our pockets, for since the old fairs were held on the Irish quarter-days, our rents fall due not as in England on Lady Day and Michaelmas but on the Gaelic festivals of 1 May and 1 November, when rents were once paid in kind, in fact in kine.

A town cannot live of itself: it is the focus of a region, and Belfast quickly came to serve the interests of an extensive market area. Strong rural and familial values, reinforced by steady immigration from the adjacent country areas and from rural Scotland, have persisted and have revealed themselves in various ways—in the strength of the family firm, echoing the family farm and its tenant right, in the pervading friendliness of a society where friendship once had economic meaning, and occasionally in the emergence of nepotism and other familiar failings. At all levels society is closely knit, so that the newcomer soon learns to mind his tongue lest he is defaming his host's second cousin. But I need not dwell on these endearing attributes, for this loyal city pays its own tribute to the Gaelic past, my Lord Mayor, in the decoration of its mace which (I quote from the official handbook) 'departs

139

entirely in its detail from all others in Ireland in that Celtic ornamentation is made use of throughout'. This proud boast makes one despair of trying to understand the personality of Belfast.

The site of Belfast has some striking topographical features and many natural advantages; and the Earl of Essex summed them up when in 1573 he described the site as one 'meet for a corporate town'. Above all it had the most sheltered haven in eastern Ireland—Belfast Lough. It could easily import many of its requirements, and still does so. It had command of the ford, and of routes into the interior, and it had space to grow: the wide valley of the Lagan, cut into sandstones, lies between hills strongly contrasted in type and age. It recalls indeed in situation but not in site or scale New York, with immensely ancient rocks on the east side of the Hudson River, corresponding to County Down, and the young pillared lavas of the New Jersey Palisades, somewhat resembling Cave Hill, on the other. Approached from either side, the valley lies hidden; come nearer, and it reveals itself filled with man's industry: the big smoke, they call it in Mourne.

Conspicuous in a valley bottom of slight relief would be a continuous low escarpment bordering the level slobland at the mouth of the Lagan—with an extension almost encircling the Bog Meadows—marking the wave-cut shoreline of late prehistoric times when sea-level stood some twenty feet higher than it does today. This former shoreline guided the plan of the town and provided vantage points where roads coming from the town centre could branch out freely on firm ground. To the west Peter's 'Hill' and Mill Street (so called from the watermills which utilized the last falls of the Farset River) where the Shankill and Falls roads had their starting points, diverging as they rose towards the hills. To the south firm ground was reached at Fountainville, where 'Sandy Row', the original road to the south and to Dublin, reached the heights of the Malone sands. As Denis Ireland put it, you passed here from the sloblands to the snoblands. I remember the appealing notice that formerly stood on the railway bridge at Bradbury Place, 'Drivers please let down the reins going uphill.' On the eastern County Down side the sloblands meet rising ground at another celebrated road junction, the Holywood Arches, and also at Mountpottinger and Ormeau.

Only occasionally, as at Skegoneill on the Shore Road, are the Triassic sandstones that underlie the Lagan Valley exposed in wave-cut cliffs along the old shore line, and these rocks have contributed little to the topographic or architectural character of the town. But they have been a hidden asset. Lying below the marine clays (the 'sleech') of the sloblands the Triassic sandstones are natural filter-beds for clear water, which once bubbled out at Cromac and not far from the University at what was, until recently, Fountainville Cottage (now demolished). Now hard sandstone water makes good beer, as Burton knows: you will recall Housman's couplet, which I have been tempted to set as an examination question in Geography: 'Say, for what were hop-yards meant or why was Burton built on Trent?' Belfast uses its well-water for brewing and many other industrial purposes, but it is perhaps characteristic of a puritanical outlook that its best advertised use is for non-alcoholic mineral waters, an industry in which it can claim to have played a pioneer part.

When Sir Arthur Chichester began to build his town on the left bank of the river he used Lagan oak for the frames of half-timbered houses, which were filled in with bricks, made on the spot. It was in style an English town, but when he came to replace the old castle he built himself a massive brick castle, thus setting the fashion for the future. Chichester is said to have baked 1,200,000 bricks for his castle. The Belfast area has no good building stone, and as supplies of timber were exhausted, it was from its own inexhaustible clays that the town came to be built.

The Irish built their thatched, clay cabins on Castle Street and Mill Street, the road leading west past the castle to the mill driven by the Farset. Its extension was to become the Falls Road. The other urban extension towards the Antrim hills followed the track leading north-west past an 'old church' (Shankill) and this attracted the English overspill from the growing town. The space between the two roads later came to be filled by factories seeking the water of the Farset which divided two communities, Protestant and Catholic, singularly alike in their speech and gestures but strongly opposed in religion and politics. If the Farset River, with its string of mills and factories, serves to demarcate the Roman Catholic Falls from the Shankill on one side, on the other side, to the south, it is separated from Malone by the sluggish Blackstaff and the Bog Meadows, which was for long an almost empty no-man's land extending to the edge of the town, at Sandy Row, an ancient north-south trackway crossing the slobland between Mill Street and Fountainville, and bridging the Blackstaff River at Saltwater Bridge, the tidal limit.

The second half of the eighteenth century was a remarkable period in the history of the town, a period when there is no evidence of conscious religious segregation. Its first monuments were the Charitable Institute (1771) and the White Linen Hall (1785). At the end of the century the spirit of revolt against established authority and privilege brought Nonconformists and Roman Catholics together in a wave of radical and republican feeling. The period has been admirably and sensitively described by Miss Mary MacNeill in *The Life and Times of Mary Ann McCracken*. The increasing segregation of the two communities in west Belfast since that time has been a significant aspect of Belfast's social geography. It seems to have aroused little academic interest, and when I inquired about its origins I could find few facts and was warned off with the remark: 'Sure everybody knows that.' When I arrived in Belfast an academic colleague, an Englishman, told me frightening stories of discrimination practised against Roman Catholics and thus prepared me for a visit to Bellevue, where, he assured me, some paths were actually reserved for Presbyterians. Incredibly I saw at the entrance to one path—it was a misty evening—a notice which I read as 'Presbyterians Only'. It took me some time to recover from the shock. It was a new experience for me to live in a town divided in this way by religion, and in looking for explanations I prepared maps, published in the *Ulster Journal of Archaeology* in 1944, showing the percentage of adherents to the three main religious groups in each ward of the city, using statistics published in the 1937 census. More recently Professor Emrys Jones, using the data for 1951, and breaking down the statistics into small enumeration districts, has published a much more detailed analysis. One explanation of the uneven distribution and of the regional concentrations relates to the sources of the immigrant population. Thus the predominance of Presbyterians in north Belfast and in most of east Belfast is linked with their easy access from strongly Scots-settled areas in mid-Antrim and north Down, while the greatest concentration of Episcopalians is in the Sandy Row and University areas which are linked with the English-settled Lagan valley. They are also stronger than average in the Shankill area (where Roman Catholics number less than 5 per cent of the total population) and in Ballymacarrett. The high concentration of Roman Catholics (over 90 per cent) in the Falls district is also partly explained by its links with the hill slopes towards Derriaghy and with the Irish hinterland beyond the hills, and historically with the first industrial suburb of the original town—as the name Mill Street indicates—which seems from the beginning to have attracted the native population. But areas of high concentration, whether of Episcopalians or Catholics, are more significantly correlated with the old industrial sectors of the city, and with wage-earners and small shop-keepers of low socio-economic ranking, whereas the more favoured residential suburbs are everywhere, except in the Upper Falls, predominantly Presbyterian.

By 1834, as industry expanded, the proportion of Roman Catholics in the town was 32.5 per cent. It reached a maximum of 34 per cent after the Famine in 1861, but had declined to 23 per cent by 1951. Segregation which was partly self-imposed by social, religious and educational demands increased with sectarian riots from 1857 onwards, and by 1886 the now familiar pattern had been established. In 1896, when the original five wards were increased to fifteen, religious frontiers were recognized and segregation was institutionalized. Smithfield, the old industrial sector near the city centre, was now almost exclusively Roman Catholic, so that an innocent observer might conclude that Belfast was Catholic at heart.

By 1800 the population was still only 20,000, but the town was the commercial centre of a wide area of textile manufacture—of native linen to which the American and West Indian trades had now added cotton, tobacco and sugar. Belfast at that period owed much of its character and outlook to these colonial contacts as well as to the industries which grew out of the soil—provisioning, salting, coopering, brewing, tanning, soap- and candle-making and milling. Dependent on water power, these eotechnic industries clustered along the tributary streams of west Belfast where their successors still stand, surrounded by the mean streets which they dominate, and which supplied the labour force. Meanwhile the centre of the city was laid out in a grid-pattern inspired by the logic of the eighteenth century, and this example of town-planning was of inestimable benefit to the city when it grew afresh in a great spurt between 1840 and 1860.

Power weaving now brought the first large mills, and the shipyards took on a new life under the impact of E.J. Harland in 1854. The full force of the industrial revolution was at last felt. Prosperity depended partly on physical advantages but also on personal enterprise and on the juxtaposition of shipyards and mills employing respectively male and female labour, and able therefore to keep wages low. To the supply of cheap labour the Great Hunger of the late forties contributed its hordes of refugees who were mainly Roman Catholics.

In turn cholera and typhus now precipitated an outward movement, for those who could afford it, to the countryside where the suburbs were to grow. Queen's College had been built in 1848 on a dry site in farmland fields on the sandy Malone Ridge. Characteristically, it was built of brick, and thanks to the genius of Sir Charles Lanyon, remains one of the city's most elegant buildings. It is said that the workmen refused to cut down some venerable thorn trees—relics of old field hedges—that were held in superstitious awe, and one of them remained directly against the Senate Room until recently. The last survivor still flowers abundantly in late May in front of the Students Union building. The College became a point of attraction for elegant terrace houses. But there was another factor in this exodus. In 1840 the government of the town was reformed—an elected mayor replaced the town sovereign—and the powers of the establishment were broken. Donegall Place, in the shelter of the Castle, had maintained an exclusively residential character down to this time, but now the shopkeepers took possession. Professional men moved on the heels of the wealthy merchants and the lesser gentry to the sandy slopes of Knock and the Lough shore but above all to the spacious southern parklands on the Malone Ridge, where they could look down on their poorer neighbours. And the shopkeepers followed: instead of living above their shops in Ann Street they were now said to live above their incomes on the Malone Road!

The parks of the vanished landlords became dotted first with lodges and then with villas. Winding roads and tree-lined avenues replaced the parklands but the parks and avenues kept their loyal romantic names—Windsor, Adelaide, Balmoral, Cranmore, Maryville, Myrtlefield. At first the villas were detached, built in late Georgian, neo-Gothic, Victorian or Edwardian style. But finally, like their owners, they tended to pair off and after about 1860 become semi-detached—little hedged estates with their parks shrunk to neat lawns. The semi-detached house spawned into acres of semi-detachery sprawling over the countryside—and these wasteful models of nineteenth-century taste and architecture are still being built by private enterprise. A fascinating byway of urban history traces the origins of the names of a town's districts, streets and houses. I recently picked up this bit of folklore about the word Malone: when King William was stopped at the Bradbury Place Toll House on his way south he was abandoned by his troopers, and he spurred on his horse past Queen's with the words: 'I'm alone!'

Rosetta is more plausibly explained because the big house it is called after was named by a keen Egyptologist who wished to commemorate the finding of the Rosetta stone in 1799. But Macedon at Whiteabbey was not a scholar's label: it betrays a robust sense of humour on the part of an ambitious merchant, Alex Stewart, who announced that he wished to be known as Alexander of Macedon.

By the end of the century, when Belfast's population was 350,000, a central business district was clearly defined—the core which is the heart of any large city, pulling people in each day and pumping them out at night. The ebbing tide of humanity meets the even more numerous flocks of starlings who come to take their place as noisy chatterers around the City Hall. In many towns the business core is a clearly defined zone of skyscrapers, but partly because of the problems arising from soft foundations, they have hardly begun to appear in Belfast. In between the core and the suburbs is a 'zone of decay' which has changed little in a century or more, except that most of the houses in the main streets were converted to shops. It may have a housing density of up to eighty per acre—an appalling figure.

This congested 'zone of decay', which is a feature of most cities, brings with it many social evils. The almost total lack of open spaces and amenities—particularly for the young and old who must stay near home—is one of the most serious. Because of its factories and its crowded domestic chimneys, it is a zone of heavy atmospheric pollution with a heavy incidence of such ailments as bronchitis. There is another tragic consequence. Road-accident figures provided by Police Traffic Control show that the risk to life and limb increases enormously in the congested districts. Worse, the percentage of children injured rises alarmingly.

The city is now tackling some of these appalling problems with vigour. They are a by-product of the very spirit of *laisser-faire* which made the city prosperous. It should be remembered in attributing blame that private enterprise had full control of housing throughout the nineteenth century (indeed until twenty-five years ago)—and its concern was, so far as the bye-laws permitted, to pack as many dwellings as possible to the acre.

Clearly much of this decayed ring must be rebuilt and more spaciously planned. But the city is faced with a problem that cannot be properly solved so long as the tangle of outmoded administrative areas persists. There has been a desperate infilling of outlying open spaces, large urban housing estates replacing little rural clachans, and like them lacking many amenities. Thus Andersonstown, in the townland of Ballymurphy, was described in 1830 as 'a village of farm-houses'. The boundary of the city has not been extended since 1896. It is like a lobster denied a new shell. The green belt lies shattered save where swamp or steep slopes have mercifully saved the Bog Meadows, the Lagan valley and the Antrim Hills from permanent spoliation. We have no National Parks or Nature Reserves, though the National Trust is playing a noble part in filling the gap.

Many of the enlightened planning proposals made twenty years ago—by the Planning Advisory Board under the distinguished chairmanship of a former Vice-Chancellor of this University, Sir David Keir—have been shelved by Stormont. The government has been pressed from many sides, not least by the city, to introduce new planning legislation. And now at last the Matthew Report—the Gospel according to St Matthew—while it is welcomed at Stormont, is critical of the Belfast Corporation. But it seems to me that the blame lies largely elsewhere. We are not living in the Middle Ages or even in the nineteenth century. There is no longer a sharp distinction between town and country. Urban limitation, like family limitation, is a debatable question but the problem is not solved by creating contiguous independent boroughs such as Newtownabbey.

It is not only the city itself but the city region that must be planned. Economic considerations are being advanced in addition to all the others—aesthetic, social and cultural—to support urban renewal, and one hopes that economic arguments will convince the hard-headed where the others have failed.

To conclude: the richly varied physical and social environment of this city—planted by the English on Irish soil and peopled by Scots and others

145

as well as by Irishmen—will surely continue to contribute to its vigour. Its very tensions could once more be a source of energy rather than strife.

I have sometimes felt that the claim made by Belfastmen—that their city has been built by unflinching determination and grit—is only half the story and anyhow should more properly be made by others. Let me take this opportunity then, my Lord Mayor, of paying a tribute to the warmer human qualities which are so much in evidence in the city's Chief Citizen. Queen's has good cause to remember with gratitude your services. And I should like to add, from my knowledge of his good works, a warm tribute to your immediate predecessor, Sir Robin Kinahan, who is an honorary Doctor of this University.

THE KINGDOM OF MOURNE

Youthful by the geologist's time-scale—for these are Ireland's youngest mountains—the Mourne country is a land old in human history, and it has retained much of the flavour of the past. I want to try and convey to you something of the nature and spirit of this little kingdom, and to illustrate how the human geographer attempts to evaluate what he calls the personality of a region.

Every picture is improved by a frame. Here the frame provided by nature is unusually clear-cut, and it is one of singular splendour. For the Mourne Mountains, rising sharply above the lowlands of south Down, stride along the whole landward side of the kingdom, their heads in the clouds and their feet in the sea at both ends. From Cave Hill above Belfast the serrated profile of the Mournes closes the southern horizon some thirty miles away: from the Dublin hills they can be seen on a good day sixty miles away to the north. The monarch of the range, Slieve Donard, rises to nearly 3000 feet only two miles from the Irish Sea, and from its summit the curving boundary of the kingdom maintains an average height of some 1500 feet until it reaches Carlingford Lough in the Rostrevor Mountains. Several of the Mourne peaks rise well above 2000 feet, and by far the most interesting is the central tor-crowned Slieve Binnian, which is intimately linked with the kingdom in legend and popular sentiment. Tradition says that Boirche, first king of Mourne, was a cowherd who ruled his kingdom from the summit of

Slieve Binnian. Thence he could keep watch over the plain beneath and on the fringing sea to the south. At its seaward ends the barony of Mourne is bounded by two mountain streams, the Cassy Water on the south-west and the diminutive Srupatrick (St Patrick's stream) on the north-east. Thus defined, the barony is in shape rather like an eye, a giant eye seven miles wide and twelve miles long, slanted up on the east. The dark hills are the half-closed lid, and the rest, the living eye, is a peopled plain sloping sharply seawards from a height of some 600 feet. The pupil is the capital of Mourne, Kilkeel, placed near the sea where roads and rivers tumbling from the mountain-foot converge. Kilkeel is the only urban centre, and its parish is coterminous with the historic kingdom and with the Anglo-Norman barony which succeeded it. 'From its smallness', wrote Walter Harris in 1744, 'it is called the half Barony of Mourne.' It is little more than seventy square miles in area and only about half of this is arable, and its total population amounts to less than 12,000. This represents, however, the high density per arable square mile of about 300. Compare this with the density figures for the fat lands of County Meath, which in some baronies are as low as 50 per square mile. Mourne is the only strictly rural area in Northern Ireland having a population density of this order and in all Ireland the figure is exceeded only by that for the Rosses of Donegal. Like many another coastal fringe it has been a congested area but it was never officially recognized as such. Today it is prosperous enough: there is little emigration, though in its day it sent sheep-farmers to Montana and stone-workers to the mines and quarries of many lands. It is characteristic of these crowded coastal fringes, here as in Donegal, that their sons, if they emigrate, hope to return. This attitude, as we shall see, is noted in an old tradition of seasonal movement.

Annalong men used to spend the spring in New York fixing the side-walks after the winter's damage, and it was said of them that they would cross the Atlantic just to see what time it was the other side. A sturdy people has contrived to maintain itself as a close-knit community of small family farms in the face of movements which have led elsewhere to continuing rural depopulation. The kingdom of Mourne has bred among its sons a rare devotion, and I want to seek its sources.

Undoubtedly the small area and the compactness and isolation of the region are contributory factors. I am not going to pretend that there are no rival loyalties, but I fancy Mourne comes first to Orangemen and Long-stonemen alike. They all belong to Mourne. The mountains, the fields and the sea have been welded into a unity by age-old economic links, and their folk have had to co-operate in the secular task of taming the wild. Great granite walls, sturdy as the hills yet delicate as crochet-work when seen against the sky, embroider the fields and stitch them to the slopes between the mountains and the sea. Shepherds and stonemen, farmers and fishermen—all have had a hand in the making of Mourne. Through the media of shopping, worship, intermarriage or political associations almost every family has relations or acquaintances throughout the little kingdom. The Twelve Miles of Mourne are a measure of affection as well as distance. It is Kindly Mourne.

Yet no-one would call grey granite a kindly rock. The great domes of the high Mournes are not volcanic, as their shapes might suggest. Granite is an igneous rock which cooled slowly underground. It was the wear and tear of millions of years that exposed the hardened rock and carved out deep valleys, leaving a ring of clustered peaks. Slow cooling gave gran-

The Professor dressing kerbstones, near Annalong, County Down, watched by E.E.E., c.1947.

ite its tough nature and crystalline quality, but the same process riddled it with cooling-joints. Thus its surface layers were broken by rain and frost into countless blocks and boulders which became the tools of that master mason, the great ice-sheet. Pressing down from the cold north, the ice dumped millions of granite boulders over the sloping plains of Mourne on the south side. After centuries of clearing by man they are still there in great numbers. The many miles of stone walls, the houses and farm-buildings, illustrate some of the economic uses to which they were put, but the stones were also turned into bread by being dressed and cast upon the waters. Without cheap transport by sea the export of granite would have been profitless. Percy French sang of 'the Mountains of Mourne that go down to the sea': many thousands of tons of Mourne granite have indeed gone down to the sea as sets and kerbs to pave the streets of Belfast and the towns of Lancashire. The great days of the stone trade were from the middle of last century to the early decades of the present one. It brought succour to a famine-stricken land and enabled its people to tide over the years between the hungry 1840s and the Land Purchase Acts when they were given a new incentive to till the soil.

Naturally this activity was greatest where the granite comes nearest the sea and where harbours are available, that is between Annalong and Newcastle, in what is called Lower Mourne, where the mountains dip steeply towards a rock-bound coast. As one goes south, the coastal cliffs still maintain heights of some fifty feet, but they are composed of sands and gravels, for here a strip of fertile glacial material, deposited at the margin of ice moving down the Irish Sea, widens out past Kilkeel to merge with the morainic deposits at the mouth of Carlingford Lough, a true fiord as its name tells us. Inside the mouth of the lough sands in turn are replaced by fine muds which floor Mill Bay and which as we shall see have played an important part in the total economy of Mourne. At many periods planters from overseas have been attracted to the fertile lands along the coast, and here there are strong colonies of Protestant settlers. But what I want to emphasize is the interdependence of these little sub-regions in the total economy of Mourne.

To picture its traditional patterns we would do well to see how and where man began his long association with this countryside. And first we turn to the sea whence he came. Between the mouth of the Boyne and the entrance to Strangford Lough the north and south flowing tides of the Irish Sea meet. This meeting of the waters means that tides run high, but at the same time there are few tidal currents. Before the days of sail, prospecting navigators would there have found themselves in a pool of still water whence they could, and did, make landings on the Irish shore. In megalithic times from about 3000 BC what has been called the Carlingford culture, identified by its long cairns, rivalled in strength if not in splendour, the round cairn culture of the Boyne. A dozen great stone monuments in the heart of the Mourne plain testify to the first colonization of the land by clearing forest and scrub and opening little patches of cultivation among the boulders. The 'Longstone' which gives its name to part of this earliest zone of settlement is one of these great boulders set ceremonially on end.

Although the long-cairn version of the megalithic faith appears to have dominated in Mourne as in the northern half of Ireland generally, the southern passage-grave culture of the Boyne valley gave the area what must have been through the ages its most conspicuous monument, for there can be little doubt that the great cairn on Slieve Donard covered a corbelled passage grave. It was this monument that provided the links with early Christianity and the Donard pilgrimage of historic times. In prehistory, as today, although the balance of the rival faiths was different, the personality of Mourne seems to have been strong enough to embrace and absorb adherents of two religious traditions.

Two thousand years later, in the earliest days of Christianity, the population still clung to the central strip of the sloping plain, as the remains of over fifty raths show. The archaeological evidence, especially the virtual absence of a Bronze Age culture, points to a striking continuity through pre-historic times; and the ruined mother-church of Kilkeel, set in its circular rath, links the past with the present. Even the speeding motorist must pay homage to it, for as it enters the heart of town the coast road makes a half circle around the walled-in site. There are hints in folklore that the first Christian missionaries were not well received in Mourne. Only St Patrick's stream, the boundary on the north-east, bears the name of the patron saint—I know of no Patrician dedications inside the kingdom—and the story goes that Patrick did not cross the stream but took off his sandal and threw it across the Twelve Miles of Mourne into Carlingford Lough, utter-ing in true Christian spirit the prophecy, 'the length of that there will never be blood spilled'. If we knew more about fifth-century Ireland we might find that isolated districts such as Mourne were speaking a non-Gaelic language at that time. At any rate the stubborn resistance of these mountain fringes to the new faith is illustrated by the legend of the conversion of Donard, which St Patrick achieved only after a protracted display of his superior powers. Conviction finally came when he restored to life a fierce bull which had been disjointed and salted down. St Donard later retired to a cell in the summit cairn of the mountain which bears his name, and for centuries it was the scene of an annual pilgrimage. 'It is believed', wrote John O'Donovan in 1834, 'that the Saint says mass every Sunday at his altar in the cairn.'

To get a glimpse of what medieval life was like in Mourne we must jump to the sixteenth century, when we have a *Survey of the Lordship*, then nomi-nally an English possession, made in 1540. One pictures a pastoral people living as throughout prehistory in the midst of the plain. The townlands named in the *Survey* fall into five strips running from the coast into the mountains, and their rents were payable in cows. Their cattle and sheep would have moved with the seasons between the high hills and the seashore, accompanied by the young folk as herders. In summer the stony soils of the lowlands dry out quickly and the rains run off rapidly with the slope, but in the hollows of the mountains are many boggy stretches where the waters lie and the grazing stock is refreshed. Here the seeker may find the remains of the sod and stone booley houses where the herders lived during the summer months. This traditional mode of life continued into the eighteenth century, for Walter Harris wrote in 1744:

In the bosom of the Mourne Mountains there is a place called the Deer's Meadow ... to which great numbers of the poorer people resort in the summer months to graze their cattle. They bring with them their wives, children and little wretched furniture, erect huts, and there live for two months, and sometimes more, and often cut their turf to serve for the next returning season; which done, they retire with their cattle to their former habitations.

This refers no doubt to the last lingering days of booleying, when the period of stay, formerly from 1 May to the end of October, had been reduced.

At the approach of winter the flocks and herds would have moved or been driven towards the shore, where they found sustenance in the saltings and in the edible seaweeds that flourish in a region of high tidal range. In some measure, this seasonal movement of stock continues, though sheep have taken the place of cattle and the herders no longer move with them. During the winter, in recent centuries, many of the men engaged in the arduous long-line fishing from double-ended yawls that needed no harbours but could be drawn up on the open beaches. In their excursions the Mournes were never out of sight or mind, for the oarsmen were guided to and from the fishing grounds by landmarks whose still remembered names read like a poem: the Two Hills, the Three Tallies, the Horsemen, the Buckie, the Blue Hills and the North Mountain Foot. In summer, their few acres of crops planted, able-bodied men, down to recent times, would seek work on the herring boats fishing the Scottish and Irish seas, or travel to England as pedlars or harvesters. They would return in autumn in time for their own harvests, saving their corn by day, and by night netting the herrings that come close inshore at this season. Salted down, the herrings provided the tasty 'kitchen' not only for Mourne but for many inland districts where the Carlingford cadgers were a welcome sight. A hardy stock, and good judges of horses, the cadgers are remembered as having been the last native Gaelic speakers in these parts. Some of their descendants are now prosperous fish-mongers or scrap-merchants in our cities.

But is was not only innocent fishing boats that landed their cargoes on the coast of Mourne, for it looks out to the Isle of Man less than fifty miles away, and down to the end of the eighteenth century the island was a smuggler's paradise. Manxmen indeed have been blamed for giving the inhabitants of more than one stretch of coast their taste for strong liquor. The coast of Down was strongly patrolled, and the first harbour at Newcastle was erected to shelter revenue-cutters, but in Mourne illicit goods could speedily be taken to hiding-places in the cover of the hills and later carried inland by tracks which are still remembered. Indeed the best-known of all the mountain walks is the storied Brandy-pad.

Of all the harvests of the sea none has left a clearer mark on Mourne life and landscape than the wrack harvest. Trails of bladder-wrack no longer litter the roads in spring and the stony beds where the seaweed was cultivated are now neglected, but shore-rights are jealously preserved while the older generation lives, for they remember the time when a good wrack harvest was a guarantee of bountiful crops. More, it brought with it the magic harvest luck, and I have been told of hillmen, clinging to their ancient rights, who would scrape up fragments of the golden weed with their hands, as if it were really gold-dust, to fill a creel. Every few hundred yards seaweed-lanes run down from the main road to the shore, and where they meet the road is an open space—where the touring motorist parks his car—in which the weed was stacked. Marks now neglected divide the foreshore into strips where each farm cut its wrack, and after the winter's storms the inblown weed was gathered on the beach and divided with complicated ritual. But, more important, the wrack was cultivated. By the time of the Great Famine over a square mile of the muddy expanse of Mill Bay had been partitioned into wrack-beds which supplied Mourne with fertilizers. Countless boulders, laboriously carried from the fields to give the weeds anchorage, are laid out in plots of which over a thousand survived a few years ago. And this marriage of land and sea was blessed with abundance; barren stones cleared from the fields became the means of restoring fertility to the soil.

The granite, we have said, was also turned into bread by being shipped overseas as dressed stone. The stone-trade has left its mark everywhere. Walk where you will, by the shore, through the fields, among the heather, along the streams, on some difficult ledge of rock where you imagine you're the first person ever to have trod, and you will find the imprints of the stoneman's tools on boulder and rock face. The tracks that wind into the mountains are mostly of his making, levelled with sturdy sledges and carts. Alas, many of the great stone monuments which their forefathers erected have fallen victims to the stonemen's hunger, a litter of waste chips their only memorial. Others are scarred but were saved from destruction by some fateful accident which is the theme of any moral tale. Down to about a century ago, the stone was split by the old method of driving a line of iron wedges into picked-out cavities. The more efficient plug-and-feathers came in time to speed up production of the square-sets which were needed to lay the tramways of our cities. No doubt there was much sweated labour, for in those days landlords and merchants were all-powerful, but it was the stone-trade that tipped the balance from famine to survival after the middle of the century. In recent years there has been a revival of granite working. It is now a highly organized and in part a mechanized trade. Its products no longer go down to the sea in ships but are taken by road to Belfast: they are expensive tombstones, serving the dead rather than the living. Kindly Mourne is becoming mournful Mourne!

But the skills of the granite men have left a legacy of sound workmanship throughout the Kingdom of Mourne. You see it in the neat farmhouses of dressed stone, in great walls that defy the elements, and in the whitewashed gate-piers that stand so erect. It is a pleasure to stroll along the farm-loanings in the assurance that the gates will open at a touch and yet close securely, for the stoneman knows the secrets of tool-making and iron-work-ing, and he takes a pride in his well-hung gates and farmyard fittings. He must have a good eye and a steady hand, and his traditional hobby is the del-icate carving of model boats which he used to race in the tarns of the hills and in the sea that guards his kingdom. He has few words, for his was a noisy occupation, carried on, in the words of W.R. Rodgers, among 'the tiny clus-tered clinks of little chisels tinkling tirelessly on stone'. But working in the open he watched the ways of nature and became knowledgeable about wildlife. He is often a bird-fancier. He delights in flowers and shrubs and will be moved to unconscious poetry in talking of the daffodils and fuchsias with which he adorns his holding.

In the course of the present century traditional ways have declined but many new needs and demands have come to quicken the life of Mourne. Reafforestation with its manifold amenities has been less successful on these steep windy seaward slopes than in other parts of the mountains. The tourist industry, on the other hand, although Newcastle and Rostrevor at the mountain-ends profit most, has brought benefits to the coast; and the hills attract walkers and climbers at all seasons. The Youth Hostel Association has enabled the young-at-heart of all ages to follow in the pioneer footsteps of that great countryman and lover of Mourne, Robert Lloyd Praeger.

But it is the inexhaustible water resources of these cloudy hills that have brought the greatest changes to the landscape. A massive granite wall three feet wide and over twenty miles long, enclosing the catchment area of the Silent Valley Reservoir, now marches conspicuously from peak to peak. It is a monument to the skill of the stonemen, but it serves no useful purpose other than as a slippery short-cut to the summits. The reservoir and its planted approaches, however, bring scenic relief to the bare hills as well as pure water to Belfast, and its construction long engaged the stonemen and gave Mourne its one ephemeral railroad. For many tourists a bus-trip to the Silent Valley is their only claim to acquaintance with the kingdom.

But the daily life of Mourne is still firmly rooted in the small family farms which have come to specialize in potato-growing. Seed potatoes and earlies are their main concern, the former profiting from the high winds which dis-courage virus disease, the latter from the mild coastal climate and from the south-easterly aspect which lessens the risk of sunburn on frosted leaves. Changes there have been and must be, for it is the ability to adjust its econ-omy to changing circumstances that has kept Mourne alive. Thus artificial fertilizers have largely replaced seaweed as potato-manure. Heavy crops are still obtained—yields of up to twenty tons an acre as against the Northern Ireland average of seven tons—but intensive production has brought the dreaded eel-worm in its wake. As an alternative to potatoes some coastal farmers are taking up the cultivation of soft fruits which need the many hands of small family farms. The fishing industry too has revived with the use of motor vessels and electronic devices, but the old harvest—herring fishing—remains more of a festival than a thing of profit. With all these changes the general pattern of settlement has changed little. Frugal living is a virtue not quickly lost. Through the ages Mourne has not been given to display. It can show no ornate churches, high crosses or other work of art. A monolithic simplicity is appropriate to a land of tough granite, which is not easily carved, and the plain longstone is perhaps its best-known monument.

Mourne clings to the old ways so long as they work and does not adopt the new merely because they are new. You will see wooden ploughs still, because they are less likely to be broken in stony soils than iron ones, and primitive slipes in the most mechanized quarries. Resistance to change among the hill-folk is balanced by the initiative of the coastal farmers who are receptive of new ideas, and in this egalitarian society where all must be good neighbours successful innovations are soon copied. The sprinkling of 'strong' farmers of Scottish descent has acted as a stimulus in many ways. One effect of the friendly rivalry between Catholic and Protestant is illustrated in the remark made to me by a Mourne man. 'Those people', he said, naming a Scots family, 'do be up at five in the morning, and for shame we must rise at seven when we'd like to lie abed at nine.' But the incomer has also been touched by the immemorial lore of the Irish countryman. I recall the joy with which a rough labourer, an import from the low country, drew my attention to a lone May tree standing by his cottage which had burst into flower in its season. 'The thorn's white over,' he said, 'you'd think the fairies was in it.'

I have aimed here not only at painting a picture and incidentally pointing a moral, but at giving an example of the method of regional survey as geographers understand it. We believe that to approach full understanding of a community it should be studied against the background of the particular physical and social environment as well as the history of the area to which it belongs. Why otherwise should there have come to be, among the many little regions which together make up Ireland, such fascinating diversities? They certainly cannot be explained in terms of race, nor fully in terms of religious beliefs or political, cultural or economic activities taken separately, but we can perhaps come near to the mystery of regional consciousness by observing human societies against the particular environments in which they live and work.

[Thomas Davis Lecture, *Radio Éireann 1944*]

THE PAHVEES OF SLIEVE GULLION

On the east coast of Ireland, facing the Irish Sea along the border between Northern and Southern Ireland in South Armagh, is a belt of wild mountain country known from the great central dome of granite which dominates it as the Slieve Gullion country. Around the cairn-crowned mountain runs a ring of lesser hills, some seven miles across, which is composed of igneous rocks intruded in the form of what geologists call a ring-dyke—the Ring of Gullion. The floor of the ring is composed of far older granites (the Newry granites), so that the whole area has a complex and fiery nature, geologically as well as historically. The pahvees or travelling men are part of the story of the Ring. In telling this story I owe much of the detail to conversations with the late George Paterson and with a gifted native of Drumintee, Michael Murphy, author of that delightful collection of essays, *At Slieve Gullion's Foot.*

The Ring is a little world of its own, a poor congested district, strewn with bogs, patches of farmland and small whitewashed cabins, looking for all the world like a slice of the western Gaeltacht transplanted to the other side of the island. Thanks to its location on an historic borderland it is smuggling country, and the folk of its tiny farms have long supplemented their meagre earnings by smuggling across the 'border'. Running across it traces of a great earthwork built over fifteen centuries ago can still be seen. Country people call it the Black Pig's Dyke, and the old folk will tell you that it was

156

carved out by the tusks of an enraged boar of monstrous proportions as he ploughed across the land from sea to sea. The archaeologist affirms that the Black Pig's Dyke was prehistoric frontier between ancient Ulster and the South of Ireland, a device to check the lifting of cattle across this eternal borderland. The Irish are believed to have borrowed the notion of constructing these 'travelling earthworks' from their raids on the frontier defences of Imperial Rome.

Centuries later, when the English invaders had brought new targets for their raids, the Irish of Slieve Gullion were still at it. Here was a hide-out of wood kernes, tories and highwaymen, who readily turned from their local adventures to join forces against the foreigners. Among them was the celebrated Redmond O'Hanlon, Prince of the Tories, a name that was later borrowed as an ironic label for politicians of the die-hard variety. Today O'Hanlon's ghost, thundering by on a steed with red-hot hooves, is a warning for law-abiding citizens, few though they may be, to keep to their beds and ask no questions when they hear noises in the night.

During the period 1916 to 1921, when the native Irish were in rebellion, a time euphemistically referred to throughout the country as 'The Troubles', the Slieve Gullion district was alive with men 'on the run'. In 1921 the partition of Ireland made it a political frontier once more. The noise of driven cattle was heard again in the hills, and the sound of muffled oars along the shore. A narrow sheltered fiord cuts like a shining sword straight and deep into the border hills, and here the Vikings in the ninth century found a familiar coast and added their lawlessness to that of the wild hills. Their descendants had clung through the centuries to the Isle of Man out there on the eastern horizon, and they kept in touch with the Irish harbour that had been named for one of their kin, the fiord of Carling—Carlingford. Folk memory recalls that the Manxmen would sail over on moonlit nights and with ancestral skills steer their pointed luggers far into the fiord. A low whistle would bring the Slieve Gullion men out of the bushes, and there would be hurried coming and going from the water's edge while the tide lasted. Across the slippery rocks hiding-holes among them were replenished with duty-free goods—rum, sherry, brandy, French wines, tobacco—and the luggers would slip back loaded with bales of wool and lengths of white linen cloth lifted from the bleach fields of fat merchants who lived in the adjacent lowlands.

True to character, the Ring is today a hide-out for the Provisional IRA.

The hilly slope where the Slieve Gullion country comes closest to Carlingford Lough is known as 'Clinchycora'. You will look for this name in vain on the map—not because it is unreal but because it is often hard to recognize the spelling of an Irish place-name from its pronunciation—but you will find the name Clontigora. If you should go there you would find a wild mountain face littered with rocks and crossed by huge stone walls. Great megalithic tombs tell of the first settlement of a pastoral people here over five thousand years ago. In the little fields and on the mighty walls you would be likely to see scraggy goats tossing their horns and looking for mischief. Ask anyone who has the Gaelic and you will learn that Clontigora signifies the grazing ground of the goats. Irish goats have a bad reputation, like ancient Greek goats or any others. 'Always kick a goat,' they say around Slieve Gullion, 'for if it's not going into mischief it's after coming out of it.' But 'bad and all as they are', they were about the only crop that could be taken from these stony hills, and they were one of the few sources of more or less honest money.

So when the sea-smuggling fell off, the men of Clontigora and other parts of the Ring of Gullion were driven back on their own resources and turned to the goats. There was quite a demand for goats in England, where goat's milk was at one time a fashionable medical cure-all, and the wily hillmen knew how to create a demand even where there was none. Soon the goatmen were searching Ireland for surplus goats, walking the roads of the west, and driving their flocks back to Slieve Gullion, grazing them free on the Long Acres provided by the roadside strips of grass. In England they would sell the goats at fairs or hawk them through the countryside. They would talk extravagantly of the virtues of goat's milk and then get rid of a billy-goat on some innocent suburban housewife, making only a small extra charge for his special milking properties. Their sales were helped by exploiting two ancient beliefs associated with goats. Horse breeders claim that the smell of a buck-goat is good for the horses, while keepers of dairy herds say that they have more luck with calving if a nanny-goat is allowed to run with the cows. I have seen plausible explanations of both these beliefs, but they are perhaps solidly rooted in the fertility cults associated with the great god Pan.

Where superstition failed, the mountain men were ready with alternative reasons for keeping a goat. 'Sure these wise animals is the best thing for keeping down weeds in the garden', and they would demonstrate to an innocent housewife the way of a goat with groundsel while carefully keeping the animal away from the vegetables. All this was good training for the Slieve Gullion men, fitting them for the larger world of trade as globe-trotting 'pahvees'. In the war years after 1939, with the introduction of severe rationing of meat, the goatmen made easy money by exporting the animals as carcasses to feed hungry England.

But it was not only goats that they dealt in. They might be 'at the fish', hawking salt herring as they roamed across Ireland. Some of them have been able to set up in business as fishmongers in the larger towns. They also 'took to the rags', as the phrase goes, picking up on their travels the incredible remnants of clothing that hang around so many Irish homes, the last shreds of jackets and skirts bought years ago at second or third hand at some country fair. The rags would be sold to paper-mills, and any other junk would be gathered to turn into cash. In this way several one-time pahvees have settled down in business in Britain as marine storekeepers and have amassed considerable fortunes.

From rags they turned logically to cloth. Farmers were always on the lookout for a cheap length of cloth to make a suit, or for the makings of a dress for their women-folk. So from buying rags many a Slieve Gullion traveller took to selling cloth. He would not reveal the source of his goods and there was always an air of mystery about the bargains he sold. There was a hint that the cloth had been smuggled through the customs: this always adds a touch of excitement to a transaction. One of the tricks of the trade was to dress up sailor-fashion, perhaps a genuine survival from the old smuggling days, and it became something of a joke later on, when the travellers had carried their trade across the world, to have the same S.S. *Slieve Gullion* printed across their sailor caps. This gave the illusion that the goods were smuggled, an illusion backed up by wealth of anecdote and whispered hints of the risks that had been run. The chances were that the cloth had been legitimately bought at a factory not far away. Those in the know dubbed them 'dry-land sailors', but the name that came to be applied to them in Ireland was 'the pahvees', a word said to have been picked up in French Canada, and meaning perhaps, men who hit the pavement? Around Slieve Gullion you will see them gaily dressed in American style after their return from a profitable tour of the New World.

And what stories they had to tell! Paddy Doran, king of the pahvees, had crossed the Atlantic thirty times and had done trade with the Eskimos as well as the Yankees and the prairie farmers. Twice he had travelled Australia, with New Zealand and Tasmania thrown in. The pahvees were by no means ordinary Irish emigrants: they were extending around the world the travels they had begun as goatmen and ragmen in Ireland and Great Britain. They came home frequently, and liked to end their days where they began them, in white-washed homes under the hills, where they could gaze out to sea and talk about their travels. They like to tell a story of a skeleton discovered at the North Pole which was identified as belonging to a Slieve Gullion man because there was a bundle of rags beside it. True to his borderland home, the pahvee has the wit and the blarney of the South of Ireland combined with the enterprise and the toughness of the Northerner. He is a Gascon for boasting, and will brag among his friends of the triumphs he has had in the fashionable suburbs of London or New York.

In some parts of the world the pahvee is still on the road: he no longer has his pack on his shoulder. He travels by automobile which he may keep hidden around the corner so that you are to believe he has come on foot straight from the boat. He will sell you cloth of good quality, stamped perhaps with the name CLONTIGORA MILLS, and there will be plenty of entertainment, and a touch of mystery, thrown in for luck. But you will do well to make sure that there is enough in the length you are offered to make up into a suit; otherwise you will be persuaded to buy it for one of the ladies of the house and purchase another length for yourself.

The pahvee must know how to tell a good tale. A Clontigora woman once told me she would not let her eldest son become a pahvee because he was incapable of telling a lie. They say that every member of the O'Hanlon clan in that district is born with a piece of cloth in his hand; and they certainly learn the patter young. In their own language, you must be able to 'spin your tale and put a good skin on it'. 'Sure that's a grand bit of staff: it will wash like a child's face and wear like a woman's tongue.' And their speech is shot through with nautical terms: 'That length is good fore and aft, port and starboard', and 'just throw your eye along the beam of this bit of material.'

But they can also, back home, tell many a story against themselves. Driving a bargain with a ship's officer in a seaboard town, one 'dry-land sailor' was persuaded to take his pack out to the vessel anchored in the bay, only to disgrace his cloth by being violently sick on the journey of a hundred fathoms. And in New York a sale of cloth was interrupted by the appearance of a cop who happened to have been born in Newry and whose native humour was awakened by seeing the name S.S. *Slieve Gullion* on the cap. 'Is Oiney O'Hanlon still skipper?' he enquired.

Here are some verses of the Pahvee Song of the S.S. *Slieve Gullion*, 'the ship that never left a dock, yet sailed in every sea'.

> I've sold to many a scholar though I cannot write my name,
> But I learnt enough of the blarney stuff to play the pahvee game,
> When selling cloth indeed in troth if you should look me over,
> You'd never twig in my pahvee rig I come from Clontigora.
>
> I've been in every country from the States to Singapore,
> I'm better known in Edmonton than round my own half-door,
> To Scots indeed I've sold the tweed for kilts that bring me bullion,
> As one of the crew of that twin-screw, the S.S. *Slieve Gullion*.

* * *
* *

Many years ago, when teaching in the USA at Bowdoin College, Maine, I was strolling one day in the quiet campus when I encountered a pedlar who

160

was doing business. He had just sold a suit-length of cloth to a somewhat naive senior colleague who was Professor of Classics, telling him he was a purser on a boat which had recently arrived from Liverpool. The purser shook my hand warmly. Dressed in a smart double-breasted blue suit, he looked every inch a sailor. He carried a bulky suitcase full of rolls of cloth. 'You'll be needing some new clothes yourself', he told me, when he heard I was an English visitor. 'I know how hard things are over there, what with rationing and all. I come from Liverpool myself.' His accent however was unmistakeably that of South Armagh. I told him I was born not far from the Mersey but that I now lived in Belfast, and I asked him if he knew the city. 'Sure every seaman knows Belfast,' he replied. 'It's a grand city. I suppose it has spread as far as Lisburn by now.'

'It has,' I replied, 'but it still has a long way to go to reach Newry. I expect you have put in there?'

'I was onc't in Newry.'

'Perhaps you've heard tell of a hill called Slieve Gullion near Newry?' I asked. 'I used to spend my holidays in that part of the country.' I spoke of Forkill and Drumintee and mentioned a few local characters with whom I had played long bullets. He showed some interest and surprise. 'After the game we went to a pub over by Carrickarnon. I wish I could remember the name of that pub.'

'That would be Barney Connolly's place', said he.

'By the way,' I said, as he was leaving, 'I never got your name.'

'O'Hanlon's the name', he replied.

ULSTER
The Common Ground

Curséd be he that curses his mother. I cannot be
Anyone else than what this land engendered me
LOUIS MACNEICE, 'VALEDICTION'

Insofar as I was brought up in Shropshire, than which there is no more English county, I can imagine that many Irishmen would want to disown me completely. But I do have this much in common with a minority of Irish people, that both my parents were Celtic speakers, brought up to speak Welsh and continuing to speak it through their lives. Perhaps more relevantly, I have lived and worked in Ireland for some fifty years, and in the early 1940s I wrote a little book called *Irish Heritage*, in which I set down observations on the customs and skills, tools and other things which seemed to me to have a distinctive Irish flavour, and at the same time very considerable local or regional character. I was flattered when a well-known Irish scholar called it an epoch-making book.

I found that running through the whole there was a single theme with many variations—and this variety is a source of dissension. I think we have somehow to live with that variety and exploit it rather than let it disturb our peace; because it is precious in that it stands in contrast to the almost universal monotony of modern culture, its dullness, its commercial exploitation and material values, its mass production.

162

This variety is potentially a great source of strength for the future. It reflects differences, not only in landscape, but in dialect and attitudes of mind, but there is common ground in the emotions which bind people to this bit of country or to that. Diversity is reflected in different religious affiliations; the most fertile areas of fat drumlins have usually been occupied by newcomers. In Ulster where you find the drumlins you will hear the drums, for the Protestant planters usually chose the most fertile lowland areas, and I suspect that people living in such closed-in lowlands with restricted horizons tend to have a limited vision and imagination. I like to contrast that kind of hidden landscape—Protestant landscape, shall I say?—with the open, naked bogs and hills which are naturally areas of vision and imagination, and which represent the other tradition in Ulster.

As a geographer I believe that these local variations are essentially environmental. It is this variety, physical and human, that distinguishes Ulster from the rest of Ireland. The great plain of Ireland stands before you as soon as you get to south Armagh. Once you leave the hills, you leave Ulster.

These local and regional differences are also found in varying degrees in the South of Ireland: in local politics, or in football matches, between Cork and Kerry, for example. On the whole however, they've been submerged, in the drive for unity within a single nation state.

It was this complex of regional and national qualities that I thought appropriate to call the Irish heritage. My only regret is that the term Ulster heritage has been almost monopolized recently by extreme Protestant spokesmen. But I would take it to mean the total inheritance irrespective of formal creeds. And it seems to me that in its complexity Ulster is the most Irish of the Irish provinces.

Now if we are to live in peace we must face hard facts. We all have a lot of myths to forget. It is our duty to explore as much as we can of the past that has made the present. It is true, for instance, that the sentiments expressed by Mr Paisley and his followers today, the formulae of 'No Surrender' and so on, are echoed almost precisely though more poetically in the words of Cuchulainn fighting the men of Ireland: 'We will stand our ground though the earth shall split and the sky fall on us.'

In quoting such heroic words I am not arguing for the necessity of political division in Ireland; it is absurd to project the modern political scene back to the Dark Ages, or vice versa. But I have met many Southerners who express a sneaking admiration for men like Dr Paisley, for their stubbornness, their tenacity, and indeed they see those qualities as characteristic of Ulster as a whole and not only of its extreme spokesman. I have often heard it said that we should find a common ground in the Ulster tradition by using more generally in our educational system the legends of ancient Ireland—

163

admittedly a very fertile field. However, the bloody goings-on and decapitations chronicled in the *Ulster Cycle* would make the most violent television play seem tame.

There is far more solid ground for a common base in the objective evidence of the science of archaeology. True, one can treat the epics as imaginative literature; true also that the tales are conventionalized and that we shouldn't judge them by modern standards, but I'd like to draw a parallel between them and their possible influence and some other records that have come down to us. They are not very different in moral tone or in anthropological meaning from the confrontations and cruelties that we read about in the Old Testament, which have been used to justify the extermination of the enemies of the Lord. It has been said of early colonists of North America, for instance, that: 'First they fell upon their knees, then on the aborigines.'

One of the characteristics of Ulster—and here I quote a Methodist minister—is that it contains the most notorious Bible belt in Protestantism. Now I would disagree only in one way: there is an even more notorious Bible belt in the heart of the eastern United States of America, in Kentucky and Tennessee, to which, historically, the Presbyterian emigrants of Ulster made a baneful contribution. Fundamentalism and Evangelicalism I regard as blind and dangerous forces. But the extreme Presbyterians have no monopoly of absolutist doctrines, and I think that is near the root of our problem. Until myths of various kinds are exposed, there is not much hope for peace.

That is the negative aspect of things. In this divided community it is our duty to stress the many common bonds.

Ulster people share, and I've often been the target of it, a rather sly, satirical form of humour and a gift of deflating repartee; for instance, the reply given by a Ballymena girl to an American GI who was getting no response to his advances: 'Say, what do you do about sex in this part of the world?' 'Well, we usually has our tay about sex.' They share the Ulster spirit of Tenant Right and resistance to civil authority. Loyalty to local traditions and regions is a common bond too, and in most other communities in these islands it overrides religious differences. Partly for this reason, I have always been keen on developing local studies in Ulster, and indeed geographers have pioneered local studies aimed at an understanding of our own environment for at least half a century. The historians have only just caught on to it, but this understanding by observation, the inculcation of local patriotisms, is an important part of our educational duty.

To revert to my own interest in this subject—our heritage—I was surprised and moved by the reception my book received in all parts of Ireland, because I believe it struck a common chord: the familiar surroundings of our childhood, the things we were brought up with; the theme of the common country life. It is an interest that takes me into houses of every conceivable kind, in all parts of Ireland. I have found very little interest in these matters in university circles, or indeed, in ecclesiastical circles. It was considered somehow improper that a university teacher should descend from his ivory tower and, as it were, muddy the wells of speculative thought with farmyard dirt.

I recall a clerical critic who took me to task for wasting my time on the craft of the spade-maker or the basket-maker, and for not concentrating on Celtic art and the work of vanished Gaelic craftsmen. Now if you look into that world you will find that these products were the work of a privileged class, producing for an aristocracy. No doubt every Irishman cherishes the belief that he is descended from ancient kings. And no doubt, there is some justification for that because they were a prolific breed, but I suggest that there is a great deal of humbug and snobbery about much of what passes for national sentiment. A friend of mine, a genuine nationalist, wrote that the last thing he would want would be to be transported back to the heroic age of the Welsh princes, which many nationalists see as a golden era: 'The odds are that nearly all those hankering after a past glorious age would find themselves slaves in that princely world.'

So my theme is the common people and the land itself, the land that they've helped to make; because the land is far older than us all, far older than all human cultures. Although I'm pleading my own cause as a geographer, I'm convinced that we've got to look to the land to understand the nature of its products, material and spiritual.

I've been taken to task for daring to suggest that the historic Plantation of Ulster is not the sole cause of its troubles. It is certainly the most obvious one, but we must live with the history of this land both before and since the Plantation, and a great deal that is characteristic of Ulster was shaped during those critical times when two peoples were coming together. It was Marc Bloch who insisted that the framework of institutions within which a society lives can be understood only in the light of the whole human environment. With this in mind, co-ordinated field studies can be used to advance our knowledge of culture-history.

If you look at the position of Ulster in Ireland or in the British Isles, or as part of north-western Europe, if you look at its natural or man-made landscapes, its hills, its farms, its little towns, you begin to sense its personality. And if you look at the historic character of that landscape as made both by man and by nature, you will find themes running through it. It is a green pastoral landscape and dominant among its people is the attitude of the man who deals in cattle, the canny conversation of a man who is trying to sell a cow. Many of you have the close nature and long-lasting qualities of Ulster linen. I wouldn't press these analogies of the cow and the linen too far, because I might be led into the cow byre or the lint hole. What I am suggesting is that there is in Ulster a very deep conserving and conservative attitude of mind, which applies to all irrespective of political affiliation. It is a conservative region and a conservative community, and it is uncompromising because it doesn't want to change.

In the long run your ancestors and your ancestral faiths have come into Ulster from overseas, and I must look at the Irish problem in the context of the gradual peopling of a remote island which was, for millennia, the end of the world. I suspect that at all periods these newcomers were resisted by the natives, and that the newcomers vowed that they would never become Irish. I think one of the problems is that the inhabitants of this land of yours ultimately—I don't mean planters only but all Irish stocks—in the terms of human history, are relative newcomers. Many parts of the world have been peopled for tens of thousands of years, but most parts of Ireland have been occupied for six or seven thousand years only. To put that in historical perspective, Jericho was already a city before human beings set foot in Ireland, so that in the perspective of human history, Irish history is brief.

The homeland was not across the Atlantic but in sight, only just across the Irish Sea, and therefore always in mind. I like to remember how St Columba wanted to get Ireland out of sight so that he could get it out of mind when he chose Iona in his mission to the land that came to be Scotland. But in the long run, however much you have thought otherwise, Ireland has absorbed you all. It has very nearly absorbed me in one generation. True, some of the newcomers still obstinately refuse to call themselves Irish. I suspect this is really because they are more Irish than they want to admit. They've inherited a land full of Irishness, full of things Gaelic and pre-Gaelic. They've inherited a material culture and an idiom that has the stamp of this country on it. And I like to think of a very paradoxical figure: an Orangeman from the Bannside, waving a British flag and pouring scorn on the Englishman because he can't get his tongue round a good Gaelic place-name like Ahoghill. The Gaelic men of Ulster seem to have resisted complete absorption for many centuries.

You cannot send those of planter stock back across the water, any more than you can recall millions of Irishmen from America. Both sides have got to rid themselves of a lot of prejudices. I'm alarmed at the gap that exists, for instance, in attitudes as well as in information, between the scholar and the ordinary citizen. I'm sure many an Irishman would be prepared to die in support of the popular view that St Patrick came to Ireland in AD 432. But scholars of the highest integrity and piety are fighting a holy war over St Patrick. None of them believes in the sanctity of AD 432. Some put the date half a century away; others want two or three St Patricks; others say St Patrick never existed. Here is the discrepancy between people searching for truth and people tied to a myth for which they might even be prepared to die.

I believe—and I come back to this—that we can all profit from the objectivity of observational study of prehistoric, or indeed historic, archaeology. In it the clash of native and newcomer has been repeated over and over again, and we should try to discover how at various times they have not only come to terms with themselves but produced great blossomings of culture. I think you will find that it is precisely this clash of native and newcomer that struck the sparks in Irish culture.

The Institute of Irish Studies at Queen's University has been preparing for publication a review of the north of Ireland in a period which may seem to you hopelessly remote; this is the Neolithic period which began—and we can now date it fairly precisely, as precisely as a good many ancient documents—to 3500 BC. This was the beginning of agriculture and animal husbandry, of the clearing of the forests, the making of fields, the building of houses, the establishment of tradition. One of the English contributors to this publication, who is perhaps the best authority on the Irish Neolithic period, uses words in describing the subdivisions of Ulster at that time which might have come from an opposition member of Stormont. He refers to the inland parts of Ulster, beyond the relatively densely populated east— and this is five thousand years ago—as 'the fringe areas West of the Bann'.

This may all seem irrelevant, but those first Irishmen were skilled craftsmen, had cattle and sheep and pigs and just as the modern farmers are coming to do again, they grew barley as their main crop. They grew barley, they drank beer, they were almost civilized human beings!

As every archaeologist knows, this corner of Ireland was among the most advanced, culturally and technically and commercially, of all regions not only in Ireland but in the British Isles. If you look at any map of the Bronze Age in the British Isles you will see how Ulster stands out. It had poor resources but it made the most of them; it was a place of great activity. And what happened was—I think this can be shown from the archaeological evidence—that people of different origins and cultures had learned to live together, to mix, to quicken each other. So Ulster, which is best known to the English today as a place of unrest and civil strife, is thought of by British archaeologists as the place where they had that brilliant Bronze Age.

There have been, therefore, at various times in the past, in this area, for reasons which still exist if they could be exploited, opportunities of contacts in many directions; there have been opportunities, not only at this earliest period I am talking about, but at other periods in Ulster history, at the end of the eighteenth century, for instance, when again extremes came together and sparked off a great cultural movement. So it is of some use, I think, to look back into these earlier periods and to become aware of how this land took its physical and human shape, not only before the Plantation but long before there was any written history.

I have no doubt that a great deal in our folklore, in our customs, in our folk music, as well as in our dialects, which are full of Gaelic idioms and forms, are the inheritance of an older time. Isn't it significant that the great festivals of the Ulster year, both Protestant and Catholic, are Gaelic festivals? The festivals we celebrate are not, for instance, Guy Fawkes but Hallowe'en, and we all pay our rents (or should do), whether we are Protestant or Catholic, not on the Scottish or the English gale-days but on the pre-Plantation gale-days, 1 May and 1 November. These things we share are things we should be aware of and make known because they are part of our common heritage. It was partly for this reason that, many years ago, some of us in Belfast got together and sought such a common bond in founding a society for the study of Ulster folk life, and through that, because this was one of its promoters, in the opening of the Ulster Folk Museum in 1964. Let me give you an example again from that particular field: the English planters were instructed to build houses 'after the English fashion'. The houses the farmers built, however, the houses they live in today, are in most respects Irish houses, that is they had to take over a lot of the native culture though they do not seem to be aware of it.

I have referred to the nature of the land. I always like to remember the wise words of the BBC garden commentator whom we affectionately called 'Old Manure'. He had one or two stock answers to any question or problem a gardener brought to him, and he would say: 'The answer lies in the soil.' There's a lot of wisdom in that. The variations in soils are what colour the culture. Ulster is a land of hard, acid soils, apart from certain fertile patches which have been, as it were, pre-empted. By and large you've got to deal with acid, sour soils—the whole of what we call the cultural landscape is a reflection of that: it favours the cattlemen rather than the farmer, the isolated dwelling rather than the village.

Topographically and geologically Ulster is a difficult country, a land of hard rocks and soft water. As soon as you begin to taste hard water you know you're getting out of Ulster. The hard rocks and the soft water are the combination that somehow make up the physical personality of Ulster. With it goes relative poverty, and a certain lack of concern for comfort and for the artistic, aesthetic side of life.

Then there's another complication. Looking at the historic regions of western Europe, the stable ones have had a permanent base of wealth and good government. Their capitals are situated in fat river basins: the London basin, the Paris basin and so on. In the only lowland basin that Ulster has to offer lies a vast puddle of water instead of a fertile plain. If you could have done away with Lough Neagh a few centuries ago, I believe you would have had the site for a local capital of more significance than Craigavon. Lough Neagh has a lot to answer for.

I remember once being asked, if I had the choice of locating a new city which might do something to pull Ulster together, where would I put it? And I immediately thought that the great period of Ulster's independence was when O'Neill held the heart of the Tyrone uplands, so I said immediately, Tullahogue or Cookstown. But I wasn't taken seriously.

Again, although Irish soil was first used for growing barley, in the long run what paid off was cattle rearing. The theme and the noise that runs through Irish history is the bellowing of bulls and the lowing of cows. This implies, for one thing, living close to your animals. Until little more than a hundred years ago, a large part of Ireland (and of Ulster) had the great majority of its people living with the cattle and other animals in single-roomed houses.

Certain cultural traits persist and can be related in one way or another to a pastoral heritage. A use of the patronymic and the strength of familial bonds reflect the pride of blood which is characteristic of the breeder of animals. Loyalty to kin outlives changing economic conditions and can on occasion prove a stronger force than truth or justice. Suspicion of external authority, especially of impersonal authority, is another factor leading to difficulties of government. Lawless, too, in having no perceptible order in its plan, was the clachan or farm-town, in contrast to the more disciplined village of England or France. The word 'throughother' well expresses this characteristic. Small units of population served by few urban centres had to be largely self-sufficient, yet were too poor and too small to support specialist craftsmen. A large proportion of the population has lived in single farms since late prehistoric times, and this type of scattered habitation is widespread: the lone tailors and skilled woodworkers were therefore itinerant. Despised as landless men, the itinerants yet had social as well as economic functions. The Irish pedlar and the Scots draper are in this tradition, as are the travelling shops and breadvans one meets on the roads of Ireland and western Scotland. The Breton onion boy is a related phenomenon.

So the solitary farm has been characteristic of rural living, in a way that it was in almost no other part of Europe. And that surely has left its mark on character—a certain roughness and independence. The pastoral custom of dividing the inheritance brought very small farms and general poverty, a lack of capital, and therefore, in the arts for instance, the natural thing for the Irish is not the communal effort of expensive orchestral music but the lone fiddler. The Arts Council, to educate the native, spends a great deal on orchestral music, ballet and grand opera, on the assumption that what is foreign is best. I suspect that the term 'cultural lag' which is often applied to Ulster was invented by an Englishman who did not understand this other island.

[Lilliput Pamphlets No.2 (Mullingar 1984): originally given as a talk at a seminar on 'Understanding Ourselves' in Benburb, County Armagh, and subsequently printed as 'The Northern Heritage' in *Aquarius* (1971), an annual religio-cultural review.]

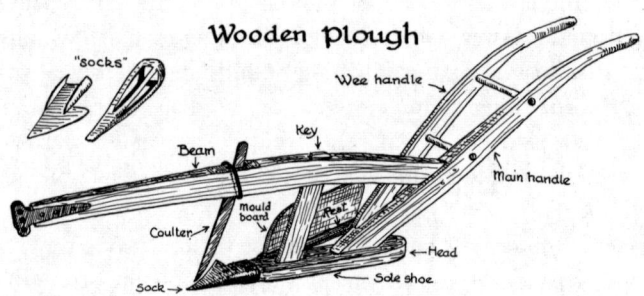

part IV

IRISH HARVEST
'Tis the Best of Land

I bent my head to meet the Atlantic gale and forced my way along a road that led between low stone walls towards the sea. The narrow road, taking the full force of the wind, was raised several feet above the level of tiny fields that had been reclaimed from the sodden surface beneath a six-foot turf bog. Peasant farmers must have cut fuel here for generations, but now the land below was cultivated and several fields were white with oats. Struggling along between the whistling walls, my head bent to bore into the gale, I saw no-one until I heard a shout above the noise of the wind from the field below.

'That's a great day!' The countryman likes to have news of the wide world and will not readily let the stranger pass without a greeting. His comments on the weather call for an appropriate formula of agreement: 'It is indeed', or 'Aye, a great day.' The clouds sped by in tattered wisps, and by ordinary standards this was anything but a great day. I returned his steady gaze with a smile and protested mildly: 'It's stormy and looks like rain.' But he stuck his stubbled chin into the threatening sky: ''Tis windy', he summed up, 'but 'tis dry.' And that, it appeared, was the best tribute anyone could hope to pay to Irish weather.

One should spend a full round year along these coasts to know the norm by which the weather is judged. And I was soon to learn that wind without rain is indeed a rare blessing in harvest time, the best that could be wished for. All the same I have felt that there is a superstitious reverence which

173

shapes the attitude of the countryman towards the elements. It will not do to give the weather a bad name lest worse follow. Praise it when you can, and do nothing to get on the wrong side of the forces that control it. So those rare days of stifling heat in July, when the milk turns sour before you have time to drink it, are merely 'warm' to the sweating haymaker, and dreary winter days of soaking rain, when all Ireland becomes a grey-green sponge, are referred to as 'soft'.

I climbed over the wall and leaped down into the sparse stubble, my feet sinking inches deep into the black stoneless bog-soil. I was wearing my heaviest nailed shoes, well dubbined against all weathers, and I confess my pride was hurt when the man in the field remarked, in a tone of pity, 'Thon articles is too thin for this country.' His enormous plated boots would have taken him dry-shod across a quaking bog. He had cut—sheared was the word he used—a few square yards of the white over-ripe oats. The month was October. There had been no harvest weather, and I offered to help him for he had no-one to bind the sheaves. His reaping-hook was curiously shaped: it had a long thin straight point, and the underside was nicked with little teeth like one of those bread-saws that seem designed to manufacture crumbs. But the saw-toothed sickle is no newfangled implement: it is descended from the rough-edged flint sickle of ancient husbandry. It must be pulled towards you across the standing straw, not slashed against it as with a hook or scythe. The scythe is a newcomer to these parts: its diffusion from the prehistoric centres of iron-working in mid-Europe to this remote Atlantic outpost required some two thousand years. It is kept almost exclusively for hay-cutting and is hung on a low straight pole or sned, from the end of which protrudes a three-inch nail, a safety device to anchor the scythe to the ground when the long keen blade is being honed.

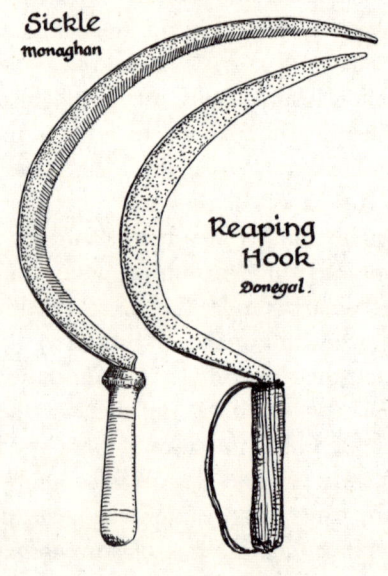

Sickle
monaghan

Reaping
Hook
Donegal.

I noticed that the scythe could have been used only with great difficulty in this little plot of corn. Every few feet the jagged and bleached stumps of ancient pine trees protruded above the ripe oats. I heard in imagination another wind singing in a long-vanished forest above our heads. Not a single living tree was in sight, save a solitary thorn, hardly more than a bush, bent almost horizontally away from the sea. Before this bog began to grow, perhaps fifty centuries ago, the last legacy of glacial conditions, a stable continental climate had kept Atlantic storms at bay and great forests clothed the rocky coast down to the water's edge. When the now familiar 'depressions' began to break across the country, rains swamped the land, and whole belts of trees were blown down, clogging the drainage. A couple of feet of vegeta-tion had accumulated to form peat before the surviving trees rotted away, to be buried by many more feet of peat. Toughened by bog acids, the stumps had outlived the deposits that had smothered them.

There came a time when the turf had been cut away for fuel to within a few inches of the rock. This was before the Great Famine, when every rood of land that would raise a crop was cultivated. The bog-floor had been heavily limed, dug over with spades and sown down to corn. They would cart the limestone to the fields, seeking it down the coast in boats, and burn it in home-made kilns, a ring of turf enclosing layer and layer about of limestone and peat. Every four years or so the land would be left to rest—to grow sour weeds—and then further crops of corn would be taken off it. So the oats were thin: there were patches where rabbits had nibbled it close, and the crop was so short that the pigmy forest of lichened pine-stumps out-topped it.

Lying ready for binding the sheaves was a number of bands which the shearer had prepared and it was my job to tie the corn as he cut it. I watched him shear the first sheaf, bent almost double to take the corn clean and save the last inch of the precious straw. Grasping each handful with the left hand and pressing it away from him to prevent the blade slipping against his fingers, he gathered a bundle of three or four handfuls with as many quick strokes. He turned on his heels to lay it down on a band lying ready for him on the ground, using the flat of the sickle-blade to hold the heads out straight and lower them gently, in order, he explained, that the corn should not be shaken out. Four such bundles made a sheaf, and now it was my turn to stoop. The knack of twisting the ends of the band together and tucking one end in under the knot came back to me from the days of my youth. Twenty years fell from me as I worked: I could do it with my eyes shut. Yet there was something unfamiliar about the feel of the band. There should have been a bunch of ears at one end. So short was the straw that in order to make a sizeable sheaf the band had been made by twisting together the heads of two handfuls of corn.

After a while the shearer, feeling the need for a pull of tobacco, lit a short clay pipe which he kept in his waistcoat pocket and turned round to inspect my work. I was pleased with the neat sheaves lying all about my feet. The knots were well-made, he admitted, but I had bound the sheaves too tight.

The way the wind would never get into them to do its drying work. He turned them over one by one with his boot, gently, and pointed out another mistake. I should have put the bands on in such a way that the joined ears lay towards the head of the sheaves. He explained that when thrashing time came all the ears would thus be at the right end for the beater of the flail. And the bands I had made were too thick: the straw would not dry under them. There was more to come. Did I not know that the butts of the sheaves should be laid into the wind, so that the heavy bottoms would have a chance of drying out? I began to see why he had welcomed the wind.

When the cutting and binding were finished there were several score of sheaves all lying like prostrate figures, heads away from the sea, paying tribute to the wind. I left promising I would return next day to give him a hand.

The wind had blown steadily all night, and we were able to stook the sheaves. I helped him build the stooks of twelve sheaves, five on each side to make a tunnel east and west parallel to the wind, finished by a capping of two inverted sheaves, the 'hooden-sheaves' or 'hudders'. As we worked he told me something of his life. He had spent many years of his youth in 'the States', in the mines of Butte, but he had come back to the old home when he heard that his father was dying. With the prospect of inheriting the farm in mind, he had never got married in America. 'A man that marries out there', he said, 'never comes back'; and he added, as he tied the two cap sheaves securely on a stook, 'sure, marriage puts the hudders on a man!'

He was still farming the place all alone. He was immensely proud of it. ''Tis the best of land,' he told me, surveying the few miserable acres of black soil won from the bog, 'the very best.' Even so will every farmer's wife on whom you call for a drink of water point out the trickle of water which she calls her springwell and tell you, proudly, 'There's no better drinking water in all Ireland!' In such sentiments you have a measure of the compelling force which drove hundreds of thousands of Irishfolk westwards across the ocean in the nineteenth century.

Before I went on my way I hoped the weather would hold for him to finish harvest. If the wind kept up, he said, he would get the corn dried quickly. It was great weather altogether. Remembering from my youth the discomfort of pitching sheaves in a high wind I suggested that with any luck the wind would drop before he began to carry the corn home. But again I was wrong. If the wind ceased there would surely be rain and his crop would never dry again so late in the year. Let it blow a hurricane! It would 'coup' over the stooks so that they lay prostrate, the sheaves with their butts to the wind for a final drying. 'The best harvest weather of all', he shouted as I left, 'is a scouring wind that will blow the stooks into the haggard.'

[*Ulster Folklife*, 14 (1968)]

FIELDS, FENCES AND GATES

The Ulster landscape, like that of the rest of Ireland and Wales and other parts of the Highland Zone, differs considerably from the landscape of Lowland England in the pattern of its farms and fields and in the fences and gates which guard them. These differences are at once apparent from the air, or from the large-scale Ordnance Maps. It is not only that farms and fields are smaller in Ulster than in England; the hedges are more overgrown but have fewer and smaller hedgerow trees, the five-barred wooden gate hung on oak posts is replaced by the iron gate swinging between massive stone piers. There are more lanes but fewer footpaths, more farms but fewer villages; and the market towns are smaller and set rather closer together. These differences are the result of social and economic evolution in different environments, and the student of folklife must take account of them. W.H. Hudson observed that every feature of the landscape, everything that we see, hear, smell and feel, enters not into the body only but into the soul, and helps to shape and colour it.

In Ulster the word 'ditch' keeps its older meaning of a raised bank, whether of earth or stone, whereas in England it means the open drain alongside (in Ulster the 'sheugh') from which the earth bank was dug. Most of the ditches which now parcel out the Irish countryside are of no great antiquity. In English-settled areas some may go back to the sixteenth and seventeenth centuries, but by and large they date from the agrarian revolu-

177

tion which affected most of the country between about 1750 and the years of the Great Famine nearly a century later. What distinguishes them is their orderly rectangular pattern and their tall thorn hedges, growing from quicks planted low down on one side of the ditch, which is normally faced with stones. This is the type of fence advocated by agricultural improvers and stipulated in landlords' leases of the late eighteenth century, and there must be many thousands of miles of hedged banks of this kind through the agricultural lowlands of Ireland. The thorns are generally allowed to grow freely without being touched—so that one might suppose that they are regarded as 'fairy thorns'—and then cut hard back to leave a poor fence full of gaps.

Very rarely does one see a 'pleached' hedge of English style. In this form of hedgecraft the thorns are periodically half-severed near the base, bent down at an angle and secured with vertical stakes around which the slanting thorns are woven to make an almost impenetrable wall. The hedger has a varied equipment of tools, not least the short-handled billhook which exhibits almost as much regional variation as the Irish spade. In Ireland its place is taken by the long-handled slasher or pruning bill, adapted to lopping and not to the controlled strokes of the pleacher. The Irish hedged ditch seems to be a compromise between the native custom of erecting earthen banks, which was done for various purposes, and the novelty of the planted hedge. Thus the hedge was planted in the bank, whereas the English hedge normally grows on the flat, and this partly explains the difference of treatment. The tall hedge and bank provide shelter for cattle, whereas the pleached hedge is associated with arable farming. Moreover, the low pleached hedge would be no barrier to the athletic black-faced sheep of the Highland Zone.

English observers, from Arthur Young onwards, too readily attributed the neglect of hedges to indolence. Rather, the hedge is regarded as a line of demarcation and a shelter-belt which can be strengthened as a protective barrier when necessary. Behind this attitude there lies a long tradition of temporary fences erected around patches of cultivation in the outfield. Alternatively, it was customary in some areas to enclose the cattle instead of the corn. Writing of the Copeland Islands, Walter Harris noted, in 1744:

They have no fences in the island, but to preserve their corn from trespasses they fold their cattle within inclosures raised of sods, and let them out to graze at proper seasons, and watch and herd them, as it is called there; and the same custom is used in the Barony of Ards, and most other parts of the county.

A similar practice prevailed in Rathlin Island into the present century, but here the enclosures were probably built of stone. The cattle were herded by day and driven at night into these 'fanks'. In general, one may suppose that the areas where cattle were enclosed—'outfields'—were destined to be cultivated for two or three years after they had been trodden and manured in this way.

Early nineteenth-century accounts tell of great hostility to the planting of hedges in some districts. When landlords put them in the tenants would pull them out, or later hack them down for firewood. This hostility to permanent fences must be seen in the light of old custom. It had been the immemorial practice, wherever the rundale system prevailed, to allow the wintering stock to have a free run of the townland between the first of November and the first of May. Earthen ditches or 'single ditches' of stone were readily breached to allow access from one farm to another. This was customary a few years ago, for example, in the Gweedore district of Donegal, and probably continues still. In summer, when the fields were required for crops, the walls were repaired and the earthen ditches 'brairded' with dead thorns and whins. Or if the fields were very small and held in scattered bits under the rundale system the animals had to be tethered or hobbled in some way and often herded as well.

The prevalence of tethering and other methods of limiting the freedom of livestock is a relic of inadequate fencing. In the old days every country child began his emancipation from his mother's skirts as a herder: we are reminded that this is the meaning of the Irish word for a boy, *buchaill*. The old folk too passed their time tending the grazing stock in the fields, so that life began and ended with the watching of cattle. The herders themselves were kept on a short tether, never leaving the cows, and the association of old and young amid the sights and sounds of nature was no doubt a means of passing on knowledge and lore and keeping alive tradition. Both young and old were put out of work when the hedged ditch replaced the bare banks and the balks of the open fields. The coming of permanent enclosure must have had many other sociological as well as economic consequences. The physical narrowing of horizons, the obstruction of the distant view, the increased privacy, were surely partly responsible for the decline in natural poetry and in the spirit of communal living which marked the course of the nineteenth century.

Since the sixteenth century, in the Pale, the ash has been the favourite tree for planting on the earthen ditch. It was enacted in 1434 'that every husbandman having a plough within the English Pale shall set by the year twelve ashes in the ditches and closes of his farm', and the custom of planting ash trees on the ditches (or preserving them if self-sown) was very widely adopted and is still maintained. The introduced beech and sycamore, cherished for their deep shade, also became popular. But Arthur Young and other visitors before and after 1800 frequently commented on the poor stunted growth of the hedgerow trees, and they attributed it to the fact that they had to grow on dry banks and to compete with untended thorns. Young comments: 'To permit a hedge to grow too long without cutting not only ruins it for a fence but spoils the trees that are planted with it.' The depredations of livestock must also be taken into account: in the sheep-farming districts a tree has a poor chance of surviving unless it has protection, and a few prickly thorn and holly trees are all that escape.

In windy coastal districts, especially where, as at Magilligan in County Londonderry, the sandy soil gives a poor foothold for hedges, the sod ditch comes into its own, and one would like to see a study of the various methods of constructing them. Some regions use a slanting herring-bone method of laying sods: I have noticed it around Ballycastle. In the wind-swept uplands, too, save where sods are thin and boulders abundant, the ditches are earthen banks which will not support thorns but become a wild tangle of whins and bramble. One of the Morgans of Hilltown told Jonathan Binns in 1836 that these large raised banks were not as wasteful as they seemed because 'we have both sides of a ditch for feeding the cattle, and whins to bruise for the horses.' Dubourdieu tells us that in County Antrim about the year 1800 the approved thorn ditch had been introduced only in the more progressive parts, and he notes that 'the banks of the fences were made formerly much larger than they are now.'

On the higher hill-slopes, and in the lowlands wherever there are many glacial boulders or rock outcrops, it is the stone ditch which predominates. Most of these walls were built during the time of the enclosures, between 1750 and 1850, but the art of dry-walling is of megalithic antiquity, and many examples of walls of prehistoric age lie buried under the peat. Anyone who has tried to build a stone wall without mortar will realize the skill required in what may seem to the onlooker to be an artless labour. Each district has evolved the type of stone fence which experience has shown to be most suitable. It is adapted to the materials available and to the local climate and economy. Single ditches, made of large boulders built up in a single row, are characteristic of many regions of good farming such as the Braid Valley and the Kingdom of Mourne. Such walls with their loose joints through which light shows look delicate as lace-work when seen against the sky. Their weakness is their strength, for they will stand up to the winds, and it is said that sheep sheltering from the rain do not get their fleeces sodden because the wind comes through. In Clare, Galway, and in particular the Aran Islands, there are no breaks in the walls for gates, but a section of wall is taken down and rebuilt as required. The 'gates' are defined by pillar stones.

A curious hybrid type of stone ditch, known in Scotland as the Galloway ditch, is also found in east Galway, but I have not observed it in Ulster. The lower part is of dry-walling while the upper part is a single ditch which overhangs slightly and acts as a deterrent to climbing sheep. The low single ditches of Rathlin Island are said to be effective because they are apt to collapse when touched, so that grazing animals give them a wide berth: they act as a primitive 'electric fence'.

Where stones are more abundant the walls are much more massive, and they are generally constructed on the principle of the 'double ditch' or 'dry fence'. Two parallel single ditches are erected and tied together with occasional 'through stones', while at the same time the cavity in between is filled with small stones, often 'bullets' gathered from the fields. If the outer skin is broken a cascade of small stones is likely to pour out, and a repair is extremely difficult. These walls are therefore more permanent than single ditches, and they may serve as nuclei for even more massive walls. Fresh skins are added from time to time until they have become in some instances ten or more feet wide. Each skin probably represents a period of renewed agricultural activity and boulder clearance, so that an old wall of this kind is a document of economic history. In Denmark, where the history of agriculture is considered as seriously as the history of kings, much information has been obtained from the study of potsherds and other relics incorporated in field fences of different periods.

If the view I have stated above is correct, such historic walls are rare in Ireland, but one sees them around the gardens and parks of old rundale house clusters. The evidence so far gleaned from archaeology does not permit us to say whether the remains of stone ditches found in excavations or still visible in places under the hill-peats were field-boundaries. Some are massive enough, but others may be no more than linear clearances from patches of cultivation, having no function as property divisions. In some hilly districts it is customary to throw 'bullets' gathered from the fields around rocky outcrops, making cairns which frequently protect a grove of fairy thorns.

There is no evidence to suggest that the cone-capped round gate pillars which are so characteristic of the Ulster countryside go back before the Plantation period. The great majority of them cannot be older than the general enclosure movement. Their origin should perhaps be sought in the massive defensive gateways of the bawns, though these may continue an older native tradition. Certainly the folklore of the farmyard entrance piers suggests native ancestry, and the method of hanging the gates is also archaic. This is the harr-hanging, which is traditional in Cornwall, Brittany and other refuge-areas along the Atlantic coasts of Europe. The gate swings not on hinges or rings-and-hooks but, in the old style, on its heel, on a projecting spud which rotates in a hollow stone. A stone eye, now generally replaced by one of iron, secures the top of the gatepost. The doors of early Irish churches and castles usually worked on the same principle.

One of the reasons for the adoption of strong piers and gates at field-entrances was to check cattle-lifting. 'A Discourse of Ireland' in the *Calendar of State Papers* (1601–3) recommends the erection of 'a strong pair of boarded gates with an iron bar across the midst' at the entrance to fields. By the nineteenth century the gates themselves had come to be made of iron, and of course this is the Irish fashion. Wakefield, writing in 1812, tells us that 'when gentlemen erect gates, they are iron, hung upon stone pillars'. He adds that wooden gates were almost unknown and that in any case they would have been stolen for use as fuel. The virtual absence of oak trees meant that good timber gates and posts were anyhow not available. I think it will be found that particular patterns of stone piers and of iron gates tend to coincide with the old landed estates. Evidently the example of landlords in erecting piers and gates was followed by the tenants. It will be noticed that they tend to occur along the roadsides, so that ostentation and visible improvement were probably factors in their erection, though it was along the highways that protection was most needed. For fields away from the roads the entrances tend to be less showy, old farm implements often serving as stop-gaps. Sampson, writing of County Londonderry in the early nineteenth century, describes a rustic forerunner of the now ubiquitous barbed-wire—a hay-rope strung with thorns. Nowadays the great piers are often neglected or replaced by characterless concrete pillars. Whatever their origin, the stout whitewashed pillars are a very attractive feature of the countryside.

[*Ulster Folklife*, 2 (1956)]

A GAME OF BULLETS

In my younger days, when engaged in exploring the Irish countryside, I used to try my hand, as opportunity offered, at any game, craft or farm handwork I came across, and was often rewarded—not for any slight help I might have given but for a display of interest—by gaining some understanding of their mysteries and picking up knowledge which I would not otherwise have gained. It was when trying my hand at a game of bullet-throwing that I discovered one use to which the stone cup-marks, so dear to an older generation of romantic antiquarians, could have been put.

The game of bullets, formerly known as long bullets, is still occasionally played in South Armagh. Under the more innocent name of bowls (pronounced to rhyme with 'howls') it is popular in Counties Cork, Limerick and Waterford, where it is catered for by numerous bowling clubs. Within living memory it was played in several other parts of Northern Ireland, notably around Belfast. Down to the Second World War it was popular on the Horseshoe Road at Ligoniel. Ballygomartin, Hannahstown and the Shore Road were also favourite meeting-places. The game is still remembered around Downpatrick and Ballynahinch and I have been told that it flourished formerly in parts of Counties Tyrone, Londonderry and Monaghan. There is great doubt about its legality because of the inconvenience and danger it brings to 'subjects upon the King's highway'. In fact it was prohibited under the Summary Jurisdiction Act of 1851, though one suspects that since the game was popular in areas of strong 'Irishness' there may have been a political motive in discouraging it, for the large gatherings at a big bullet match could readily be regarded as subversive. The name 'bullets' has no hostile significance but it does suggest that the stone or iron balls which give the game its name were originally missiles, and I have wondered whether its distribution in Ireland may be partly explained by the presence of military barracks where small cannon-balls might have been procured for peaceful use. A hard-surfaced road would also be needed, and the older examples would probably have been planned for military use, though many of those made before about 1760 were dead straight and are unlikely to have attracted bullet-throwers. Certainly some early nineteenth-century observers attribute its introduction to English colonists, and it is known that 'long bullets' was once a popular game in northern England and parts of Scotland. Indeed it has a wider distribution, for a similar ball game is practised in north Germany.

In County Cork international bowling events are held in which teams from north Germany and Holland compete with Irish teams under the aegis of An Bol-Chumann na hEireann. The ball may be delivered underhand or overhand, and this is the main difference between the northern and southern versions of the game in Ireland. But it must not be supposed that the underhand delivery of the North is any less violent or less skilful than the overhand throw of the South. Nor do the games differ in other respects whether in the thirst engendered by the exercise or the attraction the competition holds for gamblers, groups of onlookers pooling their resources to back a favourite player. The most popular contests are between two throwers; when two pairs of players compete the game is known as a double score or a partners. The team 'score' may derive from the average number of throws required to complete the game over a normal course of about two miles of road. The player who covers the distance in the least number of throws is the winner. To ensure that chances are even only one bullet is used in a match, and since it must be returned after every throw the game proceeds at a leisurely pace, especially when, if it leaves the road, the bullet may bury itself in a field or lie hidden in the 'sheugh', the roadside ditch. If it is recovered the throw is measured to the point on the road nearest the bullet's resting place. This point, or the place where the bullet comes to rest if it stays on the road, is marked by a grass sod which is the butt for the player's next throw; and one knows where a game has taken place by the litter of grass strewing a country road. As in cricket or baseball, the ball-thrower's skill depends on spin or 'screw' as well as on direction and speed of delivery. Thus a player will roughen one side of the iron ball by rubbing it in roadside grit; but he could hardly achieve the cricketer's shine by rubbing it in his groin! The game was played mostly in summer and autumn.

John Mogey 'at the bullets', Drumintee, County Armagh, April 1945.
Michael Murphy (below) *making a stone bullet in a cup-marked boulder at Ballinyamaddy, and bullet-throwing at Drumintee* (photograph by John Mogey).

It was out of season, on a spring day many years ago near Forkill, in County Armagh, that I tried my hand at bullet-throwing. The year was 1945. Michael Murphy introduced me to a character known as Paddy the Goat (so called because he had made his living 'at the goats', buying and selling), who was a local bullet-champion. 'In my young days', said Paddy, 'it was all bullet-throwing in these parts. Now it's nothing but skittles and pitch-and-toss', and he cast a contemptuous eye, accompanied by a quid of tobacco, towards a group of young men who were listlessly throwing pennies against the chapel wall. 'Bullets was a man's game: the young fellows going about now aren't up till it at all.'

When I told him I would like to see how the game was played he promised to arrange a score at Drumintee for Sunday evening, Paddy and I to be the throwers. We first went to the police barracks to put ourselves right with the law, and when we explained the circumstances, the 'polis' were most understanding and promised to turn a blind eye on the proceedings. In the event they not only showed up in strength but kept the road clear for us and took a keen interest in the game.

Evening in these parts begins at noon, and news travels fast. By mid-afternoon a crowd of thirty or forty men and boys had assembled at the cross-roads and were talking about games played on this course many years before. I noticed that there were no women or girls: bullets was indeed a man's game. I learnt that the balls, nowadays of iron, were formerly made of stone, and could in emergency be fashioned on the spot. Michael led me aside to a large granite boulder by the roadside and pointed to an artificial cup-shaped hollow on the flat upper surface. I took it to be an example of a 'cup-mark', one of those mysterious smooth depressions found in many parts of the world, dating from many periods and normally associated in Ireland with dolmens (giants' graves) and standing stones, including Christian crosses and grave-slabs. This example, I was told, had been used for making stone bullets. Michael picked up a small boulder to use as a hammer-stone and selecting a roundish granite pebble, placed it in the cup and demonstrated how, by repeated blows, it could be rotated in the cup and shaped into a round ball about 2.5 inches in diameter. The bullet we used, an iron ball, was rather smaller and weighed two pounds.

A stir of excitement moved through the assembled crowd as Paddy prepared to make the first throw from the butt, a sod placed at the crossroads. Advice was freely offered as he gave his jacket to an admiring acolyte, swung his arm to loosen up, and took a couple of trial runs up to the butt. 'Open up the road', was the cry on all sides as men posted themselves high on the roadside banks to watch the throw and to keep the course clear. Paddy took a quick run up to the butt, and his movements were so rapid that it was difficult to see the finer points of his delivery. The right arm moved rigidly backward from the shoulder in lightening circles, then stopped suddenly as the elbow hit the hip so that the ball was hinched forward on its flight. Paddy's face was drawn into tight lines of strain as he put all his strength and skill into the delivery. He came out of his state of rigid tension with a slow smile, 'She's right', was all he said as the acolyte came up with his jacket. The road curved as it went downhill, and the bullet, striking the inside curve, kept to the road and trundled on for a distance of more than 100 yards. Everyone said it was a great throw. A sod was placed on the road at its resting place and the bullet was returned to the starting point for me to make my first throw. Acting on advice, I decided to hinch the bullet into the air in the hope of clearing the bend and striking the road beyond. It was an ill-advised attempt. The weight of the bullet nearly wrenched my arm from its socket, and I did not make enough distance to clear the bend. There was a loud crack as the ball struck a boulder in the hedgebanks and bounded away into a clump of whins. After much searching the whins were set alight to expose the ground, but despite all our efforts the bullet could not be found, and although Paddy was willing to start again if a new ball could be procured my single throw had left me so exhausted that I was ready to concede victory.

It would surely be the shortest game of long bullets ever played. So we pressed the rough stone ball made by Michael Murphy into service. I made my second throw from my mark on the road but it failed to reach Paddy's first mark and as my third throw still fell short of it he was declared winner under the unwritten law that a competitor dropped out if he had failed in three throws to arrive at the point reached by his rival in two; he had not even had his second throw.

Back at the crossroads we listened to stories of epic matches recorded or remembered down the years. My mind was carried back to descriptions I had read of bullet-matches of long ago. I remembered the account of a celebrated match played at Drumballyroney in County Down in the year 1812, when the contestants were the locally-renowned athletic uncles of the famous Brontë sisters. 'Every ounce of elastic force in the great muscular frames was called into action, and there was a profusion of strange strong language.'

I remembered also how, nearly a century earlier, the Rev. Philip Skelton of Derriaghy, near Belfast, a champion thrower, had 'received a blow with a three-pound ball just over his left eye' which in his own words, 'flattened the projecting part of my skull and greatly shattered an excellent constitution'. I had been fortunate to escape unscathed, for the ball which flattened the reverend's skull had bounded back on striking a roadside boulder.

As a schoolboy in Shropshire I had frequently followed the clearly marked runs of the corncrake in hayfields, found their nests and—I am ashamed to say—stolen their eggs. The bird was already becoming rare in many parts of Britain, its decline attributed mainly to the introduction of the mowing machine. Imagine my astonishment therefore when on arriving in Ireland in 1928 I was greeted on sailing into Belfast Harbour not, as I had expected, by the clamour of shipbuilding, but by bare gantries standing in acres of grass and echoing with the cries of great numbers of corncrakes. Yet, the noisy birds in the shipyards were not visible; indeed, later, looking up my favourite naturalist writers, I found that neither Gilbert White nor Richard Jefferies—both keen observers in the south of England—had ever seen the bird in the act of craking. They did however comment on its apparent ventriloquism and on the paradox that its continuous craking is combined with a 'strong desire' for concealment. Jefferies suggests that it 'threw its voice' by directing it, for example, along a furrow, but there may be another explanation for its ventriloquism. Many years later I was to have the opportunity to observe, and help record, the shy corncrake in its act of craking.

At the time I was doing live broadcasting from the Ulster countryside for the BBC, and on one such occasion undertook to do a description, deep underground, of the geological features of the limestone caves at the Marble Arch, County Fermanagh. The BBC recording van was driven as far as the entrance to the caves, and I took an assortment of cables and ropes with me. Signals were given me, as to when to start and to stop talking, by means of an agreed number of tugs on one of the ropes. It was not an easy task, for in order to reach the finest stalactites and stalagmites I had to wade through a number of subterranean streams and pools. The BBC was later to boast that no previous broadcast had come from so deep underground.

I was in full spate when I received urgent notice to stop, but I had to reach the surface to be given an explanation: a cuckoo had flown into a nearby tree, and they wanted a recording of a cuckoo because the BBC had none. The emergency led me to recollect the folklore of the cuckoo, and was a reminder of how important a date in the country calendar was the bird's return from its wintering home in Africa. In Greece, the arrival of the cuckoo is said to have marked the ripening of the first figs. In various parts of the British Isles, several wild flowers which appear then are named cuckoo flowers, many of them yellow in colour and associated for that reason with butter making. In Scots Gaelic the bird is called 'the lady of tears'. In parts of our islands the term 'gowk' is applied to the cuckoo and to anyone regarded as stupid. And that unprepossessing fish of shallow salt water, the ballan-wrasse, which has many local names, is in some parts of England known as the cuckoo-fish.

Passing through Tyrone on the way home from Fermanagh, the air was full of the craking of corncrakes, and as the bird had become very rare in England I suggested that we make a recording for the BBC sound archive. Occasionally, when driving along country roads, I had seen a corncrake flying heavily across the road from one field to another, disturbed perhaps by the noise of the car, but I had still to see one in the act of craking. Now, at a bend in the road, just over the roadside hedge, we heard, saw and recorded—again for the first time—a corncrake in full cry, and I believed I could now understand why the crake was so elusive. The bird was standing bolt-upright, like a booming bittern as illustrated in the bird books, its bill pointing skywards so that the call could be heard in all directions. I thought I had discovered the secret of the bird's ventriloquism, but of course the bird was probably standing upright merely to keep a wary eye on the strange object, the microphone, hanging over its head. I recall here a conversation about this time with the late Lord Brookeborough, who, whatever one thinks of his political views, was a keen observer and lover of the Irish countryside. He compared a garrulous member of the Stormont Parliament to a corncrake: 'He goes on and on and on, and you never know which field he's in!'

Country people have various interpretations of the calls of wild and domesticated birds. I was given the following descriptions of bird language in Drumintee district of South Armagh. The song-thrush goes:

Poor Hughey, poor Hughey,
Come in to your tea,
Come in to your tea.

The Hen:

I lay an egg everyday,
And go bare-footed, bare-footed.

The Cock replies:

Why don't you buy brogues,
Why don't you buy brogues.

In the Hilltown district the rooster replies:

Well then, I can't help it, help it.

In folklore the domestic hen is reputed to be something of a newcomer to Ireland. Every night, when the hens chatter together before falling to sleep, they complain about the rain and their constantly wet feet and they decide to fly back home in the morning—to Norway—and are silenced only when the rooster advises them to wait one more day, when the weather may improve. They are still waiting, and complaining.

It seems likely that the domestic hen reached Ireland from Norway: alternatively, the word translated as Norway may mean 'foreign parts'. Similarly it is a mystery why the magpie should be called, in Gaelic, 'the Frenchman'. The name given to the snipe—God's goat—is more understandable. The snipe is also called 'Man in air', and its bleat is regarded as a sure sign of rain. W.H. Hudson, in one of his books, puts words of advice to the cattle thief into the bill of the cooing wood-pigeon on the Welsh border: 'Two cows, Taffy, Take two cows Taffy, Take two cows Taffy, two'.

COUNTING TIME

In the pagan Celtic world the year was divided ecologically into quarters and halves, the latter beginning at times that became, in the Gregorian Calendar, the first of May and the first of November. The other dividing points came on August the first and February first. The primary division is a reflection of a pastoral economy and culture and is related to the climate and natural vegetation of maritime Europe. While rain falls and the grass is green throughout the year, and there are therefore no sharp divisions between the seasons, May and November are the critical months. In May the countryside is bright with the creamy blossoms of the May-bush, and with the golden buttercup and Mayflower which carry the promise, for stockmen, of a bounteous supply of milk and butter. There is an abundant supply of grass and of leaf-browse, which was a significant component in the food of cattle before the natural vegetation was cleared. In November the leaves fall and the hill pastures wither; and grazing animals were taken down to the shelter of the homesteads in the valleys. Surpluses of one kind or another were readily available at these turning points of the year: wild nuts and berries, young animals, butter and soft cheese, skins and hides; and it was customary for the overlords to claim their dues at these times. With the coming of a money economy they were converted to payments in cash so that 1 May and 1 November became the rent or gale days. Even in proudly British Ulster ground-rents fall due not on the English rent days but on the Irish gale days—a striking illustration of the tenacity of Irish custom.

The quarterly division of the year was replaced, with the coming of Christianity, by a division into months and seasons beginning on 1 January and marked by many Saints' Days. The most popular of the Christian festivals, however, won prestige by taking to themselves traditions belonging to the old festivals celebrating the beginning of the native quarters. The round of the year turned about these critical hinges. They were also weak places where evil forces could get in, and these must be appeased by practising sympathetic magic of one kind or another to ensure good luck for the coming quarter-year. These practices included the lighting of bonfires, dressing up in straw costumes, playing games (some of them quite obscene and clearly designed to promote fertility), the blowing of horns, hunting the wren, bull-baiting, and above all by assemblies on hill-tops. These hill-top gatherings were popular in many parts of the country, particularly in early August, when wild berries could also be gathered and the first-fruits of 'harvest' (autumn) celebrated. At these times too certain very unchristian rites of divination were practised.

The most famous and notorious, and to this day the most popular of all Irish pilgrimages, involves an arduous climb to the summit of Croagh Patrick in County Mayo, a mountain which has many legendary associations with St Patrick but it has its objective not a Christian site or shrine but a prehistoric hilltop cairn. Moreover the most popular time to make the pilgrimage is not St Patrick's Day but the first Sunday in August, marking the pagan quarter-day festival of Lughnasa which became Lammas.

The divisions of the year I have been describing might be called ecological. Similarly the old-fashioned countryman, in counting time, goes not by the clock and the calendar but by observing sun, moon, wind and tide, and by noting the times when significant events occur in the world of nature, or in the routine of seedtime and harvest, and the rhythm of stock-rearing. I recall a visit I made to a hillside farm in the Mournes where I called from time to time. I tried to recall the date and the time of year of my last visit, but the woman of the house cut me short: 'I remember well: t'was the day after our white cow went to the bull.' Fair-day is another point of reference, or some phenomenal spell of weather. Many a countryman of an earlier generation dated the events of his youth from 'The Big Wind' of 1839.

The advent of the first clock was another point of reference. The American sociologist, Lewis Mumford, wrote somewhere that the clock, not the steam-engine, was the master machine of the industrial age, a view which equates time with money. In Ulster it was the linen-towns of the Lagan Valley, depending at first on water-power, that came to experience 'the tyranny of the timepiece'. In the expanding commercial centres of Holland

and England, the timepiece was already an item of furniture by the end of the sixteenth century. From the middle of the eighteenth century large (grandfather) clocks, with their elaborate cases, were being manufactured in the urban centres of the Lagan Valley, South Down and North Armagh, as the names on their ornamental faces tell us: Lisburn and Banbridge, Newry, Armagh and Dundalk. In the early nineteenth century the Ordnance Survey Memoirs for the parish of Racavan in the Braid Valley, Country Antrim, relate that the great ambition of the linen-weavers was to possess a clock. 'It is referred to affectionately as "she", and there is a great collection at the setting up of "her".' Thus when a countryman uses the phrase 'she's very fast', one must not assume that he is referring to some girl.

I have been told that the clock was traditionally placed on or against the south wall of the house—and the later small alarm-clock kept in a 'keeping-hole' similarly located—because this was the side where the position of the sun, or the length of the shadows it cast, had previously been observed to get an indication of the time of day. But it is not clear why the clock should have had a feminine gender. One might think it was the domestic hen, rather than the rooster, that the clock had replaced, but did not the term cock-crow tell otherwise? For I have been told that old-fashioned countrymen, if they wanted to be sure of rising early, for instance to attend a distant fair, would bring the rooster indoors.

A delightful story is told of the coming of the first clock to a remote part of County Donegal. Neighbours would assemble around it to hear it strike, nodding their heads at one another over their pints; and there was great consternation when, at the end of the first week, the unwound clock failed to strike. There was much discussion and head-shaking until it was decided to open the clock case and investigate. When a dead mouse was found inside, one of the onlookers observed: 'And how would ye expect the article to be going, and the wee engine-driver lying there dead all the time!' But the clock never became the master of the Irish countryman: not for him, as for Tristram Shandy, did the regular winding of the clock regulate the functions and duties of domestic life.

THE THREE DROWNING WAVES
A Story of Port, County Donegal

Three glens strikingly different in character open westwards to the Atlantic in the hilly peninsula of Slieve Tooey in the far south-west of Donegal. The most isolated is Glenlough in the north, for there is no road in the glen and no road into it, though traces of a track, overgrown with peat and littered with blocks of quartzite, will lead you to the high lip of the glen from the south-east; you must then make your own rough way past two dark corrie lakes, where they say there is good fishing, to the few acres of sour hard-bitten 'improved' land in the level floor of the glen before it falls sharply to a pebbled beach half a mile beyond. In the solitary thatched farmhouse in the glen live a man and his son, whose only work for most of the year is to watch the sheep which graze in a broad circle among the heather surrounding the improved acres. I asked the herd-boy if the sheep didn't invade the fields at nights and why he bothered to herd them at all. He said that every night they grazed the fields and ruined the hay crops but that it would be far worse if they were busy by day as well.

A ruined byre a hundred yards away had once been made habitable and was briefly occupied in 1936 by Rockwell Kent, the American artist. Here in the following year came Geoffrey Grigson with Dylan Thomas to live for a few quarrelsome weeks. There is a brief account of their sojourn in Constantine FitzGibbon's biography of Dylan. How the soft plump town-bred Welsh poet survived in this wilderness, and how he carried in his food and refreshment is a mystery which only Geoffrey Grigson could explain.

To the south is the famous Glen of Columbkille (St Columba) a place of pilgrimage and of tourism, well known for its early Christian and megalithic remains and for the bold enterprise of Father McDyer in establishing his co-operative schemes and his folk-village. Between Glenlough and the Great Glen of Columbkille is the narrow rocky valley, now deserted in its lower reaches, leading to Port. The approach from the sea is almost blocked by a fantastic assortment of rock pinnacles, draped in spray, resembling an armada of approaching ships vainly attempting to avoid shipwreck. A storm beach of brown and white quartzite pebbles, looking like the petrified eggs of some monstrous sea-fowl, is piled high and fills the mouth of the valley. Between the beach and the sea cliff, on the north, a dark stone pier juts into the darker water, and alongside, half buried in a spill of beach pebbles, is a slipway up which heavy fishing boats are dragged into shelter behind the storm beach. On a green shelf on this north side of the deep glen is a clustered clachan of abandoned houses, roofless, their stone walls shining as if bathed in a ghostly moonlight, having the look of old bleached bones. Around them are the tumbled walls of little fields crossed by old lazy-beds, and a linear pattern of water-channels. All the fields are cropped to the quick by sheep and rabbits.

In one of the houses there once lived one Paddy Byrne, and this is his story. He had been fishing as one of a boat's crew on a day when a great storm blew up. As the boat was approaching Port the straining oarsmen were horrified to see, coming to overtake them, 'the three drowning waves'. Said the master of the boat: 'Men, there's nothing we can do save prepare ourselves to meet our Maker.' They were becoming resigned to their fate when Paddy Byrne stepped forward to the stern of the boat and stood facing the first of the three waves, a knife in his raised hand. Just as it was about to break and swamp the boat he flung the knife into the wave. The men at their oars saw with amazement that it parted and passed by harmlessly on this side and on that. Then Paddy Byrne took his oar with the others and said: 'Pull, men, as hard as you can, and we have a chance!' The second and third drowning waves were nearly on them as they reached the pier, and as the boat slipped into its shelter the waves crashed and spent themselves harmlessly on the beach.

The boat was pulled up. Paddy Byrne went home to his supper and as night came on he left the house saying he wanted to visit a sick cousin who lived some miles away at Larracanaseara. He had not gone far along the road when a stranger on horseback overtook him and invited him to lay his hand on the saddle as a help on his journey. It was a good travelling horse and they covered the ground well. By and by the horseman asked him to climb

up beside him, and together they travelled on till they got near Larracanaseara, where Byrne told him he had business. But just before they got there
the horseman said: 'I want you to come with me to see my daughter who is
lying very sick, and you are the only man who can cure her.' Byrne replied
that he had no skill in the healing art and could not see that his visit would
do any good but the man persisted and in the end Byrne said he would do
as he was asked and would see the girl. So the horseman turned off the road
at a pillared entrance and followed a winding drive till they came to a grand
house. Here they dismounted and went through the door into a large hall.
'She's in there', said the stranger, pointing to a door on the left, 'go you in.'
Byrne went in and saw a lovely girl lying in bed, groaning in pain, and as he
looked at her she said, 'You're the only one who can save me.' And she threw
off the bed clothes and lifted up her nightdress, and there sticking into her
side, was the knife he had thrown at the drowning wave. 'Pull it out', she
pleaded, and as he did so the girl stopped groaning and was completely
restored.

The stranger then invited Byrne to take food and brought him a bowl of
porridge. It was the best porridge ever he tasted, and he asked where the oats
that made the meal were grown. 'The grains were all the top pickles of the
corn', said he, 'grown at Mullaghmore in the County Sligo.' Then Paddy
Byrne knew for sure that the fairies was in it for it is their custom to steal
the top grain of every head of corn. Sure everyone knows this is why the top
pickle is always missing at harvest.

*This story was told to me by the late John Doherty, the well-known fiddler from
Upper Kilrane, near Glenties. County Donegal.*

part V

JOHN CLARKE
The Potato King

Many tributes have been paid to the work of John Clarke of Mossside in North Antrim, a potato breeder of world renown who well deserves the title of Potato King. He began his experiments in the mid-1920s, and raised thousands of seedlings before producing the first of a dozen disease-resistant varieties, which he named 'Ulster Monarch', not long before the outbreak of the Second World War. To other varieties he gave the names 'Ulster Chieftain', 'Ulster Cromlech' and 'Ulster Leader', and they played a considerable part in providing hungry war-time Britain with essential supplies of food.

Little seems to be known, however, about the man himself and his experimental methods, which I had the opportunity of observing at first hand thanks to a visit I paid to his little farm in the company of Dr Radcliffe Salaman, Fellow of the Royal Society, and Director of the Potato Research Institute at Cambridge. This was in 1945 when O'Solanum (as we called him) was engaged in writing his great book, *The History and Social Influence of the Potato*, published in 1949. We had met previously at meetings of the British Association for the Advancement of Science and had discussed various traditional methods of potato-growing such as the Irish 'lazy-bed'.

I had no warning of Dr Salaman's visit. He rang me up from the docks one morning in August 1945 to say he was in Belfast and 'would I rescue him?' I knew that at that time he was much involved in securing adequate supplies of food for the uncertain post-war years, and in fact a search for new high-yielding, disease-free stocks of potatoes was the object of his visit.

I assumed he would want to see my agricultural colleagues at the University or 'the men from the Ministry', but when I enquired he replied: 'There's only one man I must see, and that's John Clarke.' So we went in search of John Clarke at Broughgammon, a townland on the basalt plateau of Antrim a couple of hundred feet above sea level and some two miles inland. I had been told that the sea winds along the coast were one factor in the relative freedom of the country around Moss-side from potato disease.

We took the car down a narrow track ('a wee rodden') across the bog, past a small bungalow, to a glasshouse from which a tall, stooping sandy-haired man of about fifty emerged. When I introduced him to Dr Salaman he was covered in confusion and stuttered an excited welcome. He showed us rows of flower-pots, each containing a seedling potato and outside in the dark peaty soil were plots where larger mature plants were producing seeds for new varieties of potatoes. The seeds were obtained from a strange assortment of plants. One saw a tomato transformed by grafting into a 'deadly nightshade' and passing in turn into something recognizable by its larger flowers as a potato plant. They are all, as every schoolboy used to know, members of the same family. Dr Salaman expressed his surprise at the obvious success of the grafts and asked Clarke what his secret was, commenting that with the sterilized scalpels and all the specialized equipment available in his Cambridge laboratories he had rarely been so successful. For answer Clarke showed us his earth-stained thumb, its nail grown to an inch-long point with sharpened sides: 'That's the only tool I use', he said; and one had the feeling that his success lay in the dirt. I recalled having heard of similar long 'potato nails' being used in Donegal for a more domestic purpose. The boiled potatoes would be placed in a 'potato ring' (made of willows, not silver) on the floor in front of the fire and the lengthened nail would be used to peel off the thick outer skin of their 'jackets'. A more professional parallel can be found in the case of a highly successful French surgeon who was said to perform his most delicate operations with a sharpened finger-nail.

John Clarke took us for a walk around his little farm, which still retained patches of the bog (the moss, he called it) from which it had been reclaimed. He showed us his collection of flint blades and scrapers gathered from the old surface under the moss. The uppermost bog layers of sphagnum peat had nearly everywhere been cut away; it was in this top layer, he told us, that finds of buried 'bog butter' and 'beets' of flax had been made. Below this layer was a layer full of fossil logs and stumps of pine which could not be cut with peat spades and lay intact in places. At one point a line of stone slabs was visible in a vertical bogface at this level. This he interpreted as an old footpath through a wet patch between two rock outcrops. A modern path across the top of the moss lay on the same line several feet above, and our guide pointed out that it could have preserved the exact course of the original path only by the persistent use of this line as the bog grew.

The bottom layer was of black peat full of twigs and small branches of hazel, birch and willow known as gall-sticks, so soft that they offered no resistance to the breast spade with which the peat was cut. The basal layer below was mainly composed of reeds and 'horse tails'. He showed us a sample of the drains he had made in some patches of the moss which remained, consisting of a narrow channel cut into the bottom of a wider one and roofed over with cut peats.

Dr Salaman was as impressed as I was by the intelligence, skill and versatility of this 'uneducated man'. He had worked for many years on his own, almost unknown to the outside world. In time, however, the Government of Northern Ireland, recognizing that the financial reward for such work is small, made John Clarke a small annual grant, not only to enable him to continue, but in appreciation of what he had achieved already for the potato industry. In July 1950, meanwhile, he was surprised and delighted to be awarded an honorary M.Agr. degree by Queen's University, its acknowledgment of a native son, and researcher, of international repute.

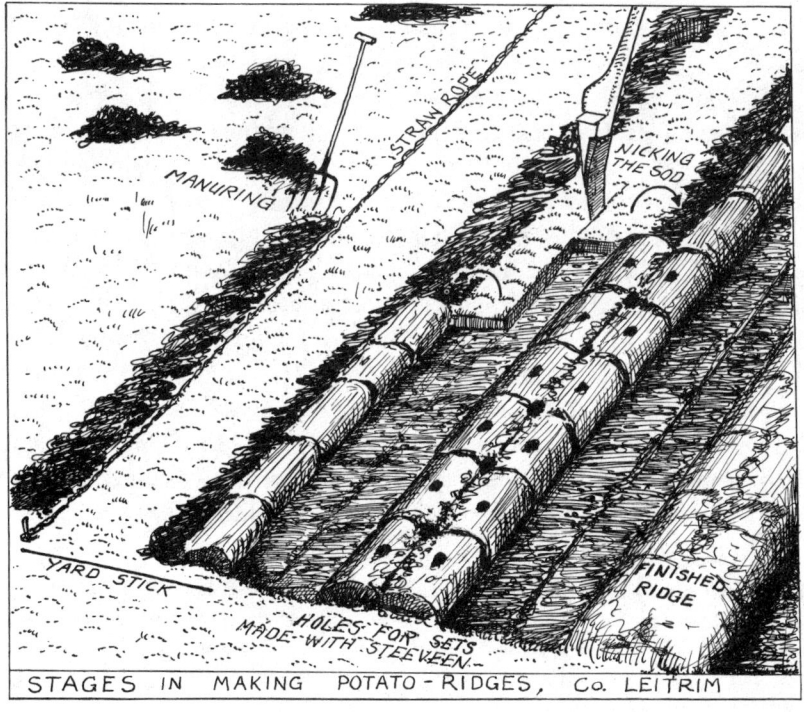

STAGES IN MAKING POTATO-RIDGES, Co. LEITRIM

WEE GEORDIE BARNETT

George Barnett, who died on 10 April 1965 in his ninetieth year, was a man of rare quality who, with little formal education, won more than local fame for his knowledge of field archaeology, botany and geology. He continued to the end not only to ask questions about the world he lived in but to explore it and to make experiments under conditions which would have daunted most of us. Slight of build and far from robust, living by himself in an ill-kept house on what seemed to be a hopelessly inadequate diet, he was sustained throughout his life by an insatiable curiosity. 'Wee Geordie' lived for most of his life at Owenreagh, in the Six Towns, County Londonderry, his farmhouse being just off the road, about three miles south-west of Draperstown, looking across the Moyola River to the Sperrin Mountains. I am indebted to Mr Sam Mawhinney, an old friend who purchased the Barnett farm after George's death, for many of the personal details which follow, and also to two other friends who knew him well, Mr James Gunn of Draperstown and Dr Desmond McCourt of Magee University College, Londonderry, and the New University of Ulster. Dr McCourt writes:

He was a natural scholar with a crystal-clear analytical mind and he was able to apply it to almost any problem. He had a burning zeal for advancing knowledge and was never happy unless he had an unsolved problem on his hands. No one could fail to be impressed by the originality of his mind. For example, he reconstructed for me, with remarkable precision, the terrain of former times in the district—woodland, bog and settlement. This he wrote in a letter,

202

in his third-grade National School handwriting, on several sheets of an old Vere Foster exercise book.

He was the second of nine children born to Mr and Mrs George Barnett of Moneyconey, the Six Towns. The Barnetts had farmed in the district for generations—Dr McCourt tells me they had moved here from the lowlands near Cookstown, probably in the 1870s—and they were presumably a planter family, but the mother, Eliza Jane McKeown, was the daughter of a butler from County Wicklow who had come to the district as attendant to visitors in the shooting season. Born on 11 February 1876, George, like all his brothers and sisters, walked to Altihaskey National School (Tullybrick). Tuberculosis took its toll of three of the family, and George himself was an ailing child. When his mother died, giving birth to twins, in 1888, a neighbour, Mary Cleary, moved in and brought up the children. He left school at thirteen or fourteen but his teachers, Mr and Mrs Charles McKenna, continued to foster his interest in natural history by lending him books. He came to know almost all the wild flowers and cultivated plants, and when I last saw him in 1963 he showed me an exercise book filled with delicate watercolour drawings of flowers collected in Glencolumbkille, Donegal, in 1959. For a time he contributed articles on natural history to the *Northern Whig*, writing under the name of J.B. McKeown. In his last years he became greatly interested in whins (gorse), observing their recovery from the cold spell of 1963: he told me he had never before seen the whins so cut back by frost.

His brothers and sisters left home in turn as they grew up, leaving him as his father's sole help on the farm. His father disapproved of his unrewarding interests and his wandering instincts, but was no doubt appeased by the boy's mechanical skills. He made his own set of carpenter's tools—planes, chisels and spokeshaves—from old scythe-blades and files, and among other things he constructed a winnowing machine and a hand-operated thrashing machine. He made ladders, rakes and chairs, and he made his own bed. Perhaps his greatest technical achievement was to make the frames of two fiddles from a tree which he felled and split into boards, using harrow-pins as wedges. He used to say that the secret of a good violin lay in the varnishes, and he spent some time experimenting with them. He sometimes played the fiddle at local dances and taught many young folk to play the instrument.

As he grew up geology captured his interest more and more. He enjoyed no farm job more than breaking—and examining—stones to mend the farm lane. Mr Sam Mawhinney relates many a story of his zeal: how, for instance, when taking a cartload of flax to Cookstown market, he noticed an unusual stone by the roadside near Lough Fea, but dared not stop to pick it up because his father was following with a second cart. He kicked it out of sight, and walked the five miles back to the spot on the following Sunday to recover it. Alas he never found it. When he had an excuse to be out at night, at a wake, for example, he would explore the countryside, returning home in time to feed the horses at dawn. He told Mr Mawhinney that at the age of fifty, when he was still 'the boy', his worldly wealth amounted to five shillings.

After his father's death, in 1931, he let the farm and went to live with a brother at Larne, where he explored the district and added to his store of geological and botanical knowledge. But after two years he returned to the Six Towns, staying first with cousins at Moneyconey and later moving into his old home, where he lived until his death. He was now free to follow his inclinations. He was very abstemious, and would spend an entire day walking the mountains with scarcely a bite to eat. Dr McCourt—a well-trained rugby wing-forward—recalls that he had some difficulty in keeping up with him. 'He moved over the hills, through bog and stream, at an incredible speed, his only sustenance being a mixture of tea-leaves and sugar. At home his staple diet was bread, butter, jam and tea. He lived on a non-physical plane more than anyone I have ever known.'

He acquired a detailed knowledge of the rocks of north Tyrone and south Derry, could spot an erratic with unfailing ease, and made an extensive collection of specimens which accumulated about the house. More than one professional geologist consulted him. J.J. Hartley, for example, in his paper 'The Geology of North-Eastern Tyrone', acknowledges his debt to the local knowledge and careful observations of George Barnett of the Six Towns. He plotted the distribution of erratics of Barnesmore granite in and around the Six Towns. He had a prodigious memory, never took notes on what he read and unfortunately left hardly any record of his many experiments and discoveries. He read whatever he could lay hands on, mainly books and articles given him by academic visitors. And he would cycle into Cookstown, when well on in his seventies, to attend lectures organized by the Workers' Educational Association.

He retained to the end a twinkling eye and a boyish sense of fun. I recall being in his house one day, talking geology. He had referred to the dressed-stone houses of Draperstown, which were 'sitting on Carboniferous Sandstone', and I asked him what we were sitting on at Moneyreagh. He replied: 'We're sitting on my old bed: underneath that there's chloritic schist!' While geologists did most to use his knowledge and recognize his work, it is his archaeological interests I want to place on record.

Of the many prehistoric sites he discovered the most celebrated is Beaghmore, that remarkable assemblage of circles, cairns and alignments which, almost hidden by peat when he found them, has since been exposed by clearance and successive excavations, and is now in State ownership. Beaghmore lies, as the crow flies across the moorlands, some six miles south-west of Owenreagh, and it is twice that distance by road, but on foot or bicycle, George Barnett was a regular visitor at all seasons—he would sit there all night to observe sunrise at midsummer—and he became convinced that Beaghmore was calendrical in purpose and was designed as a lunar observatory. If this seemed near lunacy to most archaeologists at the time, it is worth recalling that our best authority, Professor Alexander Thom, claims that 'we can be perfectly certain that some of these stone circles were set up as lunar observatories.' George Barnett's plan of the site was made with a plane-table constructed by himself from first principles.

I cannot help feeling that George Barnett may have been right in his hunch that Beaghmore was calendrical. Living close to nature, he had an instinctive approach to the life of prehistoric man. His knowledge came largely from experience, experiment, observation, and traditional lore. I remember asking him what Irish countrymen meant by 'the long eleventh of June'. He was surprised that I did not know it was the Summer solstice, and when I argued that this fell on 21 June he replied: 'We count the first of the long days.' There is in fact very little change in the length of the midsummer days from 11 June to the end of the month. He went on to speak of the 'hungry days', and said that in former times countryfolk, hoarding their meagre supplies of food and anxiously waiting for the new potatoes, would count the number of days they would probably have to wait from the long eleventh of June.

His interest in calendrical monuments led him to construct, in his rambling garden, a model of Beaghmore. This he replaced, in 1962, by a full-scale replica of Stonehenge. The sarsens, because of their great size, were made of wood, he painted them white: the 'blue stones' were painted blue, and he had a wooden sighting arrow swivelling on an upright post with which he made observations. What an extraordinary erection to come across in the wilds of Tyrone!

I should like to be able to add that he felled and trimmed the timber for this model with his own stone tools, but this I cannot affirm! Certainly he made many experiments with stone axes in the 1940s, putting his geological knowledge to the service of archaeology by selecting various fine-grained stones and grinding and polishing them into axes. He got the best results, he said, when he boiled the rough-outs in animal fat. So as not to mislead future archaeologists he would cut the word FAX (fake) into the specimens he made. Using both his own and genuine polished axes which he had found, he experimented with various methods of hafting them and—it must have been before Danish archaeologists had succeeded in felling trees with flint axes—tried them out on growing trees. He finally succeeded in felling a hedgerow ash tree with an axe ground asymmetrically so that one face was nearly flat. And he fashioned from it some stools which he used in his kitchen. He came to the conclusion that the normal symmetrical stone axe could not have been used for tree-felling. No matter how sharp the edge, and how successful the first incision, axes of this shape 'bounced off' the wood. They could have been used, of course, for ring-barking and deadening trees. He made many experiments, and conscientiously used only stone tools in making his axes.

Towards the end of his life he helped Mr James Gunn to collect folk material for a museum at Draperstown. He was a storehouse of lore, and was always ready to talk to the enquiring student. He was fond of composing poems—I have one entitled 'My Bonny Moorhen' and others 'Glenelly' and 'Rosey O'Neill'—and could recite them at length. Given further education he might have become an Irish Gilbert White. Yet one wonders whether book learning would not have dulled his curiosity and killed his initiative.

The district in which he lived is predominantly Roman Catholic, and one would have guessed from his sense of values, his indifference to worldly possessions, and his reverence for the past and for traditional ways that George Barnett was of native Irish stock. Certainly no one could have been better loved than he was. 'His funeral to Six Towns churchyard was the largest ever seen in the district', wrote Mr Mawhinney. 'They came from the mountains and lowlands, from cities and towns to pay their last respects to Wee Geordie. Soon there was a beaten path to his grave made by visitors.' Who will pretend to understand Ireland, to reconcile its bigotry and its compassion? This proud Irishman was a Presbyterian. 'A firm believer in predestination, he knew the Bible well, was a non-smoker and took no interest in the ladies at any time.' Another of his interests was panning for gold—in the Moyola River. Mr Mawhinney wrote: 'If there are any minerals on Heaven's eternal shore, Geordie will find them.'

[*Ulster Journal of Archaeology*, 3rd Series, 29 (1966)]

MISS MARY McMURRY (MAISIE) GAFFIKIN

Miss Maisie Gaffikin's name will be familiar to readers of the *Ulster Journal of Archaeology* from its frequent appearance in the early volumes of the present series, but only those who were associated with her in the years before the war of 1939–45 know the full value of her enthusiasm and her devoted work for archaeology. By her death on 25 September 1959, many archaeologists both here and throughout these islands lost a firm friend and one who was in her active years a most generous colleague. Miss Gaffikin lived at Newcastle, County Down, where she had a host of friends, ranging from archaeologists and academic folk to people from every class and walk of life who shared her interest in games and sports or in bridge, music, flowers and embroidery. Above all she enjoyed open-air sports of all kinds: hockey, golf, angling, shooting, stag-hunting. She was president for several years of the Irish Ladies' Hockey Union, and her sister Elsie (Mrs Charters) was a well-known international player. But in the years 1930 to 1940 archaeology came first among Miss Gaffikin's interests, and not unnaturally when the family moved to Newcastle, the sandhills were her special playground, whether as golfer or archaeologist.

When I first met her, Maisie Gaffikin was beginning to enlarge her love of field sports into an interest in field studies and prehistory. Both sides of her family had shown historical interests. Her mother's father, John Horner (1858–1919), was a Belfast business man who built up a vast collection of spinning-wheels and other textile gear which he presented to the Belfast Municipal Museum in 1909. He was author of a book entitled *The Linen Trade of Europe during the Spinning-Wheel Period* (1920). Miss Gaffikin's father was in the linen business and had been a keen cricketer and rugby football player. I remember him telling me that he played for the first international rugby team Ireland ever fielded. The family lived in grand style at Ardglass Castle before the decline in the fortunes of the linen industry in the 1920s, when they moved back to Belfast. The Gaffikins had also thrown up a local historian in the person of Thomas Gaffikin, author of a booklet on *Belfast Fifty Years Ago* (1894). Miss Gaffikin's grandfather, I have been told, was the builder of Queen's Elms, opposite Queen's University, which became a hall of residence: the present Students' Union stands on the site.

When the family returned to Belfast in the late twenties, Miss Gaffikin began to develop her interest in field studies and became an active member of the Belfast Naturalists' Field Club. In the early 1930s she was the moving spirit of the archaeological survey organized by the Club, and devoted her resources, energy and enthusiasm to preparing distribution maps of field monuments and portable antiquities. She visited many of the museums of the British Isles in her search for Ulster material. About this time she approached the University to enquire whether they offered any courses which she might take, but the only archaeology then taught was that of the classical world.

She found a ready helper, however, in the Professor of Anatomy, Thomas Walmsley, who, with characteristic kindness, arranged to give a special course on the elements of anatomy and prehistoric archaeology, which she persuaded her close friend, Mrs Norah Anderson of Ballee, near Downpatrick, to share with her. When Dr Oliver Davies and the present writer began a series of archaeological excavations, starting at Goward near Hilltown in 1932, these two were our most willing helpers. Altogether Miss Gaffikin must have taken part in nearly a score of excavations, mostly on megalithic sites. With the present writer she combined to publish the results of the Field Club survey in a paper on 'Megaliths and Raths', which included distribution maps of these monuments which she had prepared (*Irish Naturalists' Journal*, vol. 5, 1935, pp.242–52). For the subject of her presidential address to the Field Club in 1938 she chose 'The Bronze Age in Ireland'. She undertook some minor investigations on her own, especially in the Dundrum sandhills, but she always preferred to help others and could rarely be persuaded to lecture on her work. Her biggest adventure was attendance at the International Prehistoric Congress at Oslo in 1936, where she presented the results of a typological analysis of Ulster megaliths. When the *Ulster Journal of Archaeology* was revived in its third series in 1938 she was a member of the sponsoring committee and continued to support the *Journal* until her many voluntary war-time activities came to absorb most of her time.

Miss Gaffikin was an amateur in the best sense of the word. She wanted always to share her interest and knowledge, and had no thought, for instance, of amassing a private collection of antiquities. When the Ministry of Finance agreed that the Ancient Monuments Council should undertake a preliminary survey of Ulster field monuments, she was one of the most enthusiastic helpers. It was almost entirely her generosity, as a car owner, that enabled me, for example, to visit nearly every prehistoric site of importance in Northern Ireland. Her natural charm and her love of people and of country ways gave her the entry to any house, from mansion to mud cottage. I owe her more than I can say for such a many-sided introduction to Ulster. She always lived up to her rollicking, galloping surname, which I had first come across in one of the characters in Siegfried Sassoon's *Memoirs of a Fox-Hunting Man*. Her mother, a lady of exceptional grace and distinction, once told me that she had written to Sassoon to enquire where he had obtained the name Gaffikin. The reply was that it was the name of an undergraduate he had known at Cambridge: this was Maisie's brother George, who was killed early in the war of 1914–18.

Maisie herself had never married. She had been one of the many Ulster girls whose betrothed were slaughtered on the Somme when serving in the 36th (Ulster) Division. They had been recruited from the Ulster Volunteer Force (Carson's Army) which had been illegally trained to fight in support of the partition of Ireland and now found itself ready to be sent to France, where they were almost wiped out. About a million men and boys, some no more than fourteen, were killed on the Somme in 1917, and in all the fighting armies on both sides lost nearly six million lives.

Maisie herself was in a sense a war casualty, but found solace in games and in archaeology.

[*Ulster Journal of Archaeology*, 3rd Series, 22 (1959)]

DISPUTING WITH DE VALERA

I once had the experience of spending an evening in Dublin with Eamon de Valera. It was in 1975, when, as President of University College, Dublin, he presented me with an honorary degree. The orator on that occasion was Dr Tomas Ó Fiaich, who said that I was the only lecturer he had heard who had made reference to the place he came from, Crossmaglen.

Dev's youngest son, Rory, was one of the company. We had both worked on Irish megaliths and carried out excavations, particularly on the long court graves of Ulster and Connacht. We held rather different views as to their origins: he believed that the large court graves, like the round passage graves, had reached Ireland direct from Western Europe, whereas I took the view that the former had come to Ulster via Scotland. Three years later, when Rory was propounding his opinions in an extra-mural seminar at Irvinestown in County Fermanagh, he tragically collapsed and died.

Some years earlier he had written me a generous letter thanking me for leading the way in the excavation and interpretation of Irish megaliths. In the course of the dinner the subject of megaliths could hardly be avoided, and I told Dev how Rory had explained his involvement in the study of stone monuments:

My father often took me with him when he was canvassing in County Clare, and I was utterly tired of hearing the same speech over and over again. To give me something to interest me father would point to a nearby standing stone or megalithic tomb and tell me to examine it.

Now Clare is full of megaliths, and my father was so long-winded that I had ample time to study a great number. That was how it all began. After many visits to Clare I must have seen nearly every megalith in the county.

I don't know whether Dev realized what I was saying; he registered no emotion at all, but I have since been told that he expected Rory to follow him into politics, and that he disapproved of his appointment as Professor of Archaeology at University College, Dublin. Whatever the truth of the matter, beyond question is the great value of Rory de Valera's *The Court Cairns of Ireland*, published by the Royal Irish Academy in 1960; and this is the review of it I was asked to contribute to *Studia Hibernica*.

*   *   *
*   *

Professor de Valera, in his monumental paper of 140 pages, has concluded a vast undertaking and carried it through with single-minded dedication to his chosen subject. I suppose I can claim to be partly responsible for it since the burden of his paper is a refutation of the theories about these monuments first advanced by some of us in Belfast a quarter of a century ago. It should be explained to the non-archaeological reader that this lengthy monograph on the court cairns has nothing to do with the rituals of the court, nor with royal breeds of dogs. Court cairn is a name invented by Dr de Valera to take the place of horned cairn, which was a term popularized nearly thirty years ago when we began excavating in the north, and which then came into the receptive subconscious of James Joyce, as readers of *Finnegans Wake* may remember. For this or some other reason the term horned cairn is now replaced by court cairn, though in fact the word cairn should also have been changed since it is the megalithic structure rather than the cairn itself that is diagnostic.

Court cairns are a highly specialized and localized variety of chambered megalithic grave: they are defined as megalithic structures taking the form of segmented gallery-graves which are provided with curved orthostatically defined entrance features (horns or courts) and which are set in long cairns usually trapezoidal in plan. Such monuments, first recognized as a class in Connacht by that remarkable pioneer Wood-Martin in the 1880s, display considerable structural diversity, but they stand apart from the more spectacular Boyne tombs and others of similar style (the passage graves) which have a terminal chamber and are invariably set in round cairns. It was in 1815 that John Bell of Newry first drew the attention of the learned world to the horned type of monument in describing the now destroyed megalith at Annacloghmullin in County Armagh, which he astutely compared with one at Ballybriest in County Londonderry. Thus, from last century, curious observers had nibbled at the intriguing problem of the court cairns from both ends of their Irish range. It was not until the 1930s, however, that a serious attempt was made, by a group of Belfast archaeologists, to classify, excavate and interpret these puzzling Irish monuments. It soon became clear that they have not only a very distinctive architectural style but a striking distribution pattern. They are virtually confined to Ulster and north Connacht. Here then, within the unmistakable unity of the West European Megalithic Culture, is a dramatic demonstration of prehistoric regionalism. How did the court-cairn culture arise? So far, no ardent regional patriot has put forward the easy solution that it all began in County Tyrone, in the centre of the Irish court-cairn region. An ingenious archaeologist might well prove this by morphological analysis and statistical juggling, but no one would take him seriously. Professor de Valera has proved to his own complete satisfaction that the culture was diffused across Ireland from north Mayo and Sligo. Is he to be taken any more seriously?

It is tacitly assumed by archaeologists that we must look to diffusion from the south to explain the origins of megalith-building in north-western Europe. The great weight of evidence from history and prehistory is in favour of cultural diffusion and not of multiple origins. So far as concerns these islands at least, nearly all students admit that we have to deal at this period with secondary diffusion, since it is common ground that the megalithic idea is not indigenous. Therefore we seek a point or points of entry where we suppose the megalithic idea must have been first planted. When the Belfast group began theorizing about horned-cairn origins they were aware that very similar monuments occur in Arran, Argyll, the Clyde and south-west Scotland, as well as in the Isle of Man and parts of Wales. In Ulster we found a strong concentration around Carlingford Lough, and when the grave goods which we excavated turned out to be very closely allied to those of the Clyde group we postulated an entry into the Irish Channel culture-area from the south. Before long the Clyde-Carlingford culture had been widely publicized by writers such as Gordon Childe, Grahame Clark, Stuart Piggott and Glyn Daniel. Of course we were no nearer the ultimate origin of the horned cairns. Nor indeed is Dr de Valera, who concludes his long enquiry with the remark: 'The origin of the Irish court cairns remains unsolved.' But he is quite convinced that the diffusion across Ireland took place from west to east. Can he convince his readers? Let it be said at once that whether he is right or wrong, he has given us, in trying to prove his point, an invaluable corpus of material for future workers to draw on. This is not the place to attempt a detailed criticism of his thesis, but it is proper in a general review to warn readers that although the arguments seem convincing and even overwhelming all is not so well proven as might appear. Dr de Valera doth protest too much, and it seems to me that he has piled up so much on such insecure foundations that in the end his edifice threatens to collapse under its own weight.

To begin with—and this was his starting-point—he lays great stress on statistics. Before he took up the court cairns we had by working outwards from County Down, recognized over one hundred sites, but we had done no field work in Connacht. It is a measure of the professor's zeal and energy that he has raised this figure to 218, and great credit must go to him for his industry in tracking down new sites and investigating old ones. He would be the first to admit that a good many sites remain to be discovered (or identified after excavation), and equally I would be the first to admit that more new cairns are likely to turn up in the west than in the east. Incidentally, his method of locating sites on the six-inch maps, while giving great precision in the map-room, is of little use in the field. Recently I tried to find on the ground a megalith which he describes at Streamstown, County Galway, and which was wrongly located by G.H. Kinahan in 1872. It is not marked on the map, and I had to measure in the winds of Connemara, with a foot-rule, 51.6 cms (imagine it!) from the western edge and 11.2 cms from the southern edge of the sheet. I found the site more by instinct than by information. But when will the Ordnance Survey do its duty by revising its maps and marking on them all these precious relics?

Does it follow, however, that the areas where the court cairns are most numerous are the points of entry? None of the known invasions or cultural innovations which can be traced in Irish history has had its starting-point on the remote and wild west coast. One is tempted rather to think of the coastlands of Mayo and Sligo as areas where old-fashioned ways persisted so long that they look like congested districts on the megalithic map. Why, if the voyagers came here from the south, did they not land on the south coast, or on the west coast south of Galway Bay? The answer given is that 'entry through the Kerry massif would be most difficult' and that the 'voyagers from the south touching our western coast … might well be forced to proceed northwards to Killala before achieving any notable success' (p.45). And why, having landed in Mayo, did they not move south-eastwards into Leinster instead of making north-eastwards into Ulster? When one considers that there is evidence of almost continuous megalithic settlement along the northern coasts of Ireland from Killala to Carlingford, is it not likely that colonists from the east reached the west by sea, stage by stage, and that the spread inland was from several coastal foci? In saying this I am not implying that the court cairn reached eastern Ulster ready-made from the south. Rather I think it likely that in this area, which had long been occupied by pre-megalithic peoples, various innovations were made, as a consequence

213

perhaps of the trade in flint, which resulted in the local development from a relatively simple megalithic tomb (such as the portal dolmen) of the ritual and architectural features of the classic court cairns. It is difficult, for instance, not to connect the trapezoidal shape of the finest cairns and the occasional subsidiary chambers with the Cotswold long barrows. Then there is the site at Ballymacaldrack, County Antrim. I named this Doey's Cairn in honour of a great Irishman, Andrew Doey, on whose farm it lay, but Dr de Valera drops the name and would like to drop the cairn as well. It is a court cairn of unusual construction which yielded a rich assemblage of grave-goods, purely Neolithic in character, and evidence of cremation rites strongly suggestive of links with Yorkshire. The sealing of the entrance was untouched and contained polished stone axes *in situ*. Yet Dr de Valera believes that the rear chambers were removed at some period and replaced by a flax-drying kiln. The argument is very involved, but even if I have mis-understood can it be imagined that the megalith would have been thus vio-lated at a period when superstitious beliefs would have been strong, or that the busy kiln-users would have left no trace of their presence? I suspect that Doey's Cairn raises awkward problems. Yet these relations with Britain have to be faced whether one thinks of ideas moving west or moving east: Dr de Valera says little about them and he gives no maps of the court cairns out-side Ireland.

The most ingenious part of the paper concerns the morphology of the galleries and courts and the question of their orientation. If the reader finds the typological jargon annoying let him remember that archaeologists like other scientists must standardize their terms if they are to communicate with one another. Even so, we could have been spared some of the tedious minutiae. I cannot think that the construction of two chambers rather than three reveals a vital difference of faith or age and I suspect that this typo-logical juggling could be so framed as to prove any thesis.

Great stress is laid on the distribution of full-court cairns, that is those in which the court feature is entirely enclosed by orthostats save for a narrow entry. They occur almost without exception on the west coast, and they are exceptional also in having no sill-stones between the segmenting jambs. These elaborate and distinctive forms are apparently regarded as the start-ing point of the whole series; and yet the more complex the style the less chance there is of finding overseas parallels. The hint that we may have to look to Malta is not very helpful.

The section on orientation is both ingenious and ingenuous. The favoured E–NE orientation is strongest in the west. The Armagh tombs are particularly offensive as being 'deviationist' or 'offending', and the explana-tion naively offered is that the builders of the dual-court cairns of south-west Ulster—those in which paired galleries face in opposite directions—became so confused as to which was 'the business end' of the cairn that their descendants, colonizing Armagh, lost the rule of orientation!

The truth is that the time is not yet come for such weighty hypotheses. What is needed is excavation of western monuments, of which only one, Creevykeel, has been fully investigated. On the whole such evidence as exists suggests a fairly late date for Creevykeel (say 2000 BC) but until we have a full series of excavations and C14 datings it is premature to lay down the sequence of tomb-types in the north of Ireland. The present paper will certainly stimulate argument and lead to fresh discoveries and ideas; and this is the justification for publishing new theories, however ill founded they may be. What matters is that facts should be carefully distinguished from opinions. There is much special pleading and much involved and even tortuous writing in this paper. The author is so wrapped up in his megaliths that there are times when he does not make his meaning clear. There is a tendency to dismiss awkward facts as 'so exceptional as to warrant little stress'. A monument such as Ballymacaldrack is cited when it suits but dismissed as unreliable when it doesn't. But what matters is that the facts are on the whole fairly given, and the many plates of tomb-plans are invaluable.

Once, indeed, Professor de Valera weakens so far as to concede that the absence of the flint hollow scraper from Scottish court cairns constitutes a difficulty in the proper sequence from Ireland to Scotland. But his conviction is generally strong enough to overcome such weaknesses. After all, if it had not been so strong this fascinating paper would probably never have been written.

[*Studia Hibernica*, 1 (1961)]

ADOLF MAHR
Archaelogist and Nazi Spy

It may be noted that earlier in this century the making of stone axes for a commercial purpose had been a minor industry in mid-Antrim. W.J. Knowles records that genuine axes made of stone from Tievebulliagh were so plentiful (he himself said that he obtained over 2500 from Glen Ballye-mon) and were so keenly sought by private collectors and museums that local farmers began making them for sale. This put an end to collecting for a time.

One of the keenest collectors of axes and other artifacts later on was Dr Adolf Mahr, Director of the National Museum in Dublin. Born in Austria, he was a good archaeologist and I came to know him well. He published a comprehensive survey of Irish prehistory in 1937. In Dublin he became a powerful force. Membership of the Royal Irish Academy is a much-prized honour to which I did not then aspire. All I know is that Mahr told me one day that I was now an MRIA. (Nowadays, quite eminent people are proposed more than once before they succeed in being elected, and I did not even know that my name had been proposed.) Mahr invented what he called 'the ether test', by which, he claimed, the presence of machine-oil on the surface of a polished axe could be detected and forgeries revealed. We often discussed archaeological topics and monuments, and I showed him many of the famous sites in Northern Ireland. Only later did I suspect that he may have been spying out the land for a sinister purpose.

216

His appointment as Museum Director in Dublin when there were, I believe, excellent applicants for the post from Britain, seemed to illustrate the strength of the hatred of all things British prevailing in Éire in the years following Partition. In fact it was another German who was first appointed, Mahr succeeding him on his early death. I could not believe the rumour that, like many other scholarly Germans, Mahr was a dedicated Nazi. But apparently he had been a young museum assistant in Germany looking for a faith, and though first tempted to join the Society of Friends, eventually he fell under the evil spell of another Adolf. I was profoundly shocked to learn subsequently that he had told a Dublin archaeologist that after the war, following the German victory, he would see I was made Gauleiter of Ulster!

Suspicion fell too on another German, a certain Herr Hoven, then living in Belfast, though officially domiciled across the border. He often called to see me, and I once asked him when he hoped to return to Germany. His unguarded reply, 'Not until early September', seems to have been prophetic, for war was declared on 3 September 1939. I should add that neither Mahr nor Hoven, to the best of my knowledge, was ever charged with spying, for legally they were residents in a neutral country.

Mahr wanted to enrich the collections in Dublin and questioned both the claims of the Belfast Museum and the quality of its staff and of the inspectorate in Northern Ireland. The senior civil servant who was in charge of historic monuments was a Trinity College historian who had little archaeology, and Mahr described him to me in this way: 'He is just a big fat elephant: he is hard to move, and ven he does move, he goes in the wrong direction.' Classical archaeology was then taught at Queen's in Belfast but no Irish archaeology, and no prehistory.

Mahr appeared to take a special interest in coastal sites, especially on the Lecale coast of South Down, but only some years later did I discover a possible explanation. In 1941 I had occasion to check the condition of some stone monuments there which I had listed earlier. I found that the roof of one of the early corbelled structures had been removed, and when I peered inside I found myself staring into the barrels of half-a-dozen heavy machine-guns, pointing out to sea. Belfast was being heavily bombed by German planes at the time (as I well remember, for the house near the University where I then lived was hit by an incendiary bomb) and I came to realize that it was the possibility of their use as defensive posts which probably explained Mahr's particular concern for these apparently innocent historic monuments along an 'invasion coast'.

IN AN ORANGE LODGE IN PARIS

Over a period of forty years, in the course of my wandering through every part of Ulster in search of ancient monuments and archaic buildings and tools, I became friendly with countrymen of many different religious and political faiths who shared my interest in the countryside. Some of them are themselves human antiquities with extreme beliefs on both sides of the religious divide. I have learnt a good deal from them, Protestant and Catholic alike. They share an interest in the old ways of the countryside, and this gives them a common Irishness. I remember a farm labourer, a fervent Protestant and Orangeman, scornful of the superstitious beliefs of his Catholic neighbours, inviting me to admire the may-blossom on the 'lone thorn' standing at the entrance to his roadside house with the remark, 'You'd think the fairies was in it.' At the same time they also have in common a simple belief in the bigoted views of their teachers.

The most remarkable illustration of this came from a small hill farmer who lived on the tilted edge of the basalt plateau overlooking the north coast of County Antrim. Under the appearance of a rough man-of-the-world—he had worked in many parts of Britain and North America and had served in the Merchant Navy—he hadn't lost his Irishness and his faith, he was a very pious Catholic.

I called on him one day when I happened to be wearing short trousers which were long by modern standards and came well below my bony knees, which anyhow had little flesh on them. He tapped me on the knee with a finger, and gave me a lecture on the perils of the flesh and the sad decline in moral standards. In a sentence which, however improbably, combined three major sources of evil, he said solemnly: 'It all began with a bad woman in an Orange Lodge in Paris.' His favourite pastime, I should add, was spying through a powerful telescope he had acquired in his sea-faring days on lady bathers undressing on the sandy beaches below.

I have wondered whether this pathetic credulity in matters of religion might, in part, explain the gullibility of both sides in accepting extreme political views. His surname was typically Scottish Presbyterian, an example, perhaps, of what is best illustrated by Eamon de Valera, that it is the children of those who 'marry-in' who become the extremists.

TURNING THE PAGES OF THE PAST

I like to question students entering my Department at Queen's on the books they have read and enjoyed most. I think some of them must have got wind of this, for I find it hard to believe that so many have found inspiration in *War and Peace* when I have never managed to finish it.

On the other hand, some students object to the questioning, and recently one of them, when I probed beyond school texts and *Readers' Digests*, protested: 'Sir!: this is most irregular.'

Those of us who grew up before the mass assault of radio and television may count ourselves fortunate in having been able to keep up our early reading habits through our teens. Apart from the accident of belonging to the pre-telly age I had the good fortune to be brought up in a country manse and had access to a library which, if excessively theological, contained many of the English classics and a sprinkling of more recent works, most of which were review copies presented by the editor of a weekly newspaper to their honorary local correspondent, my father.

Among these was Nansen's *Farthest North*. Thus I was introduced to the literature of travel which has been one of my main professional and personal interests. It happens—and I think it is no accident—that the best books of exploration are inspired in their writing.

A not unusual restriction then placed on Sunday reading, that it must have some bearing on the Sabbath—though in our family profane books were not locked away as in some houses—first brought me in touch with another traveller, George Borrow. *The Bible in Spain* was strong meat to a youngster but I had only to show the title to inquisitive Sabbath-keepers to get away with it. This led me to *Lavengro*, *Romany Rye* and, of course, to *Wild Wales* and to Ford and other writers on Spain.

I felt I had a personal link with Borrow not only because I knew some of the scenes he described but also because old members of my father's previous congregation in the Welsh church in Shrewsbury used to speak of a tall, spare stranger who once slipped into a back pew: it was said to be Borrow brushing up his Welsh before one of his marathon walks into the Principality.

In my mid-teens I came across a work which has continued to be my favourite bedside book. It was Rev. Gilbert White's *Natural History of Selborne*. I can still recall the excitement of this discovery, the thrill of finding that a country clergyman had written so naturally, so intimately and so observantly about the birds and beasts and flowers and the untutored customs of the people of his beloved corner of the county of Hampshire. I can never see a magpie drop out of the chestnut tree in my garden in Belfast without remembering White's phrase: 'They flutter with powerless wings and make no dispatch.' The beauty and economy of his style, a style familiar to me from the reading of the Bible which was part of our life, must have left its mark, for a reviewer of my first book on Ireland, *Irish Heritage*, compared its 'unassuming and direct style' with that of the *Natural History of Selborne*.

I read every book of Richard Jefferies, William Cobbett and W.D. Hudson that I could come by. My favourite was *A Shepherd's Life*, through which I was introduced to Salisbury Plain, an area in which I later spent a year engaged in archaeological fieldwork. But Hudson's South American books also attracted me, and led me to Bates' *On the Amazon*, Darwin's *Voyage of H.M.S. Beagle*, and Bent's *Naturalist in Nicaragua*.

From Latin America my reading moved to the Levant and Arabia with Kinglake's *Eothen* and Charles Doughty's *Arabia Deserta*. Doughty was the last great writer to model his prose consciously on the Bible, and for this reason and also because his style is in the tradition of the strong prose writings of the Elizabethan explorers he made a deep impression on me. Later, when T.E. Lawrence wrote *The Revolt in the Desert*, the ground he covered was well-trodden holy ground, for the Hills of Moab were as familiar to my generation as the Mountains of Mourne to Ulster folk.

Another writer whom I recall with delight is Edward Whymper, scrambling in the Alps and the Andes. And from the high slopes of the Andes memory turns to the Pacific and to Herman Melville. Melville moved me

221

not only by the splendour of his prose and the majesty of his theme but also by his mastery of biological and technological details. But the detail that comes to mind as I write betrays my landlubberly instincts, for I think of the moment when the whalers felt home-sick for New England as they sniffed from afar the scent of new-mown hay blowing off the Andes.

I suppose it was this early interest in books of travel and in intimate descriptions of different ways of life that led me to geography and to a special concern for understanding the life and personality of the little countries, the *pays* and the *paysan*. Certainly it explains the kind of novel I like best. My preference is for the regional writer, for Thomas Hardy, Mary Webb, Brett Young, Winifred Holtby, Henry Williamson, R.D. Blackmore and, with some reservations, Rudyard Kipling, R.L. Stevenson, H.G. Wells, Arnold Bennett and D.H. Lawrence.

In French, too, my preference is for the older regional writers such as Balzac and Georges Sand. I often wish I could express my feelings towards a *pays* in the form of a novel. I suppose for one of my training the nearest I shall come to it may be a narrative account of my experiences in Ireland, after the fashion of Lloyd Praeger's *The Way That I Went*. Of this book, by the way, a famous English scientist remarked that he would rather have written it than all his own scientific books.

Of the general novelists I have mentioned, the one who gave me most pleasure was Mary Webb, because she wrote of scenes I knew, in the borderland of Wales, in an idiom I understood. The posthumous fame achieved by *Precious Bane*, which was first published in 1924, owed much to Tom Jones, who was the first professor of Economics at Queen's University. I have been told that Mr Stanley Baldwin, as he then was, asked his Cabinet under-secretary for a book he could take with him on a walking-tour into Wales. Tom Jones handed him *Precious Bane*, and Baldwin's introduction to a new edition of the book brought it well-deserved fame.

In these recollections of books that have influenced me I have made no mention of those which stand somewhat apart from the central line of development of my reading. Examples which come to mind are Edmund Gosse's *Father and Son*, and Samuel Butler's *Notebooks*.

Unlike many academics, I have never been addicted to thrillers, but I remember vividly a book in this genre which was part of my early Sunday reading and which, like *The Bible in Spain*, presumably won respectability by its title. It was called *The Adventures of Latimer Field, Curate*. I have never seen the book since, but I recall it with more awe if with less pleasure than *The Adventures of Sherlock Holmes*. I wonder if any of my readers remember it?

[*Belfast Telegraph*, 28 November 1960]

epilogue

ECOLOGY AND CULTURE IN IRELAND

Estyn Evans and 'The Trilogy of the Humanities':
An Appreciation by John Campbell

'You remind me so strongly of my dear lamented Fleure, who startled us by beginning lectures on almost any subject with the Ice Age.' E. Estyn Evans to C.O. Sauer, 4 May 1971[1]

'arrives my need/for antediluvian lore' Seamus Heaney[2]

Emyr Estyn Evans (1905–89) established the Department of Geography at Queen's University, Belfast in 1928, became the University's first Professor of Geography in 1945, and eventually, in 1968, the Director of its new multidisciplinary Institute of Irish Studies. On his arrival in Belfast, a youthful twenty-three year old and a newcomer to Ireland, Evans could scarcely have suspected that his entire professional career, in fact the rest of his life, would be spent there, or that henceforth his research and teaching would be largely devoted to interpreting the life and landscapes of Ireland.

Yet his intellectual pre-formation already ensured what were to be the fundamental, lasting and distinctive features of his cultural geography. Born at Shrewsbury in English Shropshire to Welsh and Welsh-speaking parents, Evans' childhood home was a Presbyterian manse in a village so close to the border that he attended secondary school in Wales, at Welshpool. Life in this Anglo-Welsh marchland gave Evans an acute awareness of the historical mingling of contrasting traditions, and thus he acquired from youth the detachment that comes from knowing both sides of a case. As he was to maintain in an early paper, and always to reiterate, such regions held considerable potential for fruitful cross-border interchange and co-operation.[3]

225

The rural sympathies this upbringing nurtured emerge in that sensuality which so enlivens Evans' geography:

I have the sharpest recollection of the sensual thrill of things seen, smelt, tasted and felt in a material world to which the doors of perception were wide open ... It was a world apart from the unreal other world of Sunday school with its deepening darkness ... I dimly felt that I belonged to the real world of nature, attracted to its beauty.[4]

Thus he found Thomas Hardy's rustic geo-piety compelling , and the evocations of his native Shropshire in A.E. Housman's lyric poetry and Mary Webb's mystic novels.[5] And later, like many a contemporary, he was doubtless confirmed in his 'frankly ... pagan' outlook by the graceful prose of Frazer's *Golden Bough*, with its revelations of religion's origins in primitive magic and ritual.[6]

When in 1922 Evans went up to the University College of Wales, Aberystwyth, his imagination was fired immediately by the lectures of H.J. Fleure, Professor of Geography and Anthropology. Indeed, Fleure was to become his revered master, and the dedicatee of his book *Irish Heritage*. A zoologist by training, Fleure had turned subsequently to anthropology, pioneering the geographical study of human physical types in England and Wales.[7] Informing this work, and the very bedrock of all his other researches and teaching, was Darwin's theory of evolution by natural selection, and that theory's equally revolutionary corollary, the inclusion of human kind, in all aspects of its life, within the natural order:

his vision has seized the world of thought. ... For him the great succession of living things have been responding to environmental influences and have been influencing their environments throughout; these ecological relations are for him the very core of the mystery of life.[8]

With Evans' love and knowledge of the countryside from boyhood, he was naturally responsive to this evolutionary credo; and, in particular, he admired Darwin's consummate skills as a field naturalist, all the more so because he too was a native of Shrewsbury, to Evans a never-failing source of pride. Under the stimulus of Fleure's teaching, therefore, Evans' thinking was set, broadly speaking, in the mould of evolutionary natural history. Alive to the possibility of cultural diffusion at all times in human history, he learnt to portray 'regional social evolution as a continuous interaction between people and their environment'.[9] On the same ecological grounds he was to share Fleure's scepticism about those universals severally proposed by developmental sociologists, positivist historians and environmental determinists: 'We must think of the world's peoples as groups seeking the good life in different ways with different difficulties and opportunities.'[10]

When Evans came to Ireland, nothing more clearly revealed his inclination to natural history than the confidence he placed in first-hand field observations. Ireland's own tradition of field natural history served to rein-force this trust, and he was to remain particularly appreciative of the topo-graphical botany of R.L. Praeger, that tradition's most illustrious current representative.[11] Quite consciously, Evans identified himself and his work with the Ulster field club movement,[12] becoming a member and ultimately president of both the Belfast Naturalists' Field Club, and the Belfast Natur-al History and Philosophical Society.[13] In this way, the inspiration he drew from the works of earlier English naturalists like Gilbert White and Richard Jefferies, was in time complemented by familiarity with contemporary stud-ies by local naturalists, most notably by the photographer R.J. Welch.[14]

In seeking evidence to reconstruct the Irish past, Evans preferred to depend primarily on field studies, on what the naturalist's alert eye could discover in the landscape, what the archaeologist's spade and trowel could disinter, and what conversation and interviews with country men and women could recover of customary practice, myth and dialect. For him, document-bound history—the history of the historian *sensu stricto*—was in scope too confining, in social and cultural range, and in span of time. In Ire-land, moreover, he felt it specially vulnerable to other failings—too great a concentration on the deeds of ruling, frequently alien, minorities, and a related tendency to misrepresentation and ideological distortion, due to his-torians' over-reliance on past accounts written to legitimate the currently powerful.[15]

So while prepared to use documents where appropriate, Evans held that a great deal was lost, or seriously misconstrued, if field evidence was ignored. This premise had as its counterpart his firm belief that 'an obses-sion with book learning has tended to divorce education from reality', and that in 'scholastic Ireland' especially there was much to commend more practical forms of instruction.[16] It is clear, for instance, that one reason Evans respected the archaeological research of Michael O'Kelly, the exca-vator of Newgrange, was because of his versatile ingenuity:

His innate curiosity has never been satisfied with orthodox views or explanations; again and again he has put forward his own theories and submitted them to experimental test. His enter-prise has been well illustrated and rewarded in his successful efforts to reconstruct ancient methods of smelting iron and in experiments to investigate, and to put to the test gastronomi-cally, the methods of operating the ancient Irish cooking places (*fulachta fiadha*).[17]

Another, parallel expression of this same basic conviction was Evans' regard for those he called 'natural scholars', talented 'amateurs' from all walks of life whose field studies were driven by an irresistible urge to know, and understand, more of the world about them. Besides some of the indi-viduals memorialized in this book—Barnett, Gaffikin, Clarke—other out-standing examples would include his long-time friend George Paterson,

227

erstwhile grocer and later curator (and virtual creator) of Armagh County Museum,[18] and Arthur Pollock of Downpatrick, night telephonist but also folk historian and archaeologist of County Down.[19] And in remarking Evans' recognition of their unique gifts, it is worth recalling evolution's sanction of individuality: in the words of Fleure, 'one of the main functions of society is the promotion of individuality, so as to guard against the fossilization of its ideas and consequent degeneracy'.[20]

Field studies certainly enabled Evans to make rapid early progress with his researches, particularly in archaeology;[21] and, as G.F. Mitchell's autobiography shows, they also quickly won him the friendship and esteem of fellow naturalists in Ireland.[22] At times, admittedly, his confidence in field evidence could appear almost exaggerated. When, for example, he was brought an Eskimo harpoon head, found by a farmer at Millin Bay on the Ards Peninsula, Evans said that to dismiss it as a chance find would be 'timid and unscientific': instead he sent it for further examination by Christopher Hawkes and his colleagues at the British Museum. They were 'absolutely certain' that it was of 'archaic Eskimo origin'; and Hawkes tentatively linked its discovery with the thirteenth-century Norwegian overlordship of both Greenland and the Kingdom of the Isles, and more specifically with the assembly of a great Norse armada in the Firth of Clyde in 1263.[23]

The trust Evans put in field studies sprang ultimately, as we have seen, from his contention that in Ireland, as elsewhere, an understanding of ecological relationships was fundamental to comprehending society, and social change. In turn, this necessarily implied an emphasis on traditional means of livelihood: the words economy and ecology, after all, have a common root in the Greek word *oikos*, meaning household.[24] In keeping, therefore with Evans' ecological approach was his insistence that the pastoral heritage had been of central importance throughout Irish history. If widely prevalent in Atlantic Europe, as shown in his Frazer Lecture, its impress in Ireland was, he asserted, especially deep and indelible, a claim amply corroborated by several more recent historical accounts.[25] Pastoralism was virtually a natural vocation, a fitting adaptation to a moist, evergreen habitat, itself the result of insularity, and Ireland's extreme maritime location on the Atlantic seaboard. Thus, an Irish farm traditionally was reckoned not by its extent, but its stocking capacity; rural settlement, and ties of kinship, were largely those appropriate to pastoralism, not crop-growing; occasional fairs sufficed for commerce in livestock, so towns were few;[26] and the key dates in the farming calendar were those associated with the breeding and keeping of stock, transhumance—the summering of herds and flocks on upland pastures—often helping to make the most of what nature offered.[27] Consequently,

The arts that spring from a rich soil and an urban environment have been slow to develop. There is no splendid architecture, no tradition of orchestral music, of famous theatres or anything requiring large endowments and capital expenditure. The pastoral heritage lays emphasis on personal qualities and kinship rather than on communal expression and civic pride, on art forms requiring little equipment.[28]

Indeed, such were this heritage's ramifications that Evans contemplated the possibility that British parliamentary democracy might not be the most suitable form of government for Ireland.[29]

If Evans' preoccupation with pastoralism, and other traditional means of livelihood was conspicuously ecological, additional, less well-known concerns of his were just as plainly natural historical in character. A case in point was his interest in, and early promotion of, research on the physical anthropology of Ireland's population.

There had been, at the beginning of this century, a widespread acceptance, scholarly and popular, that 'race' determined levels of intelligence, social progress and cultural attainment. Furthermore, the still lively evolutionary debate fostered the notion that racial traits were attributable to a people's natural environment, so that attempts by historians, ethnologists and geographers to explain history against its geographical background were then legion. The Belfast-born historian and diplomat, Viscount Bryce, for instance, envisaged the history of the Scotch-Irish in terms of this assessment of their pedigree: 'they unite the tenacity, perseverance, and shrewdness of the Scotsman of Alban with the fire, dash and geniality of the Celt of Erin'.[30] His fellow-countryman and contemporary, Leopold Bloom, was to offer precisely the same kind of explanation in a cabman's shelter conversation:

Spaniards, for instance ... passionate temperaments like that ... It comes from the great heat, climate generally ... My wife is, so to speak, Spanish, half, that is ... She has the Spanish type. Quite dark, regular brunette, black. I, for one, certainly believe climate accounts for character.[31]

Racial and geographical studies were thus inextricably linked; and so it was to Evans' great advantage that his teacher, Fleure, was among the modern scientific pioneers of British physical anthropology. Following him, Evans dismissed outright the idea of pure races and severely criticised the simplistic, prejudiced racial explanations of history commonplace earlier in the century. He rejected any portrayal of Irish history as the product of a putative 'Celtic race'; and argued that more physical anthropological survey should be undertaken in Ireland, for its own sake as an objective analysis of the island's population, but also as a means to detect the vestiges of those peoples responsible for earlier cultural innovations. Accordingly, his first research student and teaching assistant, John Mogey, carried out a field survey of human physical types in County Antrim; and among the types he found were lineal descendants of the first Irish men and women, responsible for the introduction of Mesolithic culture into the north of Ireland.[32] His findings were supported not only by Antrim's wealth of Mesolithic artefacts, but also by the survival, along the lower Bann and on Lough Neagh, of fishing gear and practices, ostensibly of equally remote antique derivation. [33] When taken together with the results of later, more extensive Irish physical anthropological surveys, Mogey's research helped persuade Evans of the lasting Mesolithic contribution to Ireland's cultural heritage: 'I like to think that a Mesolithic heritage may explain, in part, the Irish fondness for lake islands, manifest in late Bronze Age lake-dwellings, in early Celtic and medieval crannogs, in many a Christian monastery and in a long poetic tradition culminating in "Innisfree".' [34]

His recognition of Mesolithic survivals—human animal as well as cultural—testifies, in turn, to Evans' acceptance of 'the doctrine of survivals'.[35] This methodological concept was widely deployed in evolutionary anthropology after its formal introduction by E.B. Tylor;[36] and, in fact, Evans' recourse to it was particularly frequent. Because he believed that Ireland, by virtue of its extreme peripherality in the Old World, and its insularity, was almost pre-ordained to act as the last refuge and rich storehouse of peoples and cultures long ago displaced, or submerged, elsewhere in Western Eur-ope. By the same token, what was true of Ireland as a whole, applied even more so, in his view, to its more remote, less well-endowed districts: 'In the north of Ireland the culture-lag, already apparent in the northeast, increases towards the west: the centuries fall away as one approaches the Atlantic, and to journey from west to east is to travel into the past.'[37]

Some have recently questioned Evans' designation of 'survivals' and more especially his presumption of their greater persistence in the west of Ireland. And it must be frankly conceded that to argue from supposed survivals has always been a procedure with its doughty critics. Since in this respect Evans is best known for discovering 'surviving' open-field agriculture (rundale), and associated settlement nucleations (clachans), in N.W. Donegal,[38] it is apposite to mention here the objection, entered as long ago as 1893, by the English historian F.W. Maitland. He raised:

a gentle protest against what I think the abuse of a certain kind of argument concerning 'village communities'—the argument from survivals. Some quaint group of facts having been discovered in times that are yet recent, some group of facts which seems to be out of harmony with its modern surroundings, we are—so I venture to think—too often asked to infer without sufficient investigation that these phenomena are and must be enormously ancient, primitive, archaic, pre-historic, 'pre-Aryan'.[39]

Leaving aside for the moment the sufficiency of Evans' Donegal investi-gation, to such criticism has lately been added a second charge—that to seek relics in the west of Ireland is to succumb to the shallow romanticism of the Celtic Revival,[40] to fall prey to its 'invention of tradition' and the glorifica-tion for nationalist ends, of a Gaelic western heartland.[41] Of culpability on this second count, surely, Evans is entirely innocent, in part because of his dismissal, already noted, of a 'Celtic race' with its own, nation-justifying his-tory,[42] and in part because in *Irish Heritage* he expressly stated: 'I have not concentrated on the Gaeltacht in seeking survivals'.[43] Also, some search for survivals in the west was undeniably warranted by the findings of such schol-ars as J.H. Delargy of the Irish Folklore Commission. Thus, in his Sir John Rhŷs Lecture, on the subject of the Gaelic story-teller, Delargy said:

it must be emphasised that these traditions in Gaelic are not necessarily to be associated exclu-sively with Celtic civilization. Apart from the huge mass of customs and beliefs in Irish as well as English, some of the wonder tales also contain unmistakeable evidence of having belonged to a pre-Celtic civilization, perhaps pre-Indo-European. A number of these tales may have been told in Ireland in Megalithic times; indubitably, certain elements in them go back in Ireland at least as far as the Bronze Age.[44]

C. Ó Danachair's studies of material folk culture have lent some further credence to this thesis of western Irish survival;[45] and without question, what Evans was sure were long-surviving artefacts—the paddle curragh, the corn-drying kiln, the hand quern, the byre dwelling, the bed outshot—did help convince him that districts like north-west Donegal were, indeed, true cul-tural refuges. Appearing, too, to uphold this verdict was his discovery there in 1937 of a local social system of nato-locality, and bilateral descent, subse-quently outlined *in extenso* by the social anthropologist Robin Fox in his book *The Tory Islanders*. Described therein 'as a living example of an ancient system ... a social fossil that still works and thrives', its links on Tory with open-field agriculture corroborates Evans' earlier contentions.[46]

Of course, in the particular case of surviving rundale, and clachan clus-ters, Evans' inference of antiquity was based also on more widely drawn evi-dence. Thus his own Donegal find was in fact only the most famous of sev-eral similar discoveries made in the western British Isles by students of Fleure;[47] and the thrust of these investigations was to be maintained by sub-sequent research undertaken at Aberystwyth.[48] Later too, several of Evans' research students, notably D. McCourt, V.B. Proudfoot and R.H. Buch-anan, did prove rundale's more extensive presence in Ireland in the recent past, although they were unable to show conclusively its antiquity, or that of its assumed concomitant, the clachan.[49] Nor could they adequately confirm Evans' further conjecture that, from at least the early Iron Age onwards, proto-typical clachans had co-existed in the rural settlement geography of

Ireland with a dispersed form of settlement, with its prototype in the free-standing raths, the farmsteads of the ancient Celts. Undeterred, Evans sought to sustain his conjecture, first, by reference to the old Irish law tracts, and their clear 'distinction between warrior herdsmen living in isolated "raths" and lowly cultivating peasants, presumably clustered together in clachans'; and, second, by appeal to the philological research of L.R. Palmer who 'believes that single farms and collective settlements were established Indo-European institutions before 2000 BC'.[50]

Nowadays, among experts on the historical geography of lands adjoining Ireland, we can find some openly critical of 'survivals', but others implicitly favourable to the sort of argument Evans advanced for north-west Donegal. Thus, R.A. Dodgshon deplores 'the myth of archaism' in his consideration of the ecology of Highland peasant farming 1500–1800;[51] whereas, with equal cogency, G.R.J. Jones for Wales, relying in part, like Evans, on early law tracts, continues to reason the case for continuity, and has long since extended its ambit to England.[52] In Ireland, meanwhile, some would now reject Evans' settlement thesis as without any solid foundation;[53] others would regard it as unproven;[54] and still others would see it, as Evans evidently did himself, as 'a wild surmise',[55] a working hypothesis worth retention by future scholars. And just how valuable a hypothesis it is, in fact, can be judged by this statement by one of today's leading authorities: 'It is probably approximately true to say that, in seventh-century Ireland, dispersed settlement was the expression of free status, nucleated settlement the expression of servile or semi-servile status.'[56]

Whatever the reality, or otherwise, of this, and other kinds of 'survivals', Evans' concern with them itself betrays a perspective on the past which, once again, can be seen as distinctly natural historical. Its backward reach, as noted already, was unhindered by the temporal constraints to which the written-source based historian is liable. Attentive to sometimes long lasting natural rhythms and cultural episodes, the past as conceived by Evans was, therefore, very decidedly that of *la longue durée*.[57] It stretched far back into—and beyond—the remotest periods of prehistory, and stressed the continual making and remaking, physical and organic, of the land itself. Indeed it was to Ireland's geography that Evans ultimately attributed the Irishness of the Irish, and, above all, the pronounced conservatism of Irish civilization, and its enormous capacity for absorbing newcomers and their cultures.[58] Again and again, for example, he reaffirmed the definite Irish proclivity for religious syncretism, and the quite remarkable persistence of 'the Elder Faiths', whether the megaliths' age-old associations with fertility, or the equally enduring faith in the sanctity of island sites, and the holiness of wells, derived from an originally (Mesolithic?) pagan belief in the vivifying power of water.[59]

As new excavations and scientific dating prove Ireland's longer prehistory—the Irish Mesolithic is now known to have begun a millennium earlier than was believed just thirty years ago—the simple fact of its increased duration weighs powerfully in favour of Evans' case for continuity and conservatism. But strengthening that case also has been the revolt of many Irish prehistorians against 'the invasion hypothesis'[60]—the notion that prehistoric cultural change in Ireland was essentially episodic and attributable to periodic incursions by new communities and/or ideas. Now these prehistorians presuppose steadier cultural change, and ascribe a larger role to indigenous circumstances—in short, they place more emphasis on continuity.[61] Small wonder then that Evans' writings often foreshadowed this new thinking; or that he should have found it possible to concur with modern views. For example, Evans had long been aware that expert opinion was uncertain as to why, and how, Megalithic civilization spread;[62] and eventually he rejected the traditional orthodoxy—of large-scale, long-distance trafficking along the Atlantic seaways—preferring instead an interpretation which allowed for greater continuity. This was Case's idea of moderately sized communities moving, probably seasonally, over only limited distances by land and short sea-crossings:[63]

the roots of regional personality in north-western Europe are to be found in the cultural experience of pioneer farmers and stockmen, quickened by the absorption of Mesolithic fisherfolk who were familiar with the Atlantic seas and who could have picked up ideas and techniques anywhere along the line. We must still reckon with a primary diffusion of crops and animals from the Near East, providing a more or less common base of material culture, while holding that the megalithic idea was expressed in different forms and different rituals from one region to another.[64]

In similar fashion, one current appraisal of Iron Age Ireland, as subject only to limited, and cumulative Celticity,[65] accords well with Evans' own, earlier estimate: 'the price of this conquest was the loss of many elements of Celtic culture or their adaptation to the Irish environment and to long-established native tradition. The art of the Celtic overlords, for example, quickly develops forms and features which are insular and distinctively Irish'.[66] When he made this statement, moreover, Evans had the reassurance of knowing that the linguistic evidence was on his side. He well knew that J. Morris Jones had long ago explored the pre-Aryan syntax in insular Celtic, reaching conclusions largely confirmed by J. Pokorny; and he was to remain an enthusiast of this research's continuation at Queen's by H. Wagner who, like his predecessors, sought a North African provenance for this linguistic sustratum.[67] In sum, there was much to support J.B. Bury's tentative expectation, voiced almost a century ago in his Cambridge inaugural: 'the Celtic world commands one of the chief portals of ingress into that mysterious prae-Aryan foreworld from which it may well be that we modern Europeans have inherited far more than we dream.'[68]

By now it should be clear that many major *leitmotifs* in Evans' work—his commitment to field studies, his concern with traditional means of livelihood, his 'race' interest, his quest for survivals, and his vision of the past through natural historical spectacles—do all appear to set him unambiguously in a British scholarly tradition which, from the late nineteenth century onwards, sought to establish a natural science of society. His first attempts to classify Ireland's megalithic monuments point towards this. Take the particular case of dolmens: their simplicity and architectural naivety suggested to Evans two alternatives: either they represented a temporally early stage, the primitive prototypes of a series of monuments which, as megalithic civilization evolved, underwent structural elaboration; or (and more probably) they marked a late stage, the degenerate end products of this same sequence of evolutionary change.[69] Yet, it must be said—and stressed—that these and like conjectures were doubtless *faute de mieux* made necessary by the nature of the subject matter, and the dearth of available evidence. Because when and where it was, or became possible, Evans clearly did prefer to make interpretations more closely approximating a judicious balance between the natural historical and the cultural historical. As, 'The portal-dolmens may perhaps be seen as the triumphant marks of a resurgent Mesolithic (or "secondary neolithic") culture which had been won over to husbandry, for the burials they contain were accompanied by native tool-kits and "Sandhills" pottery.'[70] To infer, therefore, that in his career Evans showed a growing predilection for cultural history is to ignore the character and circumstances of his early (largely archaeological) research; and, more importantly, to overlook the fact that his passion for natural history had never precluded strongly humanistic sympathies—evident in his study of languages (Latin and French) at school and university; in his familiarity with the classics of French human geography and of the *Annales* school of historians; and, preeminently, in his high regard for the teaching of the mature Fleure, in his late forties when Evans first encountered him. For by then Fleure was championing 'the trilogy of the humanities'.

The Trilogy of the Humanities in Education,[71] a talk given in 1918, was the most complete and probably best known exposition of Fleure's argument—the imperative need forthwith to combine the perspectives of anthropology, history and geography. So vital did Fleure consider their combination that he felt bound to renew his advocacy on many occasions during the inter-war years:

Anthropology must emphasize the discipline of type, History the discipline of time, Geography the discipline of place, and all three must cooperate among themselves, and with other studies as well to record more adequately and to interpret more fully and more usefully the course of human experience, individual and social, past, present and possible.[72]

To Fleure, the outbreak of the Great War was not unconnected with a perniciously analytical and materialistic trend in thought, and his humanistic trilogy he saw as one means to the realization of a more spiritual and integrated world view. The promise was of a 'new humanism' whose creation 'is not a matter of simple transference of principles from biology to the humanities; [since] we all recognize the differences that mind has made'.[73] In this candid recognition of mind some might perceive divergence from the strictly scientific tenets of late-Victorian natural history, but Fleure—and many of his contemporaries—would not have thought so,[74] though unquestionably the trilogy did bring about a change in the sorts of work he did.[75] By 1935 he had fixed on *human ecology* as the best description of what his trilogy entailed;[76] and just two years later Evans would equate his own endeavours with this same humanized natural history:

The term 'human ecology' has come into use to fill that gap in our scientific nomenclature which has been somewhat hesitantly occupied by the name 'human geography' ... It is an inevitable extension of the ecological study of plants and animals, which, for the human ecologist, fall into place as part of the interacting environment out of which and in which man has evolved. In this view it is false to attempt to interpret the present without a knowledge of the past: history cannot be isolated from geography any more than geography can be divorced from anthropology.[77]

So, from his very earliest years in Belfast, 'my brand of anthropogeography' meant for Evans a search for 'the common ground between the natural world and cultural history'.[78] Its aim, therefore, was a natural history, and hence those diagnostic hallmarks extensively discussed already. But it was also something more than that: it was a natural history which took mind into account by weighing the respective contributions of habitat, heritage and history; and these three terms offer, therefore, appropriate headings under which to round out this consideration of his treatment of Ireland.

Evans' position on humankind's relations with habitat faithfully expressed his humanism. While, on the one hand, he was fully cognisant of the natural realities, and frequently deplored their neglect by historians, on the other hand, he always held that human adjustment to environment was active, not passive, that culture was the invariable medium of environmental appraisal, that resource presupposed the resourceful. On the largest view, this was to insist on the significance of Ireland's setting, as part of the insular and peninsular Atlantic zone of Europe, stretching from north Portugal to Norway.[79] Which meant *pari passu* frankly acknowledging the consequences of Ireland's position within the British Isles: 'Lying as it were in the lap of the larger island, Ireland's contacts with the outside world, whether social, cultural, economic or political, became largely concentrated in one direction, and an obsession with—or reaction against—links with Britain was correspondingly sharpened.'[80] And if this sounds fatalistic, then read the estimate of P. Vidal de la Blache, founder of modern French geography: 'Trop voisine de l'Angleterre pour lui échapper, trop grande pour être absorbée par elle, l'Irlande est victime de sa position géographique.'[81]

Envisaging Ireland as integral to Atlantic Europe implied also a need to revise the conventional sub-division of the British Isles into a Highland Zone in the north and west, and a Lowland Zone in the south and east. Fleure would have added a third, Atlantic Zone, including Ireland;[82] and certainly Evans thought this valid, as much of Ireland was lowland, because its peripheral uplands had been much fragmented and lowered by quickened denudation and, perhaps most of all, because throughout history—and prehistory—its insularity had been synonymous with the maritime diffusion of populations, artefacts and ideas.[83] Thus he contended that during prehistory parts of Ireland had lain within the orbit of sea-focussed cultural provinces, like the Larne-Oban culture of the Mesolithic, or the Clyde-Carlingford of the Neolithic, which his own extensive digs among the Ulster court graves had helped to define.[84] And in this latter instance, to be sure, the case Evans argued against R. de Valera for eastern maritime entry does appear to have been vindicated by subsequent archaeological research. For on the present, albeit limited and perhaps imperfect radio-carbon evidence, the court graves are of more recent date with increasing distance inland from Carlingford Lough.[85]

Nowhere did Evans disclose the mark of the natural environment better than in local studies in which he marshalled patiently gathered field observations. *Mourne Country* (1951), for example, was the result of such intimate familiarity, and was largely written 'at a little window on the seaward slope of Slieve Donard, where I had only to lift my eyes to see the hills and watch the coloured seasons climbing from the golden whins to the glowing heather and the snows'. His portrait depicts what Fleure would have called 'a region of difficulty': a compact, granite-cored, soaring massif, further isolated by its southerly projection, and for long therefore culturally recalcitrant, as resistant to early Christianity as it was later to the Anglo-Normans. Nonetheless, over the centuries, human toil and ingenuity had slowly made its sea-girt fringes tractable, almost fertile, and to the well-being of communities there the granite quarry and sea fishery had latterly added their contribution, making Mourne, at last, 'a beggar's mantle fringed with gold'.[86]

As this and other transformations demonstrated, ecological conditions changed continually: cultures could enrich—or indeed impoverish—their natural environments, and in the process themselves alter greatly. An instance of enrichment Evans often cited was the advent of oats in Ireland, probably in early Celtic times: its bounteous harvest under overcast skies and on acid soils, he felt, may have been an important factor in the agricultural revival of the Early Christian period: 'Among the older cereals the cultivation of wheat (presumably autumn sown) would have left the land exposed to leaching through the wet winter months. Not only were oats spring-sown but they were also food for man and, including the straw, for beast'.[87]

Of the environmental harm done by human intervention, he believed there was nothing in the island's past to compare with its experience of repeated deforestation. In part this loss of tree cover was due to renewed depredations by grazing livestock, and in this regard at least, Ireland's pastoral heritage had exacted a heavy ecological toll.[88] Evans indicated, as well, that climatic change could sometimes supervene, and accentuate damage initiated by human agency; as had probably occurred when the impoverishment of upland soils by late Bronze Age farmers coincided with the climatic deterioration of the sub-Atlantic phase, with the resultant extensive growth of peat bog.[89] Even so, thanks to human inventiveness, the bog became thereafter a resource of great variety, though in Evans' judgment some of its uses were only derivatively utilitarian. Thus he was inclined to interpret 'bog butter' as originally a form of sympathetic magic; for in his view, the depositing of butter in bogs was a practice probably Celtic in origin, likely associated with the transhumant movement of herds, and intended to induce more abundant herbage for summering cattle. Of the more prosaic, orthodox interpretation of this practice, he conjectured: 'the utilization of the preserving qualities of the bogs was a secondary discovery hit upon by the chance recovery of an underground ritual offering'.[90]

By heritage Evans understood 'the unwritten segment of human history, comprising man's physical, mental, social and cultural inheritance from a prehistoric past, his oral traditions, beliefs, languages, arts and crafts'.[91] In Ireland, as mostly elsewhere in the world, 'the people without history', and the principal bearers of heritage, were the peasantry. And in all Evans said of the Irish peasantry, what he conveyed most impressively was his sincere respect; for a rural heritage whose sheer resilience witnessed its close adaptation to habitat, and the embodiment of values conducive to social permanence and stability. On occasions, indeed, he pointedly chose to discuss customs, superficially crude, which on a closer, more sympathetic scrutiny, he proved were not without some reason or justification. Such a custom was 'ploughing by the tail', the practice of attaching a horse to the plough (or harrows) by its tail. Regarded by the English as self-evidently barbaric, and made illegal by them as early as 1635, what appeared its senseless cruelty later provoked in Ireland denials that the practice had ever existed, let alone continued, and an accompanying counter-charge of English falsehood and black propaganda designed to malign the Irish. The practice was, however, well authenticated; and, as Evans explained, was suited to the use of light wooden ploughs, drawn by equally light horses, on stony morainic soils: 'it had the advantage that the horse would stop if the plough struck a rock, thus saving the share, the traces and the ploughman from injury'.[92]

What this example incidentally reveals, moreover, are themes pervading much else Evans wrote on material folk culture, namely, the fitness of an artefact to its purpose, the significance of ecological context, and the desirability of practical knowledge gained from actual use. Take, for example, his comments on the half-door characteristic of the Irish peasant house, variously, a source of light and ventilation, a regulator of draught to the fire, a barrier to unwanted animals, as well as a convenient arm rest for those engaged in conversation, or mere contemplation.[93] Or, again, consider the following explanation of the enormous geographical diversity of spade types across rural Ireland:

Local craftsmen supplied the precise requirements of the district, a balance of many factors, such as conditions of soil and slope, methods of digging, types of crop, stature and physique, cemented by usage and superstition and so interwoven with other culture-elements that the whole acquired a high degree of resistance to change.[94]

The better to reveal such aspects of folk artefacts, Evans typically supplemented his written descriptions with pen-and-ink sketches, and dimensional line-drawings. These had the further advantage of showing how artefacts reflected the raw materials selected and used. In addition, the illustrations made it easier for Evans to concentrate attention on form as the least changing of an object's components. It enabled him, for instance, to propose antecedents for the simplest present-day corbelled structures—pig sties, well covers, sweat houses and the like—in a vernacular tradition with its roots in megalithic architecture.[95] Equally striking were those instances where he revealed that perpetuation of form had survived the overseas transfer of an Irish tradition, as, for example, in the case of the Scotch-Irish house on the forested Appalachian frontier of the early United States. Drawing in part on the work of Henry Glassie, he demonstrated that here the Scotch-Irish, by adopting and adapting the log-house from their German neighbours in Pennsylvania, were able to reproduce most of the morphological features of their old houses in the north of Ireland—a single room wide, one (or one-and-a-half) storey building, with gable-end chimney, opposed front and back doors (half doored), and a kitchen/living room focussed on the open hearth.[96]

Paradoxically, Evans' well-rounded accounts of material folk culture have led some—the poet John Hewitt included—to complain of a corresponding inattention to non-material culture.[97] These rebukes are, however, ill-conceived. In the first place, Evans held that in literary Ireland scholars had for too long discounted the material conditions of ordinary daily life, so that now, with rural craftsmanship in decline, it was all the more urgent to rectify this marked defect.[98] Thus he consciously sought to redress a previous imbalance in cultural description but did not deny the need for a balance to be struck.[99] The critics also err in not appreciating that Evans saw culture as all of a piece, a seamless whole whose constituents, material and non-material, interpenetrated inextricably. To exemplify: he argued that the folklore attaching to certain shrubs and small trees—the rowan, holly, elderberry and whitethorn—originated as long ago as the third millennium BC when Ireland's first farmers were clearing the forest; for palynologists had found that the shrubs and small trees venerated by custom were the very same that flourished as weeds in the first forest clearances, being as such 'a token of the fulfilment of harvest and the promise of renewed life'.[100] Indeed, in all Evans' wrote of the overriding historical importance of the common man and woman, there can be few statements more impressive than his declaration: 'The crafts of arable farming, of animal husbandry and the home industries have done more to shape our instincts and thoughts than the trampling of armies or the wrangling of kings which fill the documents from which history is written.'[101]

In the knowledge of this, and similar, statements, it is no exaggeration to claim that a geography of *mentalités* is at least pre-figured in Evans' cultural geography. And this claim is additionally justified because Evans did not restrict himself to links between material and non-material culture. For he appreciated that 'the astonishing virility'[102] of Irish folkways depended on their enduring responsiveness to expressions of reason and unreason in traditional society, on their capacity to resolve, or alleviate, the anxieties, tensions and contradictions intrinsic to any social order. Can this be doubted after readinghis descriptions of the hellraising commonplace at Irish fairs and customary at Irish wakes? Or when, with reference to the Elder Faiths, he quoted the advice given to M.J. Murphy by a County Tyrone countryman, 'Leave old thorns and priests alone; give them their dues and leave them alone'? Or, again, where he cited the following boast by a practitioner of traditional cures in County Cavan: 'Some people waste time quacking around with doctors before coming to me for the cure'?[103]

Of the trilogy of the humanities, history was the least elaborated upon by Evans: there is no chapter on history in *The Personality of Ireland*, whereas habitat and heritage merit a chapter each. He was nevertheless fully persuaded of history's significance and he warmly welcomed the emerging corpus of scholarship in Irish social, cultural and economic history. Most evident was his understanding of how much Ireland had changed from the eighteenth century onwards. Thus, in his several essays on the rise of Belfast, he remarked the heightened tempo of city life from that century; and by adverting to the influence of aristocrats like the Donegalls, and industrialists like E.J. Harland, he came closer to *histoire événementielle* than in most else he wrote. Arguing in the same vein, but with wider purview, he emphasised just how different was the New Society established in Georgian Ireland. This had, he stated, 'almost entirely an imported culture', reliant on foreign artists and silversmiths, architects and stuccadores: consequently, 'it turned its back on the Irish heritage ... which was preserved in the impoverished "hidden Ireland" of the Gael.' And yet, as he further asserted, that native heritage would not be denied, and would long defy suppression:

If the New Society left a lasting mark on Irish life and landscape, the gentry stock came in time to be profoundly affected by the older Irish heritage and to provide leaders for the nationalist cause; and in the end, in the last hundred years, some of its members were to prove their Irishness by making brilliant contributions to creative writing.[104]

What this passage also makes plain is that Evans' relative neglect of history was due, in no small measure, to the enormous potency he ascribed to Ireland's heritage. In his judgment, it had required the Great Famine of the 1840s, and its traumatization of the Irish peasantry, finally and most terribly to subvert that heritage: 'The famine ... was a great social watershed and it marked the end of an era that might well be termed prehistoric.'[105] It was a conclusion latterly vindicated, as Evans himself noted, by modern research on the history of Irish Roman Catholicism. For the Famine is now seen as a principal cause of the 'devotional revolution', and its conversion of the Irish people from their hitherto limited religious observance into one of the most pious societies in Christendom. During the preceding hundred years, so this argument goes, modernising forces had seriously compromised the Irish language, and other elements of the Irish heritage, thereby weakening the traditional foundations of Irish identity.[106] The cataclysm of famine accelerated the process: by undermining popular belief in the efficacy of the pagan Elder Faiths, it removed yet another set of traditional props and means of identity. So an ideological substitute became all the more necessary and urgent, and this the Catholic faith provided: 'The old ideal that there was a common Irish identity indifferent to religious belief was thus superseded by the concept that Catholicism was the essence of Irishness.'[107]

240

This suggests something more however: that if theocratic Ireland emerged from subversion of the Irish heritage, then Evans' personal experience of that heritage's lingering vestiges must have made him a better historian. For to become aware of the powerfully disruptive forces responsible for expunging those vestiges was to know the quickening pace, and growing scale of contemporary social change.[108] Thus his folklife studies convey the distinct sense of 'an Ireland that is passing away':[109] of the products of rural craftsmen displaced by machine made, mass-produced goods; of lore and legend of immemorial antiquity finally obliterated by the combined and cumulative effects of emigration and urbanisation, universal education and the mass media, improved rural communications and the all-pervading money economy. And confronted by this thoroughgoing, irrevocable social transformation, Evans could not remain unmoved. Though far from sanguine about peasant proprietorship, and wary of peasant tendencies to political illiberality, he felt bound none the less to voice his deeply held physiocratic sympathies. In characteristic evolutionary idiom, he indicted urban life for its 'specialisation and artificial values', and explained why he preferred the mores of vanishing peasant society: 'The peasant, in continuous touch with the whole cycle of production, can sense the wholeness of life and derive therefrom satisfaction and self confidence'.[110] It followed that an end to the peasantry, and mores conducive to social maintenance and continuity, necessarily threatened stability in the wider social order: 'there are spiritual and aesthetic as well as economic dangers in rural depopulation and decay.'[111]

In consequence, Evans could contend that in an increasingly urban-industrial society, there were the soundest possible grounds for trying to keep people in touch with their roots, for finding and preserving the best of tradition, for preventing the countryside's disfigurement. And clearly therefore his preoccupations never were purely academic; but practical also, with the enhancement of social well-being as their ultimate aim. When he asked, in *Irish Heritage*, 'without an understanding of the past how can we plan for the future?',[112] this broader objective could not have been plainer.

An active involvement in public life better enabled Evans to accomplish this social purpose. Thus his pioneer archaeological surveys, and megalithic digs, greatly encouraged the creation, in 1949, of the Archaeological Survey of Northern Ireland. He was for many years a leading member and eventually chairman of the Province's Ancient Monuments Advisory Council; and he sat too on its counterpart in the Republic of Ireland. Indeed, the chief reason for his preparing the inventory of sites listed in *Prehistoric and Early Christian Ireland* (1956) was to ensure that as many as possible were officially recognized and accorded some degree of state protection.

Evans was also a vigorous advocate of rural planning, and the protection of the natural environment. As early as 1947, his report on *The Ulster Countryside* for the Northern Ireland Government's Planning Advisory Board, proposed the designation of national parks and nature reserves as ways of conserving scenic heritage and wildlife. But its recommendations were only tardily accepted, in the 1965 Amenity Lands Act, and faced with such governmental intransigence, he had no choice but recourse to other, non-legislative bodies.[113] One of these was the National Trust, and among the several properties he pressed the Trust to acquire was Murlough Bay, the scene of the Casement commemoration recounted earlier in this book.[114] Another alternative channel was the *ad hoc* Ulster Countryside Committee in whose formation he was prominent, and whose advice—as in *Building in the Countryside* (1974)—invariably received his strong endorsement.

But above all it is the Ulster Folk and Transport Museum at Cultra, County Down, that stands as the finest monument to Evans' endeavours to rescue for posterity a fast disappearing rural tradition. Of Evans' crucial role in its foundation there can be no doubt: in the words of the Museum's first director, 'While its establishment in 1958 involved the combined efforts of a group of individuals, no one member of that group has more right than Estyn Evans to cite the museum as a personal achievement.'[115] In defining the institution's function, Evans drew no distinction between the scholarly and the social: it should demonstrate to the region's people, now living in a cosmopolitan world, the depth of their roots in the local countryside, and show how traditional beliefs and practices, seemingly parochial, had parallels in other traditions World wide. In seeking to attain these goals, moreover, the Museum has realised, as Evans knew it must, a further, and in the event prophetic purpose: to reveal to Protestants and Catholics alike that apparently separate ethnic heritages are in fact commonly grounded in a longstanding, shared experience of Ulster's diverse habitats.[116]

In concluding this epilogue, and attempting to gather its main threads, the meaning Evans attached to 'geographical personality' offers a suitable theme. A metaphor found generally in regional descriptions by human geographers, and scholars in cognate disciplines, its wide employment has fostered a range of connotations.[117] To the prehistoric archaeologist C. Fox, geographical personality was solely an attribute of a region's habitat, and concerned the natural obstacles and opportunities presented to its first human inhabitants. To the human geographer Vidal de la Blache, however, 'personality' resided essentially in landscape, palpably in the many faces of France, and its regions, as modelled by successive human cultures. While to historical ethnologists, like W. Pessler and his fellow German *Kulturkreise* theorists, what made for 'personality' was a unique amalgam of spatially associated material and non-material cultural traits.[118] As for Evans' own usage three things are evident. First, his numerous references to 'regional personality' suggest how apt he considered the metaphor; and clearly he was happy to apply it to regions both small and large—to the Slieve Gullion country, Mourne, Ulster, and Ireland as a whole. Second, when he divined the 'personality' of these, and other, regions, there were often traces of each of those connotations outlined above; and this was to be expected given his avowed intention to meld habitat, heritage and history. And third, the distinctiveness of Evans' regional delineations lay not only in his integration of these several facets of 'personality', but relied also on his going beyond and deeper, to albeit tentative identifications of typical psychological dispositions. For to Evans, it would appear, regional 'personality' inhered ultimately in the personality of a region's people—hence those occasional references to 'mental outlook' in his early book on France,[119] and the similar allusions to 'regional consciousness' in his writings on Ireland.[120]

As to the inspirational sources of this psychologism, three at least seem plausible. His mentor Fleure would be one; for he too described countries as personalities, referred frequently to *genius loci*,[121] and was himself much indebted to that great British regionalist, P. Geddes[122]—directly, and through Geddes' student, A.J. Herbertson, who wrote once on 'regional consciousness, heredity and environment'.[123] Then Evans' susceptibility to the powerful sway of French thought should be remembered: to the more psychologically inclined of its human geographers and their works, but to the historians of the *Annales* also, because as one commentator has said: 'the study of mentalités was an aim common to both Marc Bloch and Lucien Febvre [and] it constituted a decisive element in the apparatus with which the founders of the *Annales* thought to renew and even to invert the historical approach to reality'.[124] Finally, if a little more diffusely, there were literary touchstones as well: Evans' boyhood favourites like Hardy, Ruskin certainly, probably Stevenson and Wordsworth, as well as Irish wellsprings of the English tradition of the regional novel. But whatever the exact sources—and not forgetting Evans' own considerable gifts—it is likely that mentality was for him the crux of the matter. How else are we to judge certain of his comments on non-material culture mentioned earlier? How else are we to interpret his belief that in political and sporting traditions lie some of most sensitive indices of Irish regional diversity? And how otherwise are we to regard his speculations on Irish national character?[125]

In *Notes towards the Definition of Culture* (1948) T.S. Eliot devoted a chapter to 'unity and diversity: the region'. There he enunciated a series of *obiter dicta* many, if not all, strongly reminiscent of observations Evans passed in his own body of work: the desirability of most people continuing to live in the place in which they were born; the significance for a culture's vigour of intensely local, as well as national, traditions and loyalties; 'the vital importance for a society of friction between its parts', including its regional parts; and the imperative need for a culture to remain open to external forces if it is to stay vibrant. And when, reflectively, Eliot warned, 'We have not given enough attention to the ecology of cultures',[126] he indicated an axiomatic relationship which Evans took as his life's work in Ireland to elucidate.

NOTES

THE IRISHNESS OF THE IRISH

1   J.C. Beckett, 'The Study of Irish History', Inaugural Lecture, Queen's University, Belfast, 1963. A book that deserves to be better known, giving a Dutch geographer's view of Ireland, is W.M. Heslinga, *The Irish Border as a Cultural Divide* (Assen 1962).

2   Grenville Cole, *Ireland the Outpost* (Oxford 1919).

3   See *Ulster Journal of Archaeology*, 3rd Series, 2 (1939), 85; 5 (1942), 98; 6 (1943), 112.

4   A.E. Hooton and C.W. Dupertuis, *The Physical Anthropology of Ireland* (Cambridge, Mass. 1955); Carleton S. Coon, *The Races of Europe* (New York 1939).

5   J.V. Kelleher, 'Early Irish history and Pseudo-History', *Studia Hibernica*, 3 (1963), 113.

6   A.T. Lucas, 'Cattle in Ancient and Medieval Irish Society', address delivered at the Dublin meeting of the British Association for the Advancement of Science, 1957.

7   A.T. Lucas, 'The Plundering and Burning of Churches in Ireland, 7th to 16th Century', in E. Rynne (ed.), *North Munster Studies* (Limerick 1967), pp.172–229.

8   Myles Dillon (ed.), *Early Irish Society* (Dublin 1954), p.20.

9   Rev. J. Ryan (ed.), *Saint Patrick* (Dublin 1958).

10 T.W. Moody and F.X. Martin (eds), *The Course of Irish History* (Cork 1967), pp.123–43.

11 *The Times*, 16 August 1967.

12 N.I. Konrad, *West and East* (Moscow 1967).

13 Dillon (ed.), *op. cit.*

14 Giraldus Cambrensis, *The Topography of Ireland*, J.J. O'Meara (ed.) (Dundalk 1951), p.87.

15 *Ibid.*, p.85.

16 AE in *The Irish Homestead*, 11 November 1916.

17 E.E. Evans, *Mourne Country* (Dundalk 1951). In this book I have tried to analyse the many ties between man and his environment. It is worth noting, in connection with the romantic literature of regionalism, that Sir Walter Scott acknowledged his indebtedness to that Anglo-Irish pioneer, Maria Edgeworth.

ATLANTIC EUROPE: THE PASTORAL HERITAGE

1   E.E. Evans, 'The Atlantic ends of Europe', *Advancement of Science*, 15 (1958), 54–64.

2   D.B. Quinn, 'The Argument for the English Discovery of America between 1480 and 1494', *Geog. Journ.*, 127 (1961), 277–85.

3   *The Book of Lecan*, cited in P. Flatrès, *Géographie rurale de quatre contrées Celtiques* (Rennes 1957), p.565.

4   Sir Cyril Fox, *The Personality of Britain*, 4th edn (Cardiff 1943). It should be added that Sir Cyril's brilliant thesis is oversimplified rather than prejudiced.

5   *The Cambridge Economic History of Europe*, J.H. Clapham and E. Power (eds), Vol. 1, Chapter 3, p.161.

6   M. Duignan, 'Irish agriculture in early historic times', *Journ. Royal Soc. Antiquaries of Ireland*, 74 (1944), 124–45.

7   G.R.J. Jones, 'Settlement Patterns in Anglo-Saxon England', *Antiquity*, 35 (1961), 221–32.

8   It is appropriate to refer here to deposits of butter in bogs. See E.E. Evans, 'Bog Butter: another Explanation', *Ulster Journal of Archaeology*, 3rd Series, 10 (1974), 59–62; and E.E. Evans, 'Dairying in Ireland through the Ages', *Journ. Soc. of Dairy Technology*, 7 (1954), 179–87.

9   C.S. Coon, *The Races of Europe* (New York 1939), pp.376–84; E.A. Hooton and C.W. Dupertuis, *The Physical Anthropology of Ireland* (Cambridge, Mass. 1955), pp.239–43.

10   P.R. Giot, *Brittany* (London 1960).

11   M. Louis, 'Les sépultures de la civilisation pastorale campignienne du Languedoc méditerranéen', *Bull. Soc. Préhist. France*, 43 (1946), 88–91.

12   R. de Valera, *Survey of the Megalithic Tombs of Ireland*, Vol. 1, County Clare (Dublin 1961), p.166. For a recent contribution to the study of place-names and transhumance in Wales see M. Richards, 'Hafod and Hafoty in Welsh Place-Names', *Montgomeryshire Collections*, 56 (1959), 13–20; and M. Richards, 'Meifod, Iluest, Cynaeafdy and Hendre in Welsh Place-Names', *Montgomeryshire Collections*, 56 (1960), 177–87.

13   G.F. Mitchell, 'Post-Boreal Pollen-Diagrams from Irish Raised-Bogs' (*Studies in Irish Quaternary Deposits*: No. 11), *Proc. Roy. Irish Acad.*, 57B (1956), 185–251; A.G. Smith, 'The Atlantic Sub-Boreal Transition', *Proc. of the Linnean Soc. of London*, 171 (1959–60), 38–49; H. Godwin, *The History of the British Flora* (Cambridge 1956).

14   P.R. Giot, *op. cit.*, p.169.

15   H.N. Savory, 'The Atlantic Bronze Age in South-West Europe', *Proc. Prehist. Soc.*, 15 (1949), 128–55.

16   T. Pennant, *A Tour in Scotland and Voyage to the Hebrides* (Chester 1774), p.29. For a full study of the use of gorse in Ireland see A.T. Lucas, *Furze: A Survey and History of its Uses in Ireland* (Dublin 1960).

17   J. Iversen, '*Viscum, Hedera* and *Ilex* as Climatic Indicators', *Geol. Foren. Stockholm Forh.*, 66 (1944), 463–83.

18   P. Flatrès, *op. cit.*, p.566.

19   R.U. Sayce, 'A Few Elements of British Folk-Culture', *Montgomeryshire Collections*, 45 (1938), 171–182.
     On the introduction of the sycamore to Britain, see E.W. Jones, 'Acer L.', *Journal of Ecology*, 32 (1944), 215–52, where Germany is favoured as place of origin. The oldest known plantations, however, appear to have been in Scotland.

20   J.P. Mahaffy, 'On the Introduction of the Ass as a Beast of Burden into Ireland', *Proc. Roy. Irish Acad.*, 33 (1917), 530–8.

21   G.F. Mitchell, *op. cit.*, p.245.

22   H. Hencken, 'Lagore Crannog: An Irish Royal Residence of the 7th to 10th Centuries AD', *Proc. Roy. Irish Acad.*, 53C (1950), 1–247.

23   A.T. Lucas, address delivered at the Dublin Meeting of the British Association for the Advancement of Science, 1957.

24 E.E. Evans, *Irish Folk Ways* (London 1957), p.35.

25 E.E. Evans, *Ulster Journal of Archaeology*, 3rd Series, 10 (1947), 61.

26 For Norway see R. Frimannslund, 'Farm and Neighbourhood Community', *Scandinavian Economic History Review*, 4 (1956), 62–81.

27 G. Story, *An Impartial History of the Wars of Ireland*, 2nd edn (London 1693), p.16.

28 S. Erixon, 'West European Connections and Culture Relations', *Folkliv*, 2 (1938), 137–72.

29 M.T. Hodgen, *Change and History* (New York 1952).

30 E. Fowler, 'The Origins and Development of the Penannular Brooch in Europe', *Proc. Prehist. Soc.*, 26 (1960), 149–77.

31 H.J. Fleure, *Some Aspects of British Civilization*, The Frazer Lecture, 1974 (Oxford 1948).

THE PYRENEES

Works referred to in the text include the following:

P. Arbos, 'La Plaine du Roussillon', *Annales de Géog.*, 19 (1910), 150–68.

O. Barré, *L'Architecture du Sol de la France* (Paris 1903).

J. Bédier, *Les Légendes épiques* (Paris 1908), Vol. 3.

J.H.P. Belloc, *The Pyrenees* (London 1923).

R. Blanchard, 'La Morphologie des Pyrénées françaises', *Annales de Géog.*, 23 (1914), 303–24.

P. Bosch-Gimpera, *Prehistoria Catalana* (Barcelona 1919).

P. Bosch-Gimpera, 'La Arquelogia Preromana Hispánica', in A. Schulten, *Hispania* (Barcelona 1920), pp.133–205.

J. Brunhes, *Géographie Humaine de la France*, Vol. 1 in G. Hanotaux (ed.), *Histoire de la Nation Française* (Paris 1920–6).

M.C. Burkitt, *Prehistory* (Cambridge 1925).

E. Cartailhac, *Les Ages préhistoriques de l'Espagne et du Portugal* (Paris 1886).

H. Cavaillès, 'Une fédération pyrénéenne sur l'ancien Régime. Les traités de lies et passeries', *Revue Historique*, 105 (1910), 1–34, 241–276.

Victor Chapot, *Le Monde Romain* (Paris 1927), chapter 4.

C. D'Almeida, *Les Pyrénées: développement de la connaissance géographique de la chaîne* (Paris 1893).

A. Dauzat, 'Les anciens types d'habitation rurales en France', *La Nature*, 26 Jan. 1924, 53–60.

J. Déchelette, *Manuel d'archéologie* (Paris 1908).

Havelock Ellis, *The Soul of Spain* (London 1927).

H.J. Fleure, *Human Geography in Western Europe* (London 1918).

H.J. Fleure and L. Winstanley, 'Anthropology and our older Histories', *Journ. Roy. Anthr. Inst.*, 48 (1918), 155–70, 171–80.

E.A. Freeman, *The Historical Geography of Europe* (London 1903), 2 vols.

Froissart's *Chronicles*, Lord Berners (trans.), G.C. Macaulay (ed.) (London 1895).

Hamilton Jackson, *Rambles in the Pyrenees and the Adjacent Districts* (London 1912).

C. Jullian, *Histoire de la Gaule* (Paris 1908–14).

E. Lavisse (ed.), *Histoire de France, jusqu'à la Révolution*, 9 vols (Paris 1901–11). In particular: Vol. 1, pt 1, *Tableau de la géographie de la France par* Vidal de la Blache; Vol. 3, pt 1, *Louis VII—Philippe-Auguste—Louis VIII (1137–1226)*, par Achille Luchaire.

E.T. Leeds, 'Dolmens and Megalithic Tombs of Spain and Portugal', *Archaeologia*, 70 (1920), 201–32.

E.T. Leeds, 'Problems of Megalithic Architecture in the Western Mediterranean', *Liverpool Annals of Archaeology and Anthropology*, 9 (1922), 29–40.

E.C. Lodge, *Gascony under English Rule* (London 1926).

J.L. Myres, in J.B. Bury, S.A. Cook and F.E. Adcock (eds), *Cambridge Ancient History* (Cambridge 1923), Vol. 1, chapters 1 and 2.

A. Oakley, *Hill Towns of the Pyrenees* (New York 1923).

H. Obermaier, *Fossil Man in Spain* (New York 1924).

A.G. Latham (ed.), *Oxford Treasury of French Literature*, Vol. 1 (Oxford 1915), Introduction.

Harold Peake and H.J. Fleure, *The Corridors of Time* (Oxford 1927), Vols 1 and 2.

P. Perret, *Les Pyrénées françaises* (Paris 1881).

W.Z. Ripley, *The Races of Europe* (London 1899).

E.C. Semple, *Influences of Geographic Environment* (New York 1911), in particular chapters 7, 15 and 16.

W.J. Sollas, *Ancient Hunters and their Modern Representatives* (London 1924).

M. Sorre, *Les Pyrénées Méditerranéennes* (Paris 1913).

M. Sorre, *Les Pyrénées* (Paris 1928).

The Geography of Strabo, transl. H.C. Hamilton and W. Falconer (London 1854–7).

G.E. Street, *Some Account of Gothic Architecture in Spain* (London 1869).

H. Taine, *Voyage aux Pyrénées* (Paris 1858).

Arthur Tilley, *The Dawn of the French Renaissance* (Cambridge 1918), chapter 5.

Arthur Young, *Travels in France* (London 1889).

OLD IRELAND AND NEW ENGLAND

1   In fact Belfast, with the exception of the small village of Newry, is the only place I can trace in Maine named after an Ulster town. The much larger city of Bangor on the Penobscot traditionally owes its name to a popular hymn tune composed by the English psalmodist William Tansur, and presumably called after the Welsh Bangor. Actually almost any part of Europe is better represented in Maine than Ulster; Éire, for instance, can claim Limerick and Waterford. The place-names of Maine would form an interesting study. Many, especially those of natural features, have kept their Indian form (Kennebec, Katahdin, Androscoggin, Sagadahoc): others reflect the aspirations of the revolutionary period (Freedom, Liberty, Amity, Unity); a large group is said to have been named by sea-captains to commemorate their travels (Mexico, China, Peru, Poland, Norway, Naples); but the majority derives from English places and families (York, Biddeford, Cumberland, Bath, Oxford). In the east are a few French names (Castine, Calais, Mt Desert), relics of Acadia.

2   Longfellow and Hawthorne, both graduates of Bowdoin College, Brunswick, were among the first, though the latter returned to Massachusetts for his subjects after his first novel, *Fanshawe* (1828). The combination of writer, preacher, farmer, fisher and craftsman is well illustrated in Rev. Elijah Kellogg (1813–1901), who was descended from McClellans and whose ancestry is evident in his writings. His many books for boys, mostly about the Maine coast, include a series, *The Forest Glen*, devoted to the exploits of a Scotch-Irish group on the Pennsylvanian frontier. The modern Maine school of writers is strongly regionalist in character, some of its work genuinely rooted in the soil, some exploiting it for sale to tourists. Interesting and genuine accounts of life in the interior of the states will be found in books by Louise Dickinson Rich, *We Took to the Woods* (London 1944), and *Happy the Land* (Philadelphia 1946).

3   This generalized account of the Abenaki is based on papers in local archaeological publications and on a chapter by F.H. Eckstorm in *Maine: A History*, L.C. Hatch (ed.), 3 vols (New York 1919), Vol. 1.

4   J. Williamson, *History of the City of Belfast in the State of Maine* (Portland 1877).

5   W.F. Marshall, *Ulster Sails West* (Belfast 1944).

6   L.K. Mathews, *The Expansion of New England* (Boston and New York 1909).

7   *Bicentenary Handbook, Brunswick, Maine* (Brunswick 1939). The name is perpetuated in a book, *The Pearl of Orr's Island* (London 1862), written by Harriett Beecher Stowe, whose *Uncle Tom's Cabin* (1852) was also written in Brunswick.

8   J. Williamson, *op. cit.*

9   Glenn T. Trewartha, 'Rural Settlement in Colonial America', *Geog. Rev.*, 36 (1946), 568–96.

10   The story of one such family is told in R.P.T. Coffin, *Captain Abby and Captain John* (New York 1939).

11   J. Williamson, *op. cit.*

12   F.H. Eckstorm in *Maine: A History*, L.C. Hatch (ed.), 3 vols (New York 1919), Vol. 3, chapter 24.

13   A colourful account of this trade is given in R.P.T. Coffin, *Kennebec: Cradle of Americans* (New York 1937).

14   J. Williamson, *op. cit.* quotes an old rhyme of the Maine coast: 'Camden for beauty, Northport for pride,/Had it not been for clams, Belfast would have died.'

15   The white-painted timbered houses of the early nineteenth century are one of the chief assets of Maine. They were built by the shipwrights and occupied by ships' captains, and are marked by a sturdy simplicity. A common feature is the flat balustraded roof, significantly called the widow's walk, where the wife would watch for the returning ships. The white wooden pillared churches are another relic of the Golden Age. The houses, it is said, were 'raised on rum'. In fact a bottle of rum was dashed against the frame of the house in the house-raising ceremonies. The West Indian trade had its perils as well as its rewards. Williamson records the death, of yellow fever in the Indies, of the three Belfast sea-captains in the year 1839. They were Joseph Houston, James Cunningham and Thomas Patterson.

16   W.F. Adams, *Ireland and Irish Emigration to the New World from 1815 to the Famine* (New Haven 1932).

17   M.L. Hansen, *The Immigrant in American History* (Cambridge, Mass. 1940).

18   M.L. Hansen, *The Atlantic Migration, 1607–1860* (Cambridge, Mass. 1940).

19   N. Hawthorne, *The American Notebooks* (New Haven 1932) under years 1837 and 1842. These descriptions recall old Irish customs. It seems that the normal Maine practice of keeping the house warm in winter, said to have been taken over from the Indians, was to pile spruce branches against the base of the walls. This is still commonly seen.

20   Another feature of the life of Maine is that education at the college and university level takes on the proportions of an industry. This is in part the heritage of the Protestant pioneers (Congregational, Presbyterian and Baptist), who were responsible for founding the Liberal Arts colleges of Bowdoin, Bates and Colby. In addition there is the large State University of Orono, near Bangor. The high proportion of students (7800 in 1948) out of a total population of 885,000 is partly accounted for by the fact that Maine draws many of its students from southern New England and even farther afield.

THE SCOTCH-IRISH

1   I have published the substance of this address in three articles: 'The Scotch-Irish in the New World; An Atlantic Heritage', *Journ. Roy. Soc. Antiquaries of Ireland*, 35 (1965), 39–49; 'Culture and Land Use in the Old West of North America', *Heidelberger Geographische Arbeiten*, 15 (1966), 72–80; 'Cultural Relics of the Ulster-Scots in the Old West of North America', *Ulster Folklife*, 11 (1965), 33–8. I wish to express my thanks to several friends in the USA for their help in discussion and field study in various parts of North America east of the Mississippi, particularly to Professors Fred Kniffen, J. Fraser Hart and Gary Dunbar, and Mr Henry Glassie.

2   William Strickland, *Observations on the Agriculture of the United States of America* (London 1801), p.71.

3   Arnold Toynbee, *A Study of History* (London 1934), Vol. 2, pp.302, 311.

4   The Pennsylvania-German Society started its publication in 1891. The Scotch-Irish Society of America, founded in 1889, seems to have grown out of a meeting held in Belfast *c.*1884, at which Professor George Macloskie and President McCosh of Princeton University were present.

5   Charles A. Hanna, *The Scotch-Irish* (New York and London 1902), Vol. 1, p.1.

6   J.G. Leyburn, *The Scotch-Irish: A Social History* (Chapel Hill 1962), p.316.

7   On this topic see Leyburn, *op. cit.* p.315, who gives a fair summary of the divergent views held about the Scotch-Irish.

8   *Ibid.*, p.321.

9   *Ibid.*, p.152.

10   D. McCourt, 'County Derry and New England' in *County Londonderry Handbook* (Coleraine 1964), pp.87–101.

11   The fullest and most recent survey is R.J. Dickson, *Ulster Emigration to Colonial America, 1718–1775* (London 1966).

12   Quoted in *Proc. of the First Scotch-Irish Congress, Columbia, Tennessee* (Cincinnati 1889), p.184.

13   The Old Order Amish number 43,000 in the USA in 1960, over half of them living in Lancaster County.

14   J.T. Lemon, 'The Agricultural Practices of National Groups in Eighteenth-Century South-Eastern Pennsylvania', *Geog. Rev.*, 56 (1966), 467–96, refutes these claims. Basing his findings on studies of tax lists and estate inventories, he claims that there were no major differences in farming practice between the Germans and the Scotch-Irish, and that the Germans were no more virtuous in their habits than other immigrants. Folkways, however, are not revealed by statistics, and Dr Lemon does not examine the causes and consequences of expansion outside Pennsylvania. Yet he is probably right in thinking that the contrasted pictures portrayed in contemporary accounts of German and Scotch-Irish settlers were influenced by English stereotypes of the two stocks.

15   Benjamin Rush, 'An Account of the Manners of the German Inhabitants of Pennsylvania', *Columbian Magazine*, 3 (1789), 22–30.

16   See 'Letters of Benjamin Rush', L.H. Butterfield (ed.), *Memoirs Amer. Phil. Soc.*, 30 (1951), 368.

17   A pioneer work, concerned with material culture as well as with political ideas and values, is T.J. Wertenbaker, *The Founding of American Civilization: The Middle Colonies* (New York and London 1938).

18   'The Farm-Housing Survey', *United States Dept. of Agric. Miscellaneous Publication*, no. 323 (Washington 1939).

19   The myth was exploded by H.L. Shurtleff. See his book *The Log Cabin Myth*, S.E. Morison (ed.) (Cambridge, Mass. 1939).

20   Mr Glassie has very kindly deposited a copy of his Master's thesis, 'Southern Mountain Houses: A Study in American Folk Culture' (submitted to the State University of New York 1965), in the library of the Department of Geography, Queen's University, Belfast. His study of 'The Types of the Southern Mountain Cabin' has now been published as Appendix C in Jan Harold Brunvard, *The Study of American Folklore* (New York 1968). See also Fred Kniffen and Henry Glassie, 'Building in Wood in the Eastern United States', *Geog. Rev.*, 56 (1966), 40–66; and Fred Kniffen, 'North American Folk Housing', *Annals of the Assoc. of Amer. Geogs*, 55 (1965), 549–77.

21   Henry Glassie, *Southern Mountain Houses*, p.73.

22   W.R. Dunaway, *The Scotch-Irish of Colonial Pennsylvania* (Chapel Hill 1944), p.185.

23   Henry Glassie, *Southern Mountain Houses*, pp.147, 154.

24   E.E. Evans, *Irish Folk Ways* (London 1957), p.86.

25   The spirit of competition found a fertile field in North America. Its original purpose in Ireland may have been magical, but it has been interpreted as providing a stimulus towards the completion of a task, such as turf-cutting or harvesting, before the weather broke. See E.E. Evans, *op. cit.* p.188.

26   E.T. Price, 'Root Digging in the Appalachians', *Geog. Rev.*, 50 (1960), 1–20.

27   Leather or rawhide articles of clothing would have been no novelty to the Ulster immigrants, for leather breeches were worn in some parts of the country in the eighteenth century. See G.R. Buick, *Journ. Roy. Soc. Antiquaries of Ireland*, 4th Series, 6 (1883–4), p.125.

28   Joseph Doddridge, *Notes on the Settlement and the Indian War* (Pittsburgh 1912), p.25.

29   Mark van Doren (ed.), *The Travels of William Bartram* (New York 1928), p.206.

30   Arnold Toynbee, *op. cit.*, Vol. 2, p.312.

31 Colonel James Smith's famous account of his travels and captivity was published in Lexington, Kentucky, in 1799. Quoted in Wilcomb E. Washburn, *The Indian and the White Man* (New York 1964), p.265.

32 See, for example, A. Irving Hallowell, 'The Backwash of the Frontier: The Impact of the Indian on American Culture', in Walker D. Wyman and Clifton B. Kroeber (eds), *The Frontier in Perspective* (Madison 1957), pp.229–58.

33 D.B. Quinn, *The Elizabethans and the Irish* (Ithaca 1966).

34 Edmund S. Morgan, *The American Indian: Incorrigible Individualist* (Providence 1958), p.7.

35 'The Cherokee Nation' was recognized by the US by treaty in 1791, although later ignored by Andrew Jackson.

36 For this and many detailed descriptions of pioneer life see H.S. Arnow, *Seedtime in the Cumberland* (Macmillan 1960).

37 Stella H. Sutherland, *Population Distribution in Colonial America* (New York 1936), Appendix p.322.

38 C.M. Arensberg, 'American Communities', *American Anthropologist*, 57 (1955), 155. See also C.O. Sauer, 'Historical Geography and the Western frontier', in J. Leighly (ed.), *Land and Life* (Berkeley and Los Angeles 1963), pp.45–52.

39 Glenn T. Trewartha, 'The Unincorporated Hamlet', *Annals of the Assoc. of Amer. Geogs.*, 33 (1943), 32–81.

40 I am indebted to Richard Pillsbury of West Virginia University for this information, and for sending me copies of the relevant town plans. He has listed fifty-six examples of street-towns (with or without 'diamonds') in Pennsylvania.

41 For example, the grid-iron town-plan which was to become the standard pattern in the New World was already known in Spanish America from about 1570.

42 Information kindly supplied by Professor E.T. Price of the University of Oregon.

43 E.E. Evans, 'The Atlantic Ends of Europe', *Advancement of Science*, 25 (1958), 34–64.

EPILOGUE

1 Letter, E. Estyn Evans to C.O. Sauer, 4 May 1971. Sauer Papers, Bancroft Library, University of California, Berkeley. On his death, *The New York Times* described Sauer as 'one of the most influential geographers of his generation'. The close resemblance between his cultural geography and Evans' can be gauged from the following lines in the same obituary: 'He taught them [his students] that geography is the study of human history at least as much as of physical terrain, that it is strongly related to biology. ... Dr Sauer maintained that all geography is essentially historical. Written documents, archaeological evidence, plant data, soil profiles, the wisdom of the small farmer—all provided him with clues for unravelling problems of human global environment.' *The New York Times* (M) 21 July 1975, p.24.

2 S. Heaney in 'Gifts of Rain', *Wintering Out* (London 1972), pp.23–5. Ref. on p.25. For Evans' 'special importance' in helping Heaney to express a 'spirit of reverence towards the past' see B. Morrison, *Seamus Heaney* (London 1982). Ref. on p.31. And clearly Evans' colouring of the modern Irish poetic imagination has been more general; as is disclosed by Paul Durcan's 'Foreword' to the 1992 Lilliput edition of Evans' *Personality of Ireland*, and by some of Michael Longley's poetry.

3 Evans, 'An Essay on the Historical Geography of the Shropshire-Montgomeryshire Borderland', *Collections Historical and Archaeological Relating to Montgomeryshire and its Borders*, 40 (1928), 242–70. That Evans continued to believe this is plain from the compliments he repeatedly paid to M.T. Hodgen's *Change and History* (New York 1952), with its thesis of an innovatory zone of hybridization between Highland and Lowland Britain.

4 Evans, 'Recollections of a Border Childhood, Autobiographical typescript', p.4. Reproduced by kind permission of Mrs Gwyneth Evans.

5 For a geographical appraisal of Webb's novels see J.H. Paterson and E. Paterson, 'Shrop-

shire: Reality and Symbol in the Work of Mary Webb', in Douglas C.D. Pocock (ed.), *Humanistic Geography and Literature. Essays on the Experience of Place* (London 1981), pp.209–20. There is a good general discussion of nature-mysticism, and its importance in inter-war geography, in D. Matless, 'Nature, the modern and the mystic: tales from early twentieth century geography', *Trans. Inst. Br. Geogr. N.S.* 16 (1991), 272–86.

6   Evans, *Ulster: The Common Ground* (Mullingar 1984), p.9. See R. Ackerman, *J.G. Frazer: his life and work* (Cambridge 1987). The juvenile J. Enoch Powell was just one on whom Frazer evidently exerted a great influence: 'I cannot imagine how different my mental and religious life would have been if the impact of J.G. Fraser (*sic*.) had come at another time or not at all.' *The Times*, 27 September 1962, p.15.

7   See, for example, H.J. Fleure and T.C. James, 'Geographical distribution of anthropological types in Wales', *Journ. Roy. Anthrop. Inst.*, 46 (1916), 35–153; H.J. Fleure, 'Biological types of man in England and Wales', *Vierteljahrsschrift der Naturforschenden Gesellschaft in Zürich*: Beiblatt No. 30, Jg. 83 (1938), 137–48; H.J. Fleure, 'Some problems of physical anthropology; presidential address', *Journ. Roy. Anthrop. Inst.*, 77 (1947), 1–5.

8   H.J. Fleure, 'The World's Societies', in E.D. Laborde (ed.), *Education of Today* (Cambridge 1935), pp.23–33. Ref. on p.26.

9   Evans, *Irish Folk Ways* (London 1957), p.xvi.

10 H.J. Fleure, 'Inter-Racial Understanding', *New Era in Home and School*, 12 (1931), 323–4. Ref. on p.324.

11 'Only one sector of Irish science showed any real buoyancy during the closing decades of the nineteenth century: field natural history. Indeed, within that area there was a local boom—a boom in which a major inspirational figure was Robert Lloyd Praeger (1865–1953) who from 1893 until his retirement in 1923 was a member of the staff of the National Library of Ireland', G.L. Herries Davies, 'Irish Thought in Science' in R. Kearney (ed.), *The Irish Mind. Exploring Intellectual Traditions* (Dublin 1985), pp.294–310. Ref. on p.308.

12 Evans 'Beginnings', in J.A. Campbell (ed.), *Geography at Queen's. An Historical Survey* (Belfast 1978), pp.5–15. Ref. on p.8.

13 A. Deane (ed.), *The Belfast Natural History and Philosophical Society. Centenary volume 1821–1921* (Belfast 1924); A.A. Campbell, *Belfast Naturalists' Field Club: Its Origin and Progress* (Belfast 1938).

14 Evans and B.S. Turner, *Ireland's Eye. The Photographs of Robert John Welch* (Belfast 1977).

15 Evans, *The Personality of Ireland* (Dublin 1992), p.13–5.

16 *Ibid.*, p.6. Though Evans was probably unaware of it, the same point had been made many years before by Horace Plunkett who, in urging the need for more vocational education, had attacked the existing educational system for producing men and women 'with a distinct distaste for any industrial or productive occupation' (H. Plunkett, *Ireland in the New Century* [London 1904], p.129).

17 Evans, 'Introduction', in D. Ó Corráin (ed.), *Irish Antiquity. Essays and Studies presented to Professor M.J. O'Kelly* (Cork 1981), pp.xxv–xxviii. Ref. on p.xxv.

18 'Introduction', in Evans (ed.), *Harvest Home. The Last Sheaf. A Selection from the Writings of T.G.F. Paterson Relating to County Armagh* (Dundalk 1975), pp.ix–xvi.

19 R.H. Buchanan, 'Arthur Pollock', *Ulster Folklife*, 17 (1971), 1–2.

20 H.J. Fleure, 'Man and his Environment', in H.J. Fleure *et alia.*, *Geography. The World and its Peoples* (London 1948), pp.305–18. Ref. on p.312.

21 Evans and M. Gaffikin, 'Belfast Naturalists' Field Club Survey of Antiquities: Megaliths and Raths', *Irish Naturalists' Journ.*, 5 (1935), 242–52; Evans, 'Introduction to Prehistoric Monuments', in D.A. Chart (ed.), *A Preliminary Survey of the Ancient Monuments of Northern Ireland* (Belfast 1940), pp.xii–xvii.

22 G.F. Mitchell, *The Way that I Followed. A Naturalist's Journey around Ireland* (Dublin 1990), pp.66–7, 77–8.

23 Evans and C.F.C. Hawkes, 'An Eskimo harpoon-head from Tara, Co. Down (?)', *Ulster Journal of Archaeology*, 3rd Series, 3 (1940), 127–33. Refs on pp.127, 129.

24 'The producing of food is one of the most fundamental of all occupations. It absorbs the greater part of people's energy, helps to determine their social relationships, and is a centre about which many of their sentiments are formed', R.U. Sayce, 'Folk-lore and Folk-Culture', *Béaloideas*, 12 (1942), 68–80. Ref. on p.75.

25 '... in ancient Irish society cows were not merely one kind of domestic animal but ... were of such overweening importance that they almost had a status as members of society. They were in the mental foreground of king and peasant, cleric and layman, warrior and poet, young and old, men and women, and they touched the lives of everyone from sunrise to sunset, and from birth to death. This is evident in the works of Irish chroniclers, hagiographers, historians, poets and everyone who put quill to parchment or paper in the country over the thousand years from the seventh to the seventeenth century', A.T. Lucas, *Cattle in Ancient Ireland* (Kilkenny 1989), ref. on p.3; 'it is much less helpful to talk of Ireland and Wales as Celtic societies. In spite of such striking similarities as the position of the poet, the major difference—that between lordship over men by means of cattle and lordship over men by means of land—is so important as to make the two societies considerably different when considered in the round.' T.M. Charles-Edwards, *Early Irish and Welsh Kinship* (Oxford 1993). Ref. on p.477; 'The predictable emphasis on cattle raising (and stealing) is hardly surprising as cattle is the most frequent species of livestock to be encountered on Irish sites from the Neolithic (*c*.4000 BC) through the medieval period', J.P. Mallory, 'The World of Cú Chulainn: The Archaeology of Táin Bó Cúailnge', in J.P. Mallory (ed.), *Aspects of the Táin* (Belfast 1992), pp.103–59. Ref. on p.119.

26 M.E. Daly, 'An alien institution: attitudes to the city in nineteenth- and twentieth-century Irish society', *Études Irlandaises*, 10 (1985), 181–94.

27 Transhumance, whether in Ireland or elsewhere in W. Europe, had a particular fascination for Evans. Besides exploring the subject himself, he encouraged others to research it. See Evans, 'Seasonal nomadism in modern Europe and ancient Ireland', *Proc. Belfast Naturalists' Field Club*, 2nd Series, 10 (1940), 94–9; Evans, 'Transhumance in Europe', *Geography*, 25 (1940), 172–80; J. Graham, 'Transhumance in Ireland', *Advancement of Science*, 37 (1953), 74–9; B. Mac Aodha, 'Souming in the Sperrins', *Ulster Folklife*, 2 (1956), 19–21.

28 Evans, *Northern Ireland: With a Portrait* (London 1951). Ref. on p.61.

29 Evans, 'The personality of Ulster', *Trans. Inst. Br. Geogr.*, 51 (1970), 1–20. Ref. on p.3.

30 J. Bryce, 'The Scoto-Irish Race in Ulster and in America. Address delivered to the Scotch-Irish Society of Pennsylvania, February 1909', in *University and Historical Addresses* (New York 1913), pp.207–25. Ref. on p.210.

31 J. Joyce, *Ulysses* (New York 1961), p.637.

32 'One of the most conspicuous elements in the sample is a group characterised by tall stature, a large, heavy, robust body with large chest-measurements and a broad bi-iliac breadth, a very long and large dolichocephalic head, and an unusually broad face. ... This group approaches very closely the Upper Palaeolithic and Mesolithic peoples of Europe ... it is certainly surprising to find such a high percentage of the type (over 20 per cent) in the modern population, and that the short-faced Cro-Magnon type should be so well represented', T. Walmsley, J.M. Mogey and D.P. Gamble (eds), 'The Peoples of Northern Ireland. An Anthropometric Survey. 2—The Town and District of Ballymoney', *Ulster Journal of Archaeology*, 3rd Series, 5 (1942), 98–118. Refs on pp.110, 112.

33 N.C. Mitchel, 'The Lower Bann Fisheries', *Ulster Folklife*, 11 (1965), 1–32; D. Donnelly, *On Lough Neagh's Shores. A Study of the Lough Neagh Fishing Community* (Galbally 1986).

34 Evans, *op. cit.*, 1992. Ref. on p.71.

35 M.T. Hodgen, *The Doctrine of Survivals* (London 1936). See also G. Boyes, 'Cultural Survivals Theory and Traditional Customs', *Folk Life*, 26 (1987–8), 5–11.

36 'These are processes, customs, opinions, and so forth, which have been carried by force of habit into a new society ... and ... thus remain as proofs and examples of an older condition of culture out of which a newer has evolved', E.B. Tylor, *Primitive Culture* (London 1871), p.16.

37 Evans, 'Donegal survivals', *Antiquity*, 13 (1939), 207–22. Ref. on p.207.

38 'One is tempted to regard the openfield system as a survival from pre-Celtic times, when the climate of sub-boreal Ireland was more conducive to simple agriculture, overlaid with Celtic influence from the late Bronze Age onwards', Evans, 'Some survivals of the Irish openfield system', *Geography*, 24 (1939), 24–36. Ref. on p.28.

39 F.W. Maitland, 'The Survival of Archaic Communities', in H.A.L. Fisher (ed.), *The Collected Papers of Frederic William Maitland* (Cambridge 1911), Vol. 2, pp.313–65. Ref. on pp.313–4.

40 K. Whelan, 'The Bases of Regionalism', in P. Ó Drisceoil (ed.), *Cultures in Ireland—Regions: Identity and Power* (Belfast 1993), pp.5–62.

41 Futhermore, at no point in this critique does Whelan make the important distinction – additionally stipulated by Hobsbawm—between tradition and custom (E. Hobsbawm, 'Introduction: Inventing Traditions', in E. Hobsbawm and T. Ranger [eds], *The Invention of Tradition* [Cambridge 1993], pp.1–14. Ref on p.2). Even more remarkable, Whelan fails to tell us whey he excludes any consideration of language from his strictures on cultural nationalism and western survival.

42 J. Sheehy, *The Rediscovery of Ireland's Past: The Celtic Revival 1830–1930* (London 1980). 'Some students of the Celtic past, it seems to me, have been slow to outgrow the Victorian mould in which the Gaelic revival was cast, and which was shaped by nationalism and racist theories', Evans, 'Archaeology and Folklife', in B. Almquist, B. MacAodha and G. MacEoin (eds), *Hereditas*, pp.127–39. Ref. on pp.135–6.

43 Evans, *op. cit.*, 1942, p.2.

44 J.H. Delargy, 'The Gaelic Story-Teller. With Some Notes on Gaelic Folktales', *Proc. Brit. Academy*, 31 (1945), 177–221. Ref. on p.209. Similarly persuaded was the distinguished Swedish folklorist C.W. von Sydow: 'A pre-Celtic, Mediterranean or Megalithic tradition must have existed in the British Isles, and the same almost certainly is to be found in the Irish Fiannúachta, which are closely related to the Mabinogion (Wales) and the Arthurian legend; moreover, the Fiannúachta have a motive relationship with the ancient Greek heroic sagas and traditions in the Near East; and, as there seems to be no question of recent literature borrowings, we must apply the Megalithic Culture as a spreading factor in order to explain the connection between the traditions.' C.W. von Sydow, 'Das Volksmarchen unter ethnischem Gesichtspunkt', in *Selected Papers on Folklore. Published on the occasion of his 70th Birthday* (Copenhagen 1948), 220–42. Ref. on p.242.

45 '… it is clearly evident that in Irish vernacular architecture there is much variation between the 'highland area' of the north and west and the 'lowland area' of the south and east. It is also evident that much of the difference is due to the influence of settlers and of ideas from across the Irish Sea. Here we may advert to Fox's thesis that the Lowland Zone of Britain, easily overrun and open to invasion tends to have new cultures imposed upon it, while in the less accessible Highland Zone these tend to be more slowly absorbed', C. Ó Danachair, 'Irish vernacular architecture in relation to the Irish Sea', in D. Moore (ed.), *The Irish Sea Province in Archaeology and History* (Cardiff 1970), pp.98–107. Ref. on p.106.

46 R. Fox, *The Tory Islanders. A People of the Celtic Fringe* (Cambridge 1978). Ref. on p.125.

47 E.G. Bowen, 'A study of rural settlements in South-West Wales', *The Geographical Teacher*, 13 (1925–6), 317–26; E.G. Bowen, 'A map of the Trehelig common fields', *Collections Historical and Archaeological Relating to Montgomeryshire and its Borders*, 41 (1930), 163–8; S. Harris, 'The Village Community of Alderney', *Sociological Review*, 18 (1926), 265–78; S. Harris, 'Settlements and Field Systems in Guernsey', in I.C. Peate (ed.), *Studies in Regional Consciousness and Environment: Essays presented to H.J. Fleure* (Oxford 1930), pp.97–112. See also S. Harris, 'Some notes on field systems in Mediterranean lands and in the Atlantic coastal lands of south west Europe', *Sociological Review*, 20 (1928), 197–212.

48 E. Jones, 'Settlement patterns in the middle Teifi valley', *Geography*, 30 (1945), 103–12; E. Jones, 'Some aspects of the study of settlement in Britain', *Advancement of Science*, 8 (1951), 59–65; G.R.J. Jones, 'Some Medieval Rural Settlements in North Wales', *Trans. Inst. Br.*

Geogr., 19 (1953), 51–72; C. Thomas, 'The Evolution of Rural Settlement and Land Tenure in Merioneth', PhD thesis, University of Wales, 1965.

49 D. McCourt, 'The Rundale System in Ireland: A Study of its Geographical Distribution and Social Relations', PhD thesis, The Queen's University of Belfast, Belfast, 1950; V.B. Proudfoot, 'Settlement and Economy in Co. Down from the Late Bronze Age to the Anglo-Norman Invasion', PhD thesis, The Queen's University of Belfast, Belfast 1957; R.H. Buchanan, 'The Barony of Lecale, Co. Down: a Study of Regional Personality', PhD thesis, The Queen's University of Belfast, Belfast, 1958.

50 Evans, 'The Atlantic Ends of Europe', *Advancement of Science*, 15 (1958) 54–64. Refs on p.63; L.R. Palmer, *Archeans and Indo-Europeans, An Inaugural Lecture delivered before the University of Oxford on 4 November 1954* (Oxford 1955). In view of Evans' resort to both legal and linguistic sources, it seems unjust to accuse him of reliance solely on 'the cold facts of land and landscape'. T.J. Hughes, review of Evans, *The Personality of Ireland* (1973), *Irish Geography*, 7 (1974), pp.137–8. Ref. on p.138.

51 R.A. Dodgshon, 'The ecological basis of Highland peasant farming, 1500–1800', in H.H. Birks *et alia* (eds), *The Cultural Landscape. Past, Present and Future* (Cambridge 1988), pp. 139–51. Ref. on p.143; R.A. Dodgshon, 'Farming Practice in the Western Highlands and Islands before Crofting: A Study in Cultural Inertia or Opportunity Costs?', *Rural History*, 3 (1992), 173–89; R.A. Dodgshon, 'West Highland and Hebridean landscapes: have they a history without runrig?', *Journ. Hist. Geogr.*, 19 (1993), 383–98.

52 G.R.J. Jones, 'The Dark Ages', in D.H. Owen (ed.), *Settlement and Society in Wales* (Cardiff 1989), pp.177–97; G.R.J. Jones, 'The Models for Organisation in Llyfr Iorwerth and Llyfr Cyfnerth', *The Bulletin of the Board of Celtic Studies*, 39 (1992), 95–118; G.R.J. Jones, review of T.M. Charles-Edwards, *Early Irish and Welsh Kinship* (1993), *Journ. Hist. Geogr.*, 20 (1994), 205–6. See also, D. Gregory, 'Settlement continuity', in R.J. Johnston, D. Gregory and D.M. Smith (eds), *The Dictionary of Human Geography* (Oxford 1994), pp.552–3.

53 J.H. Andrews, 'The ethnic factor in Irish historical geography', paper given at the Annual Conference of Irish Geographers, Dublin 1974; R.A. Butlin, 'Some observations on the field systems of medieval Ireland', *Geographia Polonica*, 38 (1978), 31–6; A. Simms, 'Genetische Siedlungsforschung in Irland mit besonderer Berücksichtigung der Siedlungsgeographie', in K. Fehn *et alia*, *Genetische Siedlungsforschung in Mitteleuropa und seinen Nachbarräumen* (Bonn 1988), pp.319–43. Refs on pp.324–5; K. Whelan, 'Settlement and Society in Eighteenth-Century Ireland', in G. Dawe and J.W. Foster (eds), *The Poet's Place* (Belfast 1991), pp.45–62. Refs on pp.45–7.

54 V.B. Proudfoot, 'Economy and settlement in rural Ireland', in L. Laing (ed.), *Studies in Celtic Survival*, BAR 37 (Oxford 1977), pp.83–106; F.H.A. Aalen, *Man and the Landscape in Ireland* (London 1978). Ref. on p.95; T.B. Barry, *The Archaeology of Medieval Ireland* (London 1987). Refs on pp.20–5; J.H. Johnson, *The Human Geography of Ireland* (Chichester 1994). Ref. on p.49.

55 Evans, *op. cit.*, 1992. Ref. on p.61; D. McCourt, 'The dynamic quality of Irish rural settlement', in R.H. Buchanan *et alia*, *Man and his habitat. Essays presented to Emyr Estyn Evans* (London 1971), pp.126–64; R.H. Buchanan, 'Field Systems of Ireland', in A.R.H. Baker and R.A. Butlin (eds), *Studies of Field Systems in the British Isles* (Cambridge 1973), pp. 580–618; T. McErlean, 'The Irish Townland Scheme of Landscape Organisation', in T. Reeves-Smyth and F. Hamond (eds), *Landscape Archaeology in Ireland*, BAR British Series, 116 (Oxford 1983), pp.52–61; G.F. Mitchell, *The Shell Guide to Reading the Irish Landscape* (London and Dublin 1986). Ref. on p.158; N.T. Patterson, *Cattle – Lords and Clansmen. Kinship and Rank in Early Ireland* (New York and London 1991), pp.88–118.

56 T.M. Charles-Edwards, 'The Church and Settlement', in P.N. Ó Cathain and M. Richter (eds), *Ireland and Europe. The Early Church* (Stuttgart 1984), pp.165-75. Ref. on p.170.

57 F. Braudel, 'History and the Social Sciences: The Longue Durée', in his *On History* (London 1980), pp.25–54.

58 Evans, 'The peasant and the past', *Advancement of Science*, 17 (1960), 293–302.

59   Evans, *op. cit.*, 1957. Ref. on p.298; M.L. Nolan, 'Irish Pilgrimage: The Different Tradition', *Annals of the Association of American Geographers*, 73 (1983), 421–38; P. MacCana, 'Placenames and Mythology in Irish Tradition: Places, Pilgrimages and Things', in G.W. MacLennan (ed.), *Proceedings of the First North American Congress of Celtic Studies* (Ottawa 1988).

60   J. Waddell, 'The invasion hypothesis in Irish prehistory', *Antiquity*, 52 (1978), 121–8.

61   That continuing discussion of 'the invasion hypothesis' among Irish prehistorians can be seen as part of a much wider and older debate is clear from the following statement by Axel Steensberg, the Danish folklife scholar and friend of Estyn Evans: 'Our main problem is not diffusion or invention but the analysis of how much of the historical evolution can safely be registered under either of these two—alas rather abstract!—headings, and how much is a composition of both'. As interesting—and as pertinent—as this statement, however, is another he makes earlier in the same paper: 'Many years ago the present author proposed that Graebner's criteria of distribution and quality should be complemented with a third criterion, that of adaptation, which is almost congruent with the modern concept of ecology'. A. Steensberg, 'Diffusion and Invention', in L. Bogdanova *et alia* (eds), *Etnografski i folkloristichni izslezvaniia: v chest na Khristo Vakarelski po sluchai 80–godishninata ot rozhdenieto mu* (Sofia 1979), pp.44–54. Refs on pp.54, and 44.

62   Evans, 'The Megaliths', *Geographical Magazine*, 17 (1944), pp.294–305. Ref. on p.296.

63   H. Case, 'Settlement-patterns in the north Irish Neolithic', *Ulster Journal of Archaeology*, 3rd series, 32 (1969), 3–27.

64   Evans, *op. cit.*, 1992, p.73. By thus—characteristically—emphasizing hybridization, Evans allowed for both cultural continuity and the impact of external influences: if never an 'invasionist', neither was he ever an 'internalist'. Both these poles of opinion are recognizable in current interpretations of the Irish Neolithic. 'Some have … argued that the new economy might have been introduced by local Mesolithic populations rather than farmer colonists. According to this hypothesis, local Mesolithic peoples in Ireland may have come into contact with farming communities on the other side of the Irish Sea, and they themselves may have obtained the new livestock and cereals from there. But all the evidence … suggests that the later Mesolithic populations of Ireland remained culturally isolated from developments in Britain and it is most unlikely that seasonal hunter-fishers would immediately adopt the complicated and radically new techniques of agriculture and a settled way of life', J.P. Mallory and T.E. McNeill, *The Archaeology of Ulster. From Colonization to Plantation* (Belfast 1991), p.31.

65   'The most outstanding characteristics of the Irish Iron Age are not its resemblances to La Tène but its native character and its continuity with the Late Bronze Age culture which preceded it', G.S. MacEoin, 'The Celticity of Celtic Ireland' in K.H. Schmidt and R. Kîdderitzsch, *Geschichte und Kultur der Kelten* (Heidelberg 1986), pp.161–74. Ref. on p.163.

66   Evans, *op. cit.*, 1957, p.7.

67   J. Morris Jones, 'Pre-Aryan syntax in Insular Celtic', in J. Rhŷs and D. Brynmor-Jones (eds), *The Welsh People* (London 1906), pp.617–41; J. Pokorny, 'Das nicht-indogermanische Substrat im Irischen', *Zeitschrift für Celtische Philologie*, 16 (1927), 95–144, 231–66, 363–94; 17 (1928), 373–88; 18 (1930), 233–48; H. Wagner, 'Near Eastern and African connections with the Celtic world', in R. O'Driscoll (ed.), *The Celtic Consciousness* (Portlaoise and Edinburgh 1982), pp.51–67. See also G.B. Adams, 'Place-names from pre-Celtic languages in Ireland and Britain', *Nomina*, 4 (1980), 46–63.

68   J.B. Bury, *The Science of History, An Inaugural Lecture delivered in the Divinity School, Cambridge, on January 26, 1903* (Cambridge 1903), pp.39–40.

69   Evans, 'Giants' graves', *Ulster Journal of Archaeology*, 3rd series, 1 (1938), 7–19.

70   Evans, 'Prehistoric Ireland. From the earliest migrations to about AD 500', in B. de Breffny (ed.), *The Irish World* (London 1977), pp.19–46. Ref. on p.37.

71   H.J. Fleure, *The Trilogy of the Humanities in Education, An Address given to the Tredegar and District Cooperative Society* (Aberystwyth October 1918).

72 H.J. Fleure, 'The Teaching of Geography', in A.W. Bain (ed.), *The Modern Teacher. Essays on Educational Aims and Methods* (London 1921), pp.173–94. Ref. on p.182.

73 H.J. Fleure, 'The new outlook in Geography', *The Journal of Education*, 71 (1939), 296–8. Ref. on p.296.

74 This was because Fleure—like many of his fellow natural scientists then—gave a Lamarckian twist to his interpretation of evolution, embracing thereby 'the idea of consciousness driving evolution' (P.J. Bowler, *The Eclipse of Darwinism. Anti-Darwinian Evolution Theories in the Decades around 1900* [Baltimore and London 1983]. Ref. on p.81).

75 Evans himself put the matter more succinctly: 'H.J. Fleure, though his training and early researches had been in a variety of natural sciences (he became a Fellow of the Royal Society), … won a wider reputation as a humanist', Evans, *op. cit.*, 1978, p.6.

76 H.J. Fleure, *op. cit.*, 1935. Ref. on pp.26–7. See also Fleure's 'Foreword' in Evans, *France. A Geographical Introduction* (London 1937), pp.vii–viii.

77 Evans, 'Human ecology: man and his environment', *New Era in Home and School*, 19 (1937), 273–6. Ref. on p.273. In the academic year 1935/36 Evans' course of extra-mural lectures in the city of Armagh had been entitled 'Human Ecology'. J.A. Campbell, *op. cit.*, 1978, p.24.

78 R.E. Glasscock, 'Obituary: E. Estyn Evans, 1905–1989', *Journal of Historical Geography*, 17 (1991), 87–91. Ref. on p.87.

79 Evans, 'The ecology of peasant life in Western Europe', in W.L. Thomas, Jr (ed.), *Man's Rôle in Changing the Face of the Earth: An International Symposium* (Chicago 19560, pp. 217–39; Evans, 'Ireland and Atlantic Europe', *Geographische Zeitschrift*, 52 (1963), 224–41.

80 Evans, 'Introduction: The Irish. Fact and Fiction' in B. de Breffny (ed.), *The Irish World* (London 1977), pp.7–18. Ref. on p.7.

81 P. Vidal- de la Blache, *Ëtats et Nations de l'Europe. Autour de la France* (Paris 1891), p.301.

82 H.J. Fleure, *A Natural History of Man in Britain. Conceived as a study of changing relations between Men and Environments* (London 1951), pp.1–15.

83 Evans, 'Highland landscapes: habitat and heritage', in J.G. Evans, S. Limbrey and H. Cleere (eds), *The Effect of Man on the Landscape: the Highland Zone* (Oxford 1975), pp.1–5. Ref. on p.2.

84 Evans, 'Prehistoric Geography', in J.W. Watson and J.B. Sissons (eds), *The British Isles: A Systematic Geography* (Edinburgh 1964), pp.177–97.

85 P. Harbison, *Pre-Christian Ireland. From the First Settlers to the Early Celts* (London 1988). Refs on pp.51–2.

86 Evans, *Mourne Country. Landscape and Life in South Down* (Dundalk 1978), Acknowledgments.

87 Evans, *op. cit.*, 1975. Ref. on p.4.

88 'In many parts of Ireland one comes upon the tradition that there was a time when a squirrel—or it might be a bird or a marten—could have hopped from tree to tree over many miles of country without touching the ground. … Such beliefs must take us back to the early seventeenth century at least, and even then there cannot have been many areas to which they could apply, so that behind them there may be a lingering folk memory of earlier times'. Evans, 'The Ulster Landscape', *Ulster Folklife*, 4 (1958), 9–14. Ref. on p.9. E. McCracken, one of Evans' former research students, considers the deforestation of Ireland in recent centuries, its causes and consequences, in her book, *The Irish Woods since Tudor Times. Distribution and Exploitation* (Newton Abbot 1971).

89 Evans, *op. cit.*, 1963. Ref. on p.231.

90 Evans, 'Bog Butter: another explanation', *Ulster Journal of Archaeology*, 3rd series, 10 (1947), 59–62. Ref. on p.61.

91 Evans, *op. cit.*, 1992. Ref. on p.3.

92 Evans, *op. cit.*, 1942. Ref. on pp.87–8. In fact, Evans subsequently suggested that the practice may date back to megalithic/Bronze Age times; and in a recent book Steensberg has presented evidence which would lend support to this contention. See, respc. Evans, 'Some

Problems of Irish Ethnology: The Example of Ploughing by the Tail', in C. Ó Danachair (ed.), *Folk and Farm. Essays in Honour of A.T. Lucas* (Dublin 1976), pp.30–9; 'Origins of the Ard and the Plough', in A. Steensberg, *Man the Manipulator. An Ethno-Archaeological Basis for Reconstructing the Past* (Copenhagen 1986), pp.129–48.

93 Evans, *op. cit.*, 1951, p.44.

94 Evans, 'A Book of Irish Spades', *The Field*, 182 (7 August 1943), 144.

95 Evans, *op. cit.*, 1957, 114–26. See also R.H. Buchanan, 'Corbelled Structures in Lecale, County Down', *Ulster Journal of Archaeology*, 3rd series, 19 (1956), 92–112. See also J. Walton, 'Megalithic building survivals' in J.G. Jenkins (ed.), *Studies in Folklife* (London 1969), 105–22.

96 Evans, 'The cultural geographer and folklife research', in R.M. Dorson (ed.), *Folklore and Folklife: An Introduction* (Chicago and London 1972), pp.517–32. Ref. on p.524–5.

97 Hewitt levelled this criticism in his poem 'On the Choice of a Title' composed on the publication of Evans' book *Irish Heritage* in 1942. See R.H. Buchanan, 'The Achievement of Estyn Evans', in G. Dawe and J.W. Foster (eds), *The Poet's Place* (Belfast 1991), pp. 149–56. Ref. on pp.155–6.

98 'Most books about Ireland are mainly a rehash of old materials though there are a few, like Dr Evans's *Irish Heritage*, which do fill a notable gap', L. MacNeice, 'About Ireland', in A. Heuser (ed.), *Selected Prose of Louis MacNeice* (Oxford 1990), pp.171–5. Ref. on p.171; 'a subject hitherto so neglected in publication', C. Ó Danachair, review of Evans, *Irish Folk Ways* (1967 reprint), *Irish Geography*, 5 (1968), 494–5. Ref. on p.494.

99 'It is typical of this country that attention concentrates on things of the spirit, and tribute must be paid to the work of the Irish Folklore Commission. ... It would need a separate commission, backed by folk museums on Scandinavian lines, to study, collect and preserve representative examples of the crafts and industries', Evans, *op. cit.*, 1942. Ref. on pp.5–6.

100 Evans, *op. cit.*, 1957, p.297.

101 Evans, *ibid.*, p.xiv.

102 Evans, *op. cit.*, 1942, p.3.

103 Evans, 'Peasant Beliefs in Nineteenth-Century Ireland', in D.J. Casey and R.E. Rhodes (eds), *Views of the Irish Peasantry, 1800–1916* (Hamden 1977), pp.37–56. Refs on p.42.

104 Evans, *op. cit.*, 1977. Refs on pp.15–16.

105 Evans, *op. cit.*, 1957, p.xiv.

106 E. Larkin, 'The Devotional Revolution in Ireland, 1850–75', *American Historical Review*, 77 (1972), 625–52; D.W. Miller, 'Irish Catholicism and the Great Famine', *Journal of Social History*, 9 (1975), 81–98; S.J. Connolly, *Priests and People in Pre-Famine Ireland 1780–1845* (Dublin 1982); K. Whelan, 'The Regional Impact of Irish Catholicism 1700–1850', in W.J. Smyth and K. Whelan (eds), *Common Ground. Essays on the historical geography of Ireland presented to T. Jones Hughes* (Cork 1988), pp.253–77.

107 Evans, *op. cit.*, 1992, p.xiii.

108 Evans, 'Changes in rural life and settlement', in T.W. Moody and J.C. Beckett (eds), *Ulster Since 1800, Second Series: A Social Survey* (London 1957), pp.67–70.

109 Evans, *op. cit.*, 1957, p.xv.

110 Evans, *op. cit.*, 1956. Refs on p.221.

111 Evans, *op. cit.*, 1942, pp.3–4.

112 *Ibid.*, p.4.

113 In its lack of adequate planning legislation, Northern Ireland post-war compared badly with the remainder of the United Kingdom; and even more so with practice in the United States, which Evans came to know at first-hand as a result of his several sabbatical visits to American colleges and universities: 'The policy of conservation—the establishment of parks, recreational areas, wild-life refuges and nature reserves—has been pursued by Federal and State governments with such rewarding rivalry that today about a quarter of the countryside is public land of one kind or another', Evans, 'The Province', in R. Common (ed.), *Northern Ireland from the Air* (Belfast 1965), pp.8–15. Ref. on p.8.

114 D. Rogers, 'History of the National Trust in Northern Ireland', in L. Gallagher and D. Rogers, *Castle, Coast and Cottage. The National Trust in Northern Ireland* (Belfast 1986), pp.113–60. Ref. on p.144.

115 G.B. Thompson, 'Estyn Evans and the development of the Ulster Folk Museum', *Ulster Folklife*, 15/16 (1970), 233–8. Ref. on p.233.

116 Evans, *op. cit.*, 1984. See also R.H. Buchanan, 'The Planter and the Gael: Cultural Dimensions of the Northern Ireland Problem', in F.W. Boal and J.N.H. Douglas (eds), *Integration and Division. Geographical Perspectives on the Northern Ireland Problem* (London 1982), pp.49–73.

117 G.S. Dunbar, 'Geographical Personality', in H.J. Walker and W.G. Haag (eds), *Man and Cultural Heritage. Papers in Honor of Fred B. Kniffen, Geoscience and Man*, Volume 5 (Baton Rouge 1974), pp.25–33.

118 C. Fox, *The Personality of Britain. Its Influence on Inhabitant and Invader in Prehistoric and Early Historic Times* (Cardiff 1932). P. Vidal de la Blache, *Tableau de la géographie de la France*, Volume 1, Part 1, in E. Lavisse (ed.), *Histoire de France, jusqu' à la Révolution* (Paris 1901–11). W. Pessler, 'Die Geographische Methode in der Volkskunde', *Anthropos*, 27 (1932), 707–42.

119 Evans, *op. cit.*, 1937. Refs on pp.46, 79, 87, 115, 156.

120 Evans, *op. cit.*, 1951. Refs on p.21; Evans, *op. cit.*, 1978. Ref. on p.9 and Evans, *op. cit.*, 1965. Ref. on p.8.

121 H.J. Fleure, 'Countries as personalities', *Nature*, 108 (1921), 573–5; *cf.* also the title of his Aberystwyth *festschrift*, I.C. Peate (ed.), *op. cit.*, 1930.

122 H. Meller, *Patrick Geddes. Social Evolutionist and City Planner* (London and New York 1990). One index of the enormous impact of Geddes' ideas—and those of his American disciple, Lewis Mumford—is the part they played in shaping the regionalist philosophy of John Hewitt. See 'Introduction', in F. Ormsby (ed.), *The Collected Poems of John Hewitt* (Belfast 1991), p.xli–lxxiv. Refs on pp.l–li.

123 A.J. Herbertson, 'Regional consciousness, heredity and environment', *Geographical Teacher*, 8 (1915), 147–53.

124 A. Burguiére, 'The Fate of the History of Mentalités in the Annales', *Comparative Studies in Society and History*, 24 (1982), 424–37. Ref. on p.428.

125 Evans, *op. cit.*, 1977, p.18.

126 T.S. Eliot, 'Unity and diversity: The region', in *Notes towards the Definition of Culture* (London 1948), pp.50–66. Refs on p.58.

THE WRITINGS OF E.ESTYN EVAN, 1926–88

1926—'Salt and Society', *The Legionary*.
—'Sir Christopher', *The Dragon*.
1927—'Bronze celt found near Carno, Mont.', *Archaeologia Cambrensis*, 82, 390–1.
—'Excavations on the Kerry Hills, Montgomeryshire' (with John E. Daniel and Trevor Lewis), *Archaeologia Cambrensis* 82, 147–60.
1928—'An essay on the historical geography of the Shropshire-Montgomeryshire borderland', *Collins Hist. Archaeological Mont.* 40, 1–30.
— 'Lost and Found', *The Dragon*.
1929—'Denmark' [in part], in *Encyclopaedia Britannica*, 14th ed.
1930—'The Pyrenees: a geographical interpretation of their role in human times', 45–68, in I.C. Peate, *Studies in Regional Consciousness and Environment: Essays Presented to H.J. Fleure*, Oxford, O.U.P.
—'The sword–bearers', *Antiquity* 4, 157–72.
1931—'A Study of the Origins and Distributions of some Late Bronze Age Industries in Western Europe' (M.A. dissertation, Univ. of Wales).
—'The late Bronze Age in Western Europe', *Man* 31, 207–13.
1932—'Ridgeways in north central Wales', *Bull. Brd. Celtic Studies* 6, 295–6.
1933—'The bronze spear–head in Great Britain and Ireland', *Archaeologia* 83, 188–202.
—'Excavation of a horned cairn at Goward, Co. Down' (with O. Davies), *Man* 33, 114–17
—'Goward Hill cairn, Co. Down' (with O. Davies), *Antiquity*, 7, 222.
—'Ridgeways in north Wales', *Bull. Brd. Celtic Studies* 7, 86–8.
1934—'Excavation of a horned cairn at Ballyalton, Co. Down' (with O. Davies), *Man* 34, 88–9.
'Excavations at Clonlum small cairn, Co. Armagh' (with O. Davies), *County Louth Archaeological J.* 8, 165–8.
—'Excavations at Goward, near Hilltown, Co. Down' (with O. Davies), *Proc. Rep. Belfast Nat. Hist. Phil. Soc.* (1932–3), 90–105.
—'Prehistoric archaeology in Northern Ireland', *Antiquity*, 8, 329–30.

261

1935—'Archaeological investigations in Northern Ireland: a summary of recent work', *Antiquaries J.* 15, 165–73.

—'Belfast Naturalists' Field Club Survey of Antiquities: megaliths and raths' (with M. Gaffikin), *Irish Naturalists' J.* 5, 242–52.

—'A Bronze Age cist containing food vessel and cremation burial found at Ballynagross, near Downpatrick, Co. Down' (with M. Gaffikin), *J. R. Soc. Antiquaries Ir.* 65, 141–6.

—'Excavation of a chambered horned cairn at Ballyalton, Co. Down' (with 0. Davies), *Proc. Rep. Belfast Nat. Hist. Phil. Soc.* (1933–4), 79–103.

—'Excavations at Aghnaskeagh, Co. Louth, Cairn A', *County Louth Archaeological J.* 8, 235–55.

—'Excavations at Clonlum, Co. Armagh' (with O. Davies), *County Louth Archaeological J.* 8, 165–8.

—'Notes on excavations in … Northern Ireland, 1934', *Proc. Prehistoric Soc. E. Anglia* 7, 411–13.

—'Ridgeways in north-west Wales', *Bull. Brd. Celtic Studies* 8, 84–7.

1936—'Doey's cairn, Dunloy', *Antiquaries J.* 16, 208–13.

—'Excavation of a chambered horned cairn, Browndod, Co. Antrim' (with O. Davies), *Proc. Rep. Belfast Nat. Hist. Phil. Soc.* (1934–5), 70–87.

—'Notes on excavations in … Northern Ireland, 1935', *Proc. Prehistoric Soc.* 1, 140–2.

—'Some recent finds of flint arrow heads', *Irish Naturalists' J.* 6, 9–11.

—'Stone Circles in Northern Ireland' (with O. Davies), *Req. Brit. Assoc. for Adv. of Sciences* (Blackpool), 395.

1937—*France: A Geographical Introduction*, London, Christophers, 183 pp. (New ed., 1959, 159 pp.; 3rd ed., London, 1966, Chatto & Windus and New York, Praeger, 192 pp.)

—'The Causeway Water, Co. Down, and its cairns', *Irish Naturalists' J.* 6, 242–8.

—'Excavations at Aghnaskeagh, Co. Louth, Cairn B', *County Louth Archaeological J.* 9, 1–18.

—'Notes on excavations in … Northern Ireland, 1936', *Proc. Prehistoric Soc.* 2, 221–3.

—'The site of Belfast', *Geography* 22, 169–77.

1938—'A bronze spear-head from Caernarvonshire', *Archaeologia Cambrensis* 93, 134–5.

—'A chambered cairn in Ballyedmond Park, County Down', *Ulster J. Archaeol.*, 3rd s. I, 49–58.

—'Doey's cairn, Dunloy, County Antrim', *Ulster J. Archaeol.*, 3rd s. 1, 59–78.

—'Giants' graves', *Ulster J. Archaeol.*, 3rd s. 1, 7–19.

—'Megalithic civilisation in Northern Ireland', *Proc. Prehistoric Soc.* 3, 338–9.

—'The multiple-cist cairn at Mount Stewart, Co. Down, Northern Ireland' (with B.R.S. Megaw), *Proc. Prehistoric Soc.* 3, 29–42.

—'Notes on excavations in … Northern Ireland, 1937', *Proc. Prehistoric Soc.* 3, 453–4.

—'Some results of recent excavations in Northern Ireland', *Q. Notes Belfast Munic. Mus. Art Gallery* 57, 7–10.

—'An urn from Aghascrebagh, Co. Tyrone', *Ulster J. Archaeol.*, 3rd s. I, 189–92.

—'Human ecology: man and his environment', *New Era* 19, 273–6.

1939—(Edited) *South Carpathian Studies: Roumania II* (with H. J. Fleure), London, The Le Play Society, 58 pp.

—'Works submitted' (published papers presented for D.Sc., Univ. of Wales).

—'A Bronze Age burial group from Kilskeery, County Antrim' (with T.G.F. Paterson), *Ulster J. Archaeol.*, 3rd s. 2, 65–71.

—'The Celts in archaeology' (with O. Davies and C. Blake Whelan), *Ulster J. Archaeol.*, 3rd s. 2, 137–47.

—'Donegal survivals', *Antiquity* 13, 207–22.

—'Excavations at Carnanbane, County Londonderry: a double-horned cairn', *Proc. R. Irish Acad.* 45C, 1–12.

—'Killin Hill', *Ulster J. Archaeol.*, 3rd s. 2, 250–4.

—'Notes on excavations in … Northern Ireland, 1938', *Proc. Prehistoric Soc.* 4, 322–3.

—'The rowing-boat curraghs of Sheephaven', *Ulster J. Archaeol.*, 3rd s. 2, 28–31.

—'Some survivals of the Irish openfield system', *Geography* 24, 24–36.

1940—(Sub-editor for Prehistoric Monuments) D.A. Chart, *A Preliminary Survey of the Ancient Monuments of Northern Ireland*, Belfast, H.M.S.O., xxiv, 284 pp.

—'Bibliography of the periodical literature relating to the archaeology of Ulster, 1939' (with B.R.S. Megaw), *Ulster J. Archaeol.*, 3rd s. 3, 170–1.

—'Conditions of life in prehistoric Ireland'. Compiled by members of the Editorial Board (E.E. Evans, O. Davies and C. Blake Whelan), *Ulster J. Archaeol.*, 3rd s. 3, 5–16.

—'An eskimo harpoon-head from Tara, Co. Down (?)' (with C.F.C. Hawkes), *Ulster J. Archaeol.*, 3rd s. 3, 127–33.

—Introductory note to E. Watson, 'Prehistoric sites in South Antrim', *Ulster J. Archaeol.*, 3rd s. 3, 142.

—'The Irish peasant house', *Ulster J. Archaeol.*, 3rd s. 3, 165–9

—'Lyles Hill: a prehistoric site in Co. Antrim', *Q. Notes Belfast Munic. Mus. Art Gallery* 64, 1–15.

—'Notes on excavations in … Northern Ireland, 1939', *Proc. Prehistoric Soc.* 5, 255–6.

—'Problems of Irish ethnology', *Irish Naturalists' J.* 7, 282–6.

—'Sherds from a gravel-pit, Killaghy, Co. Armagh', *Ulster J., Archaeology* 3rd s. 3, 139–41.

—'Seasonal nomadism in modern Europe and ancient Ireland', *Proc. Belfast Naturalists' Field Club* 2nd s. 10, 94–9.

—'Transhumance in Europe', *Geography* 25, 172–80.

—'Wooden trough from Tyrone', *Irish Naturalists' J.* 7, 246–7.

1941—'Bee transhumance', *Geography* 26, 76.

—'Cist-burial at Loughry, Co. Tyrone', *Ulster J. Archaeol.*, 3rd s. 4, 145–8.

—'Correspondence' [on Folk tales from Cadian, County Tyrone], *Ulster J. Archaeol.*, 3rd s. 4, 76–7.

—'The flachter', *Ulster J. Archaeol.*, 3rd s. 4, 82–7.

—'Grooved hammer-stones from Co. Antrim', *Ulster J. Archaeology*, 3rd s. 4, 27–30.

—'An interpretation of Irish culture'. Compiled by members of the Editorial Board (E.E. Evans, H. C. Lawlor and C. Blake Whelan), *Ulster J. Archaeol.*, 3rd s. 4, 12–18.

—'Report on some sherds from Mount Druid', *Ulster J. Archaeol.*, 3rd s. 4, 55.

—'Survey of Ancient Monuments. Additions' (contributions by E.E. Evans), *Ulster J. Archaeol.*, 3rd s. 4, 35–44.

—'A sandhill site in Co. Donegal', *Ulster J. Archaeol.*, 3rd s. 4, 71–5

1942—*Irish Heritage: The Landscape, the People and their Work*, Dundalk, W. Tempest, Dundalgan Press, xvi, 190 pp.

—'Clermont cairn', *County Louth Archaeological J.* 10, 77–9.

—'Coin hoards from Ulster: a hoard of coins from Rathlin Island', *Ulster J. Archaeol.*, 3rd s. 5, 66.

—'A baking stone from Fermanagh' (with O. Davies), *Ulster J. Archaeol.*, 3rd s. 5, 76–7.

—'A food-vessel from Ballynagarvy, Co. Antrim', *Ulster J. Archaeol.*, 3rd s. 5, 95–7.

—'Pumice stone and neolithic sherds from Dundrum, Co. Down' (with A. McI. Cleland), *Ulster J. Archaeol.*, 3rd s. 5, 11–13.

—'The stone houses, Ticloy, Co. Antrim' (with E. Watson), *Ulster J. Archaeol.*, 3rd s. 5, 62–5.

—'The fireside', *County Louth Archaeological J.* 10, 196–9.

—'Four bronze axes', *Ulster J. Archaeol.*, 3rd s. 6, 106–7.

—'The horned cairns of Ulster' (with O. Davies), *Ulster J. Archaeol.*, 3rd s. 6, 7–23.

—'Recent excavations', *Ulster J. Archaeol.*, 3rd s. 6, z3.

—'Ten years' achievement: a summary of archaeological research in N. Ireland' (anon. editorial), *Ulster J. Archaeol.*, 3rd s. 6, 1–6.

1943—'"Greengrow the Rushes oh!" Rush-wort', in *The Field*, August.

1944—'Belfast: the site and the city', *Ulster J. Archaeol.*, 3rd s. 7, 5–29.
  —'A bronze axe from Co. Down', *Ulster J. Archaeol.*, 3rd s. 7, 98.
  —'A gold ornament and other Bronze Age finds from Rathlin', *Ulster J. Archaeol.*, 3rd s. 7, 61–4.
  —'The megaliths', *Geogr. Mag.* 17, 294–305.
  —'Souterrain at Ballyhornan, Co. Down', *Ulster J. Archaeol.*, 3rd s. 7, 102–4.
  —'Two food-vessels from Co. Tyrone', *Ulster J. Archaeol.*, 3rd s. 7, 105–8.
  —'Survey of Ancient Monuments', Third list of additions and corrections (contributions by E.E. Evans), *Ulster J. Archaeol.*, 3rd s. 7, 117–21.
  —'Unrecorded finds', *Ulster J. Archaeol.*, 3rd s. 7, 122.
1945—'A famine relic', *Ulster J. Archaeol.*, 3rd s. 8, 49.
  —'Field archaeology in the Ballycastle district', *Ulster J. Archaeol.*, 3rd s. 8, 14–32.
  —'Potatoes and man', *County Louth Archaeological J.* 34–6.
  —'An urn from Culmore, Co. Antrim', *Ulster J. Archaeol.*, 3rd s. 8, 39–42.
1946—'Folk museums', *Ulster Countrywoman*, June, 5–6.
  —'Newly discovered souterrains, County Antrim', *Ulster J. Archaeol.*, 3rd s. 9, 79–83.
  —'The origins of Irish agriculture', *Ulster J. Archaeol.*, 3rd s. 9, 87–90.
1947—*The Ulster Countryside:* report of the Planning Advisory Board on Amenities in Northern Ireland, Belfast, H.M.S.O. (Members of Committee on Amenities; E.E. Evans and others).
  —'Bog butter: another explanation', *Ulster J. Archaeol.*, 3rd s. 10, 59–62.
  —'Foreword', 5–6, in H.A. Boyd, *Rathlin Island, North of Ireland*, Ballycastle, Scarlett.
  —'Some newly reported bronze implements', *Ulster J. Archaeol.*, 3rd s. 10, 66–8.
1948—'General Introduction', pp. v–vi, in D.A. Hill; *The Land of Ulster: The Report of the Land Utilisation Survey of Northern Ireland. Part I. Belfast Region*, Belfast, H.M.S.O.
  —'Lands and peoples of the world: Western Europe', 97–121, in *Geography: The World and its Peoples*, London, Odhams Press.
  —'A lost Mourne megalith – and a newly discovered site'. *Ulster J. Archaeol.*, 3rd s. 11, 43–7.
  —'Strange iron objects from Co. Fermanagh', *Ulster J. Archaeol.*, 3rd s. 11, 58–64.
  —'Northern Ireland,' in *Hutchinson's Pictorial Encyclopedia*.
1949—'Archaeological research in Ireland, 1939–1948', *Archaeology* 2, 69–72.
  —'Northern Ireland: the land and the people', *Geogr. Rev.* 39, 316–17
  —'Old Ireland and New England', *Ulster J. Archaeol.*, 3rd s. 12, 104–12.
1950—'Antrim'; 'Belfast'; 'Donegal'; 'Down'; 'Fermanagh'; 'Ireland' [in part]; 'Londonderry'; 'Louth'; 'Monaghan'; 'Northern Ireland' [in part]; 'Tyrone' [and other articles] in *Chambers's Encyclopaedia*, New ed. (Revised ed., 1967).
  —'Rath and souterrain at Shaneen Park, Belfast, townland of Ballyaghagan, Co. Antrim', *Ulster J. Archaeol.*, 3rd s. 13, 6–27.
  —'Worked flints from boulder clay in Belfast', *Ulster J. Archaeol.*, 3rd s. 13, 42–3.
1951—*Mourne Country: Landscape and Life in South Down*, Dundalk, Dundalgan Press [12], 226 pp. (2nd ed., 1967, xvii, 244 pp.)
  —*Northern Ireland: With a Portrait (About Britain* 13), London, Collins, 92 pp.
  —'Ancient fish weirs on the Co. Down coast', *Ulster J. Archaeol.*, 3rd s. 14, 48.
  —'R.A.S. Macalister and the archaeology of Ireland', *Ulster J. Archaeol.*, 3rd s. 14, 2–6.
  —'Some archaic forms of agricultural transport in Ulster', pp. 108–23, in W. F. Grimes *Aspects of Archaeology in Britain and beyond: Essays Presented to O.G.S. Crawford*, London, H. W. Edwards.
1952—'The physical background – the region and its parts', 15–28; 'The human background – prehistoric: Mesolithic, Neolithic and Bronze Ages' (with E.M. Jope), 75–87.
  —'The human background – protohistoric: the prehistoric Iron Age, early Christian and Viking periods' (with E. M. Jope), 88–97, in *Belfast in Its Regional Setting: A Scientific Survey*, Belfast, British Association for the Advancement of Science. Local Executive Committee.

—'Two Belfast raths', *Ulster J. Archaeol.*, 3rd s. 15, 84–6.

1953—*Lyles Hill: A Late Neolithic site in County Antrim* (Archaeological Research Publications [Northern Ireland] no. 2), Belfast, H.M.S.O., viii, 71 pp.

—'Archaeology in Northern Ireland, 1921–51', *Ulster J. Archaeol.*, 3rd s. 16, 3–6.

1954—'Claude Blake Whelan', *Ulster J. Archaeol.*, 3rd s. 17, 6.

—'Dairying in Ireland through the ages', *J. Soc. Dairy Technol.* 7, 179–87.

—'Joseph Skillen', *Ulster J. Archaeol.*, 3rd s. 17, 2.

—'The rural house', *The Landmark* 2, 5–6.

—'Three bronze spearheads from Tattenamona, County Fermanagh' (with G. F. Mitchell), *Ulster J. Archaeol.*, 3rd s. 17, 57–61.

—'Ulster's place in British archaeology', *Trans. Lancashire Cheshire Antiquarian Soc.* 64, 19–23.

1955—'The black man and the white thorn', *Ulster J. Archaeol.*, 3rd s. 18, 109–12.

—'The growth of Belfast' (with E. Jones), *Tn. Plann. Rev.* 26, 93–111.

—'The Ulster farmhouse', *Ulster Folklife* I, 27–31.

1956—'The ecology of peasant life in Western Europe', pp. 217–39, in W. L. Thomas Jr. (ed.), *Man's Role in Changing the Face of the Earth: An International Symposium*, Chicago, Univ. of Chicago Press (revised ed., 1960).

—'Fields, fences and gates', *Ulster Folklife* 2, 14–18.

1957—*Irish Folk Ways*, London, Routledge & Kegan Paul, xvi, 324 pp.

—'A. H. Davison', *Ulster J. Archaeol.*, 3rd s. 20, 1.

—'Changes in rural life and settlement', pp. 62–70, in T. W. Moody and J. C. Beckett (eds), *Ulster Since 1800, Second Series: A Social Survey*, London, British Broadcasting Corporation.

—'Professor S. P. O'Riordain (with E. M. Jope), *Ulster J. Archaeol.*, 3rd s. 20, 2–3.

—'The Ulster farmhouse: a comparative study', *Ulster Folklife* 3, 14–18.

1958—'The Atlantic ends of Europe', *Advancement of Science* 15, 54–64.

—'The ecology of the rural house in Ireland', pp. 47–55, in N. Anderson, *Recherches sur la famille, volume III: seminaires 1956 et 1957 du Séminaire International de Recherche sur la Famille et de l'Institut UNESCO des Sciences Sociales*, Cologne, Göttingen, Vandenhoeck & Ruprecht.

—'Excavations at the Deer's Meadow' (with V. B. Proudfoot), *Ulster J. Archaeol.*, 3rd s. 21, 127–31.

—'The Ulster landscape', *Ulster Folklife* 4, 9–14.

—'The Cultural Landscape of Celtic Countries', *Scots. Geog. Mag.*, 3, 189–90.

1959—'A fairy millstone', *Ulster Folklife* 5, 64.

—'Miss Mary McMurry Gaffikin', *Ulster J. Archaeol.*, 3rd s. 22, 2–4

—'A Pennsylvanian folk festival', *Ulster Folklife* 5, 14–19.

—'Rural settlement in Ireland and Western Britain' (with others), *Advancement of Science* 15, 333–45.

—'A shell industry in County Londonderry', *Ulster Folklife* 5, 60.

—'Social Sciences: Geography', 25–8, in *Pursuit of Knowledge: A Collection of Essays on Current Research*, Belfast, Queen's Univ.

—'Preface', to Padraic Gregory, *Complete Collected Irish Ballads*.

1960—'Dicuil', in *Encyclopaedia Britannica*.

—'The peasant and the past' (Presidential address to the Anthropology section of the British Association), *Advancement of Science* 17, 293–302.

1961—'The evolution of rural settlements in Scotland and beyond' (with R. A. Gailey), *Ulster Folklife* 7, 63–5.

—'Northern Ireland, Ireland: The People' and 'Europe: Ethnology', in *Encyclopedia Britannica*.

1962—'Irish court cairns' (with O. Davies), *Ulster J. Archaeol.*, 3rd s. 24/25, 2–7.

—'Foreword', to Max Heslinga, *The Irish Borders as a Cultural Divide*, Assen.

1963—'Introduction' and 'Chapter 1 (Prehistoric and historic background)', pp. 19–44, in L. Symons, *Land Use in Northern Ireland: The General Report of the Survey*, London, Univ. of London Press.

—'Ireland and Atlantic Europe', *Geogr. Z.* 52, 224–41.

—'Northern Ireland'; 'Belfast' (and other articles) in (Grolier) *Encyclopedia International*.

1964—'Bann'; 'Erne'; 'Europe' [in part]; 'Mourne Mountains', in *Encyclopaedia Britannica*.

—'County Londonderry: archaeology', pp. 49–62, in *County Londonderry Handbook*. [Coleraine, County Londonderry County Council.]

—'Dame Dehra Parker', *Ulster J. Archaeol.*, 3rd s. 27, 2.

—'Prehistoric geography', pp. 177–97, in J. Wreford Watson and B. Sissons (eds), *The British Isles. A Systematic Geography*, London, Nelson.

1965—'Cultural relics of the Ulster-Scots in the old west of North America', *Ulster Folklife* 11, 33–8.

—'Folklife studies in Northern Ireland', *J. Folklore Inst.* 2, 355–63.

—'Historic cities and boroughs: Belfast', *Munic. Rev.* 36, 24.

—'Introduction', *Florin Guide to Northern Ireland*. Shell Petroleum Co.

—'The Province', pp. 8–15, in R. Common, *Northern Ireland from the air*. [Dept. of Geography, Queen's University of Belfast.]

—'The Scotch-Irish in the new world: an Atlantic heritage', *J. R. Soc. Antiquaries Ir.* 95, 39–49.

1966—*Prehistoric and Early Christian Ireland: A Guide*, London, Batsford, xiv. 241 pp. (New York, Barnes & Noble.)

—'Culture and land-use in the old west of North America', *Heidelberg Geogr. Arb.* 15, 72–80 (*Festgabe fur Gottfried Pfeiffer*).

—'General introduction: geographical', pp. vii–xv, in *Northern Ireland, Archaeological Survey. An Archaeological Survey of County Down*, Belfast, H.M.S.O.

—'George Barnett: an appreciation', *Ulster J. Archaeol.*, 3rd s. 29, 1–5.

—'Some cruck roof-trusses in Ulster', *Ulster Folklife* 12, 35–40.

1967—'Flax-scutching', *Ulster Folklife* 13, 78–9.

—'H.J. Fleure', in *International Encyclopaedia of the Social Sciences*.

—'The geographical setting', pp. 1–13, in J.C. Beckett and R.E. Glasscock (eds), *Belfast: The Origin and Growth of an Industrial City*, London, B. B. C.

—'Lady Dorothy Lowry-Corry', *Ulster J. Archaeol.*, 3rd s. 30, 1.

—'Preface', 17–18, in M. Rogers, *Prospect of Erne ...*, [Enniskillin] Fermanagh Field Club.

1968—*The Irishness of the Irish*, Belfast, The Irish Association for Cultural, Economic and Social Relations, 8 pp.

—'Archaeology in Ulster since 1920', *Ulster J. Archaeol.*, 3rd s. 31, 3–8

—'A cist burial at Carrickinab, Co. Down' (with A. E. P. Collins), *Ulster J. Archaeol.*, 3rd s. 31, 16–24.

—'Ireland' [in part]; 'Northern Ireland' [in part]; 'Lough Neagh', in *Encyclopaedia Britannica*.

—'Irish harvest', *Ulster Folklife* 14, 3–5.

—'A late seventeenth-century farmhouse at Shantallow, near Londonderry' (with D. McCourt), *Ulster Folklife* 14, 14–23.

—'The "Larne" material in Lord Antrim's collection at the Ashmolean Museum, Oxford', *Proc. R. Irish Acad.* 67C, 9–34.

—'Geography', in *Undergraduate Studies in Science*, Q.U.B., 49–53.

1969—'A Cardiganshire mud-walled farmhouse', *Folk Life* 7, 92–100.

—'The Scotch-Irish: their cultural adaptation and heritage in the American old west', pp. 69–86, in E.R.R. Green (ed.), *Essays in Scotch-Irish History*, London, Routledge & Kegan Paul.

—'Sod and turf houses in Ireland', pp. 70–90, in G. Jenkins, *Studies in Folk Life: Essays in Honour of Iorwerth C. Peate*, London, Routledge & Kegan Paul.

—'Emeritus Professor Herbert John Fleure', *Geogr. J.* 135, 484–5.

—'Foreword', 3–4, in Institute of Irish Studies, *Somerville and Ross: A Symposium*, Belfast, Queen's Univ.

—'Geography', in *Undergraduate Studies in Science*, Q.U.B., 51–5.

1970—'The personality of Ulster', Institute of British Geographers, *Transactions*, 51, 1–20.

—'Recent Irish craftwork', in *Irish Craftmanship*, Irish Section, World Crafts Council, Dublin, pp.17–22.

—'The academic status of folklore in Britain', *Journal of the Folklore Institute*, 7, 105–9.

—'Introduction', in A. Gailey and A. Fenton (eds), *The Spade in Northern and Atlantic Europe*, Belfast, pp.1–9.

1971—(with D. McCourt) 'A late seventeenth-century farmhouse at Shantallow, near Londonderry, Part 2', *Ulster Folklife*, 17, 37–41.

—(with S.J. Loughlin) 'A County Tyrone tanyard', *Ulster Folklife*, 17, 85–7.

—'The Northern heritage', *Aquarius*, *a*n annual religio-cultural review, 4, 51–6.

—'T.G.F. Paterson', *Ulster J. Archaeology*, 3rd Series, 34, 1–2.

—'Introduction', to *Facts from Gweedore compiled from the notes of Lord George Hill, MRIA. A Facsimile Reprint of the Fifth Edition of 1887* (Belfast), pp.v–xxii.

—'Foreword', to M.W. Heslinga, *The Irish Border as a Cultural Divide. A Contribution to the Study of Regionalism in the British Isles*, 2nd rev. ed. Assen.

1972—'The cultural geographer and folklife research', in R.M. Dorson (ed.), *Folklore and Folklife: An Introduction*, Chicago and London, pp.517–32.

—'Foreword', in J.H. Gebbie (ed.), *An Introduction to the Abercorn Letters (as Relating to Ireland, 1736–1816)*, Omagh, pp.vii–viii.

1973—*The Personality of Ireland: Habitat, Heritage and History. The Wiles Lectures for 1971* (Cambridge); Enlarged, revised, pbk edns (Belfast 1981; Dublin 1992).

—*The Personality of Wales*, Cardiff, Annual Radio Lecture, BBC Wales, 26pp.

—'Traditional houses of Rathlin Island', *Ulster Folklife*, 19, 13–19.

1974—'Folk housing in the British Isles in materials other than timber', in H.J. Walker and W.G. Haag (eds), *Man and Cultural Heritage. Papers in Honour of Fred B. Kniffen*, *Geoscience and Man*, 5, Baton Rouge, pp.53–64.

—'Planning for recreation: the Bann valley', *Built Environment*, 3, 83–4.

1975—'Archaeology and folklife', in B. Almquist, B. MacAodha and G.MacEoin (eds), *Hereditas. Essays and Studies presented to Professor Seamus Ó Duilearga*, Dublin, pp.127–39.

—'Highland landscapes: habitat and heritage', in J.G. Evans, S. Limbrey and H. Cleere (eds), *The Effect of Man on the Landscape: The Highland Zone*, Research Report No 11, The Council for British Archaeology, Oxford, pp.1–5.

—'Introduction', to E.E. Evans (ed.), *Harvest Home. The Last Sheaf. A Selection from the Writings of T.G.F. Paterson Relating to County Armagh*, Dundalk, pp.ix–xvi.

—'An archaeological miscellany', *Ulster Journal of Archaeology*, 3rd Series, 38, 12–18.

1976—'Reminiscences of Sandy Row', *Ulster Folklife*, 22, 88–90.

—'Introduction to Ulster', Section 4, in R.P.O. Beach (ed.), *Touring Guide to Ulster*, Basingstoke, pp.35–44.

—'Some problems of Irish ethnology: the example of ploughing by the tail', C.O. Danachair (ed.), *Folk and Farm. Essays in Honour of Dr A.T. Lucas*, Dublin, pp.72–89.

—'The Bull-Roarer', *Ulster Journal of Archaeology*, 3rd Series, 39, 71.

1977—(Ed, with B.S. Turner) *Ireland's Eye: The photographs of Robert John Welch*, Belfast.

—'Introduction: The Irish. Fact and Fiction', and 'Prehistoric Ireland, From the Earliest Migrations to about AD 500', in B. de Breffny (ed.), *The Irish World. The History and Cultural Achievements of the Irish People*, London, pp.7–18 and pp.19–46.

—'Peasant beliefs in nineteenth-century Ireland', in D.J. Casey and R.E. Rhodes (eds), *Views of the Irish Peasantry, 1800–1916*, Hamden, Conn., pp.37–56.

—'The protection of ancient monuments', *Bulletin of the Group for the Study of Irish Historic Settlement*, 4, 7.

1978—'Beginnings', in J.A. Campbell (ed.), *Geography at Queen's. An Historical Survey*, Belfast, pp.5–15.

1979—'The ballad as a commercial aid', *Ulster Folklife*, 25, 123.

—'Digging for defeat', *The Annual Review of the Queen's University Association*, 44–6.

1980—'Gleanings from County Cavan', *Ulster Folklife*, 26, 1–7.

1981—'Introduction', to D. Ó Corráin (ed.), *Irish Antiquity. Essays and Studies presented to Professor M.J. O'Kelly*, Cork, pp.xxv–xxviii.

1984—*Ulster: The Common Ground*, Lilliput Pamphlets, 2, Mullingar, Co. Westmeath.

—'The Irish countryman', in A.O. Kouwenhoven, G.A. de Bruijne and G.A. Hoekveld (eds), *Geplaatst in de tijd*, Amsterdam, pp.130–45.

1986—'Foreword', to C. Thomas (ed.), *Rural Landscapes and Communities. Essays presented to Desmond McCourt*, Dublin, pp.9–10.

1988—'The early development of folklife studies in Northern Ireland', in A. Gailey (ed.), *The Use of Tradition. Essays presented to G.B. Thompson*, Holywood, Co. Down, pp.91–6.